CONTENTS

AMERICAN DRAMA
AND ITS CRITICS

PATTERNS OF LITERARY CRITICISM

General Editors

MARSHALL McLUHAN
R. J. SCHOECK
ERNEST SIRLUCK

AMERICAN DRAMA
AND ITS CRITICS
A Collection of Critical Essays

Edited and with an Introduction by
ALAN S. DOWNER

The University of Chicago Press
Chicago & London

Library of Congress Catalog Card Number 65-24424

THE UNIVERSITY OF CHICAGO PRESS, CHICAGO 60637
The University of Chicago Press, Ltd., London W. C. 1

INTRODUCTION

An Essay of Dramatic Criticism

The curtain had fallen on a summer theater's revival of a Broadway melodrama of the late twenties. While the television star who had appeared in the leading role beamed and perspired at the applause of his middle-aged fans, the four men in the last row silently left their seats and walked Indian file to the nearby pine-paneled lunchroom. They took paper cups of coffee to a booth in the far corner of the room and looked balefully at the other members of the audience who began to drift in, laughing and talking eagerly about the evening's entertainment.

"Listen to those fools," said Jean. "They *liked* the play."

"No," said Gerald. "They liked the performance. And as a performance it wasn't bad. That TV fellow has real style, or at least a pleasing personality, and the director kept everything moving at a good clip."

"But the play," Jean protested. "All that hokum about gangsters and night-club dancers. It was nothing but a patchwork, a lot of scenes from old Warner Brothers movies edited together. Ten minutes of thrill, ten minutes of gags. The characters were pasteboards. No idea, no development, nothing but the old Wilkie Collins formula: 'Make 'em laugh, make 'em weep, make 'em wait.' "

"Well," said Gerald, "that's entertainment. Or don't you think the theater should be concerned with entertainment?"

Arthur crushed his paper cup with the palm of his hand. "Look," he said, "there's more to it than that. This play looks pretty silly in 1964. Our gangsters have their minds on higher things than stealing a truckload of Canadian whiskey, and our night-club performers are protected by unions and agents and unemployment insurance. Our melodramas derive from Krafft-Ebing. But in 1928? This play was made out of the newspaper headlines of its time."

"To revive a common critical phrase of the same time," said

Jean, " 'So what?' We don't have absolute monarchs in this country, but we don't come away from *Oedipus* or *King Lear* feeling that the whole thing was silly."

"Now there's an argument," said Alexander, who had been content to listen with a bemused smile. "Let's compare bread and bricks, or a Chevrolet and a canoe. Very useful. The critics of the twenties saw this play for exactly what it was: an exciting entertainment made out of the materials (or the fantasies) of its day. They didn't waste energy evaluating it against Greek tragedy or anything else."

"That's the whole trouble with dramatic criticism in this country," said Jean. "Then and now. Always. If the critics know anything about the traditions of dramatic literature they keep it a secret. Every play gets reviewed as if it were a unique creation, independent of all its predecessors in the two thousand years of the dramatic repertory; and every critic observes and analyzes from his isolated little seat on the aisle. It's all personal, idiosyncratic, and the judgment is more often colored by an indigestible meal than by a well-digested knowledge of the principles of dramatic criticism."

The jukebox was beginning its third repetition of a clangorous popular tune. The four men left the lunchroom and walked toward the lake where soft waves lapped against the stone-lined shore. Alexander, drawing on his jacket against the late August chill, asked ironically, "Principles of dramatic criticism?"

"Jean means ol' man Aristotle and his chillun," suggested Gerald. "Somebody once compared using Aristotle as a critical mentor to turning to Hippocrates when you need an appendectomy."

Jean sighed. "Directly ahead, ladies and gentlemen, you will see Moot Point. And it won't settle anything to say that science is a constantly unfolding or developing discipline, while the principles of art are eternal. Surely there is no other instance in history—aside from religion—where the principles elucidated by one man, Aristotle, have been tested and found to be unchanging truths by every succeeding generation. Don't forget it was the Aristotelians who made possible the rebirth of the drama in Europe after the Dark Ages, and brought form and order out of the chaos of the seventeenth-century French theater."

"It was also," Arthur pointed out, "the Aristotelian Nahum

Tate who brought form and order out of *King Lear* in the English theater of the Restoration. And suppose the Elizabethan playwrights had listened to the classically minded Sir Philip Sidney? You remember Lope de Vega said that he had the greatest respect for the giants of Greece and Rome, but when he came to write a play he would lock up the rule books behind seven locks."

"You're confusing the issue," said Alexander. "Creation and criticism are two different things. Stick to criticism."

"That's not easy to do," said Gerald. "Criticism as an art is generally something done in the study. It's a matter of a lamp, a pipe, a book, and some reference works. You can hold the whole object to be criticized in your two hands; if you put it down for some reason, you know that you can pick it up at any time and it will not have changed. But dramatic criticism is a vastly different matter. In the first place, you can't hold a play in your hands. And even if you could—if you were Dr. Samuel Gargantua—put it aside for a day or two and you will find it another thing when you return to it."

"You don't have to be Gargantua," said Jean, "to hold *Macbeth* in your hands."

"The text of *Macbeth*, granted," Gerald replied. "But the dramatic critic has to be concerned with much more than the text. The text is only the blueprint of the work to be evaluated."

Jean sighed once more. " 'The drama is not literature,' " he quoted.

Gerald replied quickly; this was familiar ground. "The drama is literature as much as it is architecture or music or oratory or dance or acrobatics. All of these elements enter into the total work, and you have to measure the contribution of each in your final analysis."

"That may be true," said Jean, "though I doubt it. Anyway, it is very clear from the history of the drama that great plays have always been literary masterpieces, too. The Greeks, the Elizabethans, Racine, Ibsen, Chekhov, Shaw. Great plays have always been great literature."

"How can you prove that?" asked Gerald, sharply. "What about the Greek plays that won the dramatic contests but whose texts have not survived? It's possible they were lost because later critics felt them inferior as literature, however triumphant they may have been with their original audiences. Many Elizabethan playwrights we now dismiss as minor were more popular than Shakespeare in their day."

Jean interrupted. "Beaumont and Fletcher are better playwrights than Shakespeare because they are less readable. Is that the proposition?"

"The proposition," said Gerald, somewhat stiffly, "is that the most valid criticism of a play takes into consideration all the elements that go into the creation of an evening's experience for the audience. And since a good many of those elements are human—the actors, for example, and the audience against whose responses they play—the critic must be aware that he is describing a work which may appear quite different on its next presentation."

"Of course," said Alexander, "but now you are talking about journalism, the newspaper reviewer who reports on experience. But what about the *critic*, Jean's friend who is concerned with the eternal aspects of art?"

"Frankly," Gerald replied, "I think he's playing a game. Look, if you grant me that theater is experience, that it is the creation of a particular group of people in a particular environment for a particular number of hours on a particular day, then the critic—or reviewer, if you will—who is doing his job must have his senses alert to what is happening on the stage, and what is happening to himself at the same time. He cannot allow other things to distract him from the experience. And his recorded reaction will become part of the history of the play and the history of the theater. We can never really know Shakespeare's *Othello* because we have no records of Burbage and his fellow players at work on it. But we can arrive at a better understanding of *Shore Acres* because Walter Prichard Eaton has left us a vivid account of Herne's final moments in the play."

"Your bill of particulars strikes me as a little extended," said Jean, "but I will go so far as to grant that a valuable contribution of one sort of dramatic critic is some record of actual performance. But it will have critical value only so far as the writer himself has a defined critical position against which his description can be measured."

"*Any* defined critical position?" asked Alexander. "This strikes me as important, because the whole nature of drama has changed several times in its history, and a critic ought to have to keep up with these changes. Sir Philip Sidney's attempts to make the popular drama of his day look foolish ended in making him look like the fool he was not. Or read that high-buttoned Victorian Clement Scott on Ibsen; at heart, Scott was denying the possibility of a drama of ideas at a time when the theater was shifting ineluctably to that genre. It seems to me the critic must first be clear about what the author is trying to do and judge success or failure in those terms."

"Anarchy, here we come!" exclaimed Jean. "Shakespeare and James A. Herne, Beaumont and Fletcher and Ibsen. Standards, avaunt! Peer Gynt's himself again!"

"I don't think I made my position clear to some of my listeners," said Gerald. "Drama is a highly specialized art form, created for the immediate reaction of an assembled audience. It exists only while the audience is present. The critic is a member of the audience, more articulate perhaps, but a man of his own day rather than Aristotle's."

"Then," said Jean, "he records the prejudices for which the play was conceived."

"If by prejudices," said Arthur, "you mean tastes and attitudes, I would agree. They are all part of the total play. And they are the part to which the man of critical principles is blind. What do you think Aristotle would do if he were to find himself in a theater in New York this fall?"

"He'd be horrified," said Jean. "He couldn't get back to the land of the shades fast enough."

"You," said Arthur, "are exactly wrong. All his disciples have been so dedicated to his conclusions that they forget how he reached them. He was as curious about the effect of a play, the experience of drama, as he was about the best ways of creating that effect. He knew that the first duty of a playwright is to move his audience to belief, not just that the artifice is true but that it is related in some fashion to their own lives. All that talk about catharsis is something more than a pun, you know."

Jean shivered, and asked in disbelief, "Are you suggesting that, if he'd had to sit through what we just watched, he could persuade himself that it had anything to do with a dramatic experience?"

"Everything that goes on in a theater," said Gerald flatly, "has something to do with a dramatic experience. I suggest that we move this discussion indoors."

The four men went into Alexander's clapboard cottage. He

put three sticks of wood into the Franklin stove, found a package of matches under his typewriter, and lighted the fire. The men stared at the flames for a minute and then Alexander exercised the host's privilege of posing the first question.

"Isn't this all rather like a traffic circle?" he asked. "Each of us has entered the line of traffic at his own point, and round we go, and off again right where we each came on."

"Best kind of discussion," Arthur commented.

"I'm serious," said Alexander. "Jean here believes that the dramatic critic must concern himself with certain immutable laws. Arthur believes that the critic must operate within the framework of the culture the play reflects. Gerald sees the playwright as only one member of a complex team offering itself for judgment. And if I have any position at all, I guess it is equally familiar; how well did the playwright achieve what he started out to do?"

"The Intentional Fallacy," said the other three in unison.

Alexander laughed. "I think we've been proving that each of our positions is a fallacy, if it comes to that. I feel rather sorry for that little fellow in his aisle seat; we've really cut him off from everything."

"Except the play," said Gerald. "Except the experience."

Jean made an impatient gesture.

"I think," said Gerald slowly, "that there is a way of testing our points of view. Testing from practice, I mean. I'm pretty sure this won't appeal to Jean, but why not look at a sheaf of criticism involving a number of writers and a span of years, but controlled by a common cultural or political entity. I would suggest, of course," he added innocently, "that we must ourselves know at first hand something of the work being criticized."

"In other words," said Jean, "recent American drama. What fun! We can do research in the contemporary criticism of the play we saw tonight, for instance."

Gerald was about to make a sharp reply, but Alexander cut in. "Neither dull nor foolish as you imply, Jean. Remember that a good many of the creative writers of the adolescent Republic deliberately set out to establish a literary tradition that would express the uniqueness of the American experience, not just in subject matter but in form and technique."

"But wasn't the first native, post-revolution play modeled on *The School for Scandal?*" asked Arthur.

"You mean *The Contrast*," said Alexander. "It certainly looks that way, although the theme was directly opposite to Sheridan's. But move ahead a little. Edgar Allan Poe attacked the great popular success, *Fashion*, partly because it aped the comic style of the British theater, but more because it was 'a counterfeit of life.' I don't think it is forcing the cards to say that he meant a counterfeit of American life. For in one of his essays he encourages American dramatists to start from scratch, to forget all the plays they had seen, to create forms and develop techniques that would express the American-way-of-life."

"Funny," said Gerald. "Eugene O'Neill made almost the same proposal to a producer who asked him to rewrite his father's great success, *The Count of Monte Cristo*. O'Neill suggested throwing everything out the window, all the conventions that had become associated with the play and its genre; seizing anything new that was expressive (he was talking about the movies), and insisting that his collaborators in the physical production use the same kind of creative imagination. Of course, he never wrote the revision, but his other plays show how little he was bound by convention. Even when he revived an old device, like the mask or the aside, he forced it to serve his purpose."

"O'Neill is a prime example of what happens to a dramatist adrift in a theater without—" Jean began.

"We're talking about criticism," Alexander reminded him. "As the politician used to say, 'Let's look at the record.' Poe was far from alone in urging the creation of an identifiable American drama. And there were a number of conscientious dramatists who tried to supply the desired commodity. But it seems to be generally agreed that the first significant American playwright was James A. Herne; surprisingly, he is also the author of the first manifesto of an American dramatic theory that bore fruit, not only in his own work, but in that of other playwrights. And it is a manifesto that developed out of practical experience as an American and as an actor, rather than from a study of aesthetic theory."

"The Untaught Genius," said Jean, "The Sensitive Savage."

"Don't forget," said Gerald, "that Herne was taken up by William Dean Howells and Hamlin Garland and other early proponents of naturalism. They made him into their Theatrical Exhibit A."

"True enough," admitted Alexander. "But if you read his manifesto you will see that their discovery of him was only an added push in the direction he was already heading. I don't mean to denigrate Howells. Like Zola, he was a successful advocate for a kind of drama he could never write himself. In his various editorial capacities he gave aid and comfort to those playwrights who created what he called 'moments of delicious veracity,' chiding those who fell back on theatrical clichés while pretending to give a truthful picture of American life. The word *truth* recurs again and again in the criticism at the turn of the century, and it is quite clear that Howells and his brethren were urging that the new drama be built upon a foundation of documentary verisimilitude."

"Meanwhile, back in Fort Lee," Jean put in, "Thomas Alva Edison was inventing the machine that could alone give full realization to such a soaring aesthetic."

Alexander elaborately ignored him and put several more pieces of wood into the stove. "Of course," he said, "Herne and Howells were only clearing away the underbrush."

"I suppose we should give them E for effort," said Arthur. "Think of the entrenched men of critical principles; for instance, William Winter, who spread purple ink like a squid to blot out any playwright who strayed from the path of romanticism."

"Winter had his virtues," said Gerald. "You might call him a critic of record; he preserves some of the greatest of American dramatic experiences, the performances of Booth and Jefferson. But I'm sure that Alex is going to point out that he was a backwater, a purple backwater, trying to look like the mainstream."

"Backwater he was," said Alexander. "The mainstream had two channels. One could be represented by the iconoclastic Huneker who ranged widely over the arts in general and looked toward Europe when he thought of drama; successors in this channel might be men like Stark Young and to some extent Eric Bentley. The other channel is represented by a critic like Walter Prichard Eaton who was not only concerned with 'delicious veracity' but with somehow bringing this into conjunction with the exciting drama of ideas that had revitalized the European theater. While he could recall *Shore Acres* with pleasure as true to American character and situation, he celebrates *The Great Divide* as, I suppose we would say today, creating a myth—"

"*You* may say it," murmured Jean.

"—a plot at once specifically verisimilar, and true in the abstract. I remind you that we are talking about criticism rather than the works criticized."

"But *Shore Acres*," Jean protested, "*The Great Divide*, and all those things by Clyde Fitch and Edward Sheldon!"

"You're making a point for me," said Alexander. "The dramatic critics, some of them, were ahead of the playwrights. And, since they were without the responsibilities or the burdens of the creative men of the theater, they were surprisingly in tune with the public, with the climate of opinion. They were missionaries from the audience to the entertainers. As much as anyone they were responsible for the renaissance of drama in the United States after the First World War. It was the dramatic critics, not the theatrical producers, who first made the new developments in European stagecraft known to American audiences; it was dramatic critics who founded *Theater Arts Magazine*, the bible of the New Theater movement as *Variety* was the bible of the commercial theater; critics were among the founding fathers of the Provincetown and the Washington Square Players."

Gerald said, "I'm one for giving credit when I can find who deserves it. I always wondered what would have happened to the New Theater movement if it had had to battle the critical principles of William Winter. Instead, it confronted a new breed of judges, who were prepared to create the climate of opinion, as Eric Bentley says, in which the playwrights could live. Some of these new critics were not many years out of college—and don't forget that it was in the first decades of this century that there was the first great awakening of interest in dramatic arts in the academy. Some of these critics, too, had had their expectations broadened and their demands toughened by service in the European Theater of Operation. So, from about 1920 onward, American playwrights began working under scrutiny that was both constant and close, sympathetic and unrelenting."

"I hate to be ghoulish," said Jean, "but remember what we saw in the theater tonight. Was that play a product of this unrelenting scrutiny?"

"Critics don't write plays," Gerald replied. "They do share some of the responsibility for what is produced, however. Think of the close relationship between O'Neill and George Jean Nathan. I'm not thinking of their personal relationship, but it is clear from Nathan's writings that artistically he assumed the role of guide, sounding board, advance man, and sometimes Lear's Fool. And Nathan's running commentary on O'Neill's career in the old *American Mercury* is a remarkable instance of dramatic criticism in process. He never loses sight of the playwright's rank in the theater of the great world, but he never allows it to cloud his judgment, either.

"Incidentally," he went on, "Nathan was a college man, and he was also blessed with a prodigious memory. His mind was filled with the details of old plays and other theatrical experiences, all categorized. He not only recognized a cliché in a play he happened to be reviewing, but he could cite, act and scene, its dozen earlier appearances. And he administered these catalogues of clichés as a cat-o'-nine-tails against any playwright who preferred the easy way to what Nathan felt was the way of truth."

"A slippery word, truth," said Jean. "Your admired theorist, Herne, holds it up as his strange device, along with all the other naturalists. But the truth of art is not necessarily the same as the truth of photography or sociology."

"It's no slipperier than any of the other critical catchwords, nature, for instance, or tragedy," said Alexander. "The validity of dramatic art lies in the experience of the audience."

"Surely," said Jean, "it also lies in what the audience brings to the experience. Did you ever thumb through those volumes of the *Best Plays* of this season or that? Most of the titles you've never even heard of. Yet their audiences presumably found them satisfactory."

Arthur laughed. "I can think of a more horrible example than that, if you want one. For a good many years, *Variety* used to end the season by publishing what it called a 'Critics' Box Score.' It listed all the New York critics, the number of times they went to bat, and the number of times they were right or wrong in estimating the success of the play with the public. It was finally abandoned after some critics protested that it was not their business to predict success. But I think it had a kind of value."

"Critical value?" asked Jean, incredulous.

"In the special area of dramatic criticism, yes. Gerry said a minute ago that dramatic criticism was a valuable record of performance. I submit that it is also a valuable record for the sociologist or historian. We can learn more about the national temper from the popular theater of the nineteenth century than we can from the works of the men generally accepted as its major writers. I think we can learn even more from the public and the critical reactions of those plays. So in our day there is little profit in criticizing Arthur Miller's failure to write a Greek tragedy in

Death of a Salesman; but we can learn a great deal about Miller from a close study of what he actually wrote; and we can learn as much about ourselves from a study of our own reactions to his plays, and the critical analyses of them. Or of Tennessee Williams or Edward Albee.

"Again, a particular instance. What a wonderful picture of the national temper of the thirties can be derived from a reading of the plays of that dismal decade, supplemented by the critical writing about them. You could begin with John Howard Lawson, who not only wrote plays but, like Herne, out of his experience and his convictions devised a poetics for proletarian drama. You can observe dramatists, persuaded by Lawson's theories, creating dramatic actions that expressed the contents and discontents of mass audiences. And then as the years pass, you can see audiences turning away from the proletarian conventions which no longer reflect their sense of truth. And you can see later playwrights—Miller is a good example—adapting Lawson's principles to new conditions and convictions. All this is clear in the critical record."

Alexander threw the remaining sticks of wood on the fire. "Yes," he said, "it has often been pointed out that this is an Age of Criticism. Perhaps that means that a good deal of the creative energy of our writers has been devoted to analysis rather than invention. That might explain Jean's unhappiness, for instance, that our critics are not content to apply established standards or principles to the works they are discussing. Dramatic criticism has become one of the lively arts, itself, and it is not unusual for the critic to appear as a person of the drama too. And his essays are not just records of the adventures of the soul among masterpieces, but of the mind and the heart. And the wit."

"Say the mind and the heart guided by the wit," Arthur suggested. "Some of the best writing about theatrical experience is to be found in those first-personal essays by Bernard Shaw and Max Beerbohm. If they did not found, at least they gave a tremendous push to, a new kind of dramatic criticism in which the faceless mask of the eternal judge is set aside, and all the flaws, and foibles, and prejudices of the critic himself take a vigorous part in the discussion. The result may be idiosyncratic, as Jean would say, but you don't have to read very much before you have a clear picture of the man who is doing the judging and the bases of his judgments. And the reader, perhaps without knowing the work that is being criticized, can react in his own turn. The collected reviews of Shaw, or Huneker, or Nathan are often more entertaining than the plays they discuss, and more enduring."

"We're back to entertainment," said Jean, wearily. "I thought we were talking about criticism."

"This is just another way in which dramatic criticism is set apart from criticism in general," said Alexander, "just as the drama is set apart from the other narrative arts. Any writing about drama that is not in itself entertaining is a betrayal of the subject. Of course it can be entertaining on different levels, just as the drama can. Drama as a term covers everything from *The Comedy of Errors* to *Antony and Cleopatra*, to take the work of just one man. Most playwrights, however, are specialists: they write tragedies or comedies or social dramas or domestic farces. But a critic is expected to have something to say about anything that confronts him; the first-personal critic therefore often comes off best. He can be frank about things that are distasteful to him, or he can fling his cap in the air (as Alexander Woollcott claimed to do) when he is pleased. And the reader is invited to make his own contribution.

"Another American instance. Our theater has always had a place and a warm affection for musical shows. Before the First World War, it was content to import from Europe, or to imitate European successes. But when the legitimate drama began to find its own path in the commercial theater, musical comedy was moved to emulation, and ultimately came up with original and influential works for the criticism of which there was no possible tradition. The best response I can think of to this new challenge to critics was in the week-to-week writings of Robert Benchley. Nobody can say they were not highly personal. Benchley started out in his assumed character of urbane commentator allowing himself to be amused by the gaudy or tawdry timepassers of the twenties. But underneath the urbanity there is an interest in originality and taste, that all this industry, this extravagance, be turned to some purpose. And when the first modern musicals arrived—the ones with character and unity, the ones that recognized the entertainment value of ideas, or tried to capture the spirit of a time or place—Benchley was ready with a sure judgment, a 'secure posture' somebody called it. More conventional critics were baffled, and expressed their frustration by pretending there was nothing there."

"Let me try once more," said Jean. "I can't deny having read people like Benchley and Nathan with pleasure, though I wonder how pertinent their remarks would seem today. But you said many of these new critics came into the theater with academic degrees. Didn't they bring with them any of that sense of the past it is the function of the academy to develop? If not the past in the field of dramatic theory, at least of dramatic practice?"

"But yes, my old one," said Alexander. "If I had to pick the two most influential volumes of American dramatic criticism of our time, I think they would be *The Playwright as Thinker* by Eric Bentley and *The Idea of Theater* by Frances Fergusson. Both are firmly based on the history of drama, both are deeply concerned with the theory of drama, and both benefit from the author's practical experience in theater playing upon the perceptions of the study. And to name these is to suggest others almost at once. There is *Form and Idea in Modern Drama* by John Gassner, who has been playreader and critic, producer, anthologist, college professor. And—"

"Bentley and Fergusson are also college professors," Gerald pointed out. "In fact I would propose that the single most important development in the recent history of the American stage has been the close association of the theater with the institutions of higher learning. Our playwrights are college men, our technicians are trained in theater departments, and most of our critics are college teachers. Not the reviewers for the daily press, of course, but those who publish in the weeklies and the critical journals. When these men undertake a comprehensive view of one of their contemporaries, Maxwell Anderson or Williams or Miller, it has the double value of a reaction to a personal dramatic experience controlled by the discipline of scholarship. It is neither the dissection of a cadaver nor vivisection with a badly honed scalpel. It is the work of a skilled professional with a commitment to his subject."

"I think you can say the same thing about many of the men we dismiss as reviewers," added Alexander. "Some are no longer at the drama desk, like Brooks Atkinson and John Mason Brown. But when Walter Kerr recently assembled some of his daily pieces into a book, *Theater in Spite of Itself*, not a few people remarked with some surprise that it developed a firm and consistent set of principles, or theory of drama, for the mid-century stage."

"Those last three names," said Arthur, "remind me that we are sharing the besetting sin of the American theater. All the critics aren't in New York—or weren't between the wars. For instance, both Atkinson and Brown cut their critical teeth under the glaring eye of H. T. Parker on the *Boston Evening Transcript.*"

Jean's interest seemed to revive. "Hell to pay," he murmured.

"What's that?" asked Arthur.

"He always signed his column with his initials," Jean explained. "I read him when I was in college. 'H.T.P.' Actors said they stood for 'Hell-to-pay.' "

"Your interest in him suggests that he was an Aristotelian," said Gerald.

"Anything but," said Alexander, before Jean could reply, "at least in the proscriptive sense. He tackled everything that came along, old and new, and in any medium. He shifted with ease from a pre-Broadway opening to classical ballet to opera. He recorded his travels through the ancient and familiar German Rhineland, or a twentieth rehearing of Mozart's *Jupiter,* or an encounter with a new playwright on an unfamiliar subject, or an old playwright in a new form with equal assurance. And each column brought fresh illumination to the work and to his readers. He was a critic *omnium horarum,* a crotchety Bostonian Thomas More."

"Still he was a journalist, a reviewer, not a critic," said Jean.

Alexander thought a minute before replying. "I would rather say that he was the ideal American dramatic critic. He brought to bear on his writing a sensitive personal response to the experience of the play, a wide knowledge of the repertory and the criticism of the repertory, an awareness of all the elements of theater and their relation or their responsibility to the author's script, a sense of his own world, and—this above all—a refusal to become jaded by overexposure."

"Well," said Jean, "I've had enough. Good night." He rose and went into the dormitory. The others, since the fire was out, yawned, and followed him with mumbled blessings.

Editor's Note

The essays in this collection have been selected to illustrate the variety of critical experiences that accompanied the development of the modern American theater as discussed in the Introduction. In general they have been arranged according to the date of publication. Chronological order, however, has been violated in several instances: the essay on Clifford Odets is properly read in connection with the essay of John Howard Lawson who formulated the dramatic theory that guided many of the playwrights of Odets' generation; since Tennessee Williams preceded Arthur Miller in attracting the attention of New York playgoers, the essays on these playwrights have been so ordered. The essay by Robert Brustein has been placed at the end of the collection because it returns to the issues of drama as literature raised in the opening essay by James A. Herne.

I

JAMES A. HERNE

Art for Truth's Sake in the Drama

Those who have preceded me in discussing the question of Art for truth's sake are largely teachers in the technical, or professional, meaning of the term; they are specialists, scientific experts, commissioners from educational bureaus, professors from universities, scientific agriculturists, essayists, chemists, students of sociology in all its complex forms, contributors to sociologic work along different lines and through all its intricate ramifications—musicians, painters, sculptors, and writers—and each has given a scientific analysis of his art, its truth and its mission.

It is not to be wondered at, therefore, that I approach the task set me with extreme diffidence, and with a reasonable doubt of my ability to properly state myself here.

It is true that I have written several plays, two of which have commanded more than ordinary attention from thinkers. I have been accorded a place among the leaders in what is known as the new drama and the new school of acting. I am not, however, a teacher, except as I may teach through my work. I am not a scientist; I cannot give you a scientific analysis of my work nor explain to you scientifically how it relates to and affects society or the home.

I am an actor who possesses the additional faculty of being able to write and produce his own plays, but still an actor and not a scientist. That I have, through my work, helped some men; that the influence of my work has been felt in some homes and thus in society, I know, but I cannot explain why. I doubt whether I shall be able to explain to you what constitutes art, in its scientific sense, or what is really meant by "Art for Truth's Sake" or its relative strength and value as over and against "Art for Art's Sake."

I know what constitutes truth in my own work; I know when I write true and when I act true; I know the value of every word

Reprinted from *Arena*, XVII (1897), 361–70.

set down for me to speak; I know the value of every inflection, of every intonation, of every look; I can pick out the false notes in my own work or in the work of any other actor or dramatist as readily as a musical director can detect the false note of a singer or of a musician, but I do not believe I can explain *how* I know all this. Mrs. Herne, to whom I said as much, replied: "A skilful blacksmith may forge a very remarkable piece of ironwork; he knows the value of every stroke of his hammer, the value of the heat and cold to which he subjects it; he knows how to turn every bit of the delicate scrollwork, and when he has completed his task he knows the value of the whole, and he appreciates its beauty. It is a work of art, but he can no more explain to you how it came to be a work of art, than he can tell you how the ancient smiths came to conceive the wonderful iron doors and gates of their castles and their churches."

"Art for art's sake" seems to me to concern itself principally with delicacy of touch, with skill. It is aesthetic. It emphasizes beauty. It aims to be attractive. It must always be beautiful. It must contain no distasteful quality. It never offends. It is high-bred, so to speak. It holds that truth is ugly, or at least is not always beautiful. The compensation of the artist is the joy of having produced it.

"Art for truth's sake," on the other hand, emphasizes humanity. It is not sufficient that the subject be attractive or beautiful, or that it does not offend. It must first of all express some *large* truth. That is to say, it must always be representative. Truth is not always beautiful, but in art for truth's sake it is indispensable.

Art for art's sake may be likened to the exquisite decoration of some noble building; while art for truth's sake might be the building itself.

Art for truth's sake is serious. Its highest purpose has ever been to perpetuate the life of its time. The higher the form of expression the greater the art. Vereschagin uses his masterly art to express truth. There is none of the "pomp and circumstance of glorious war" in his battle pictures. They reproduce war as it is. Tolstoy uses his art for truth's sake; so do Howells and Enneking and Hardy and Sudermann; and so does Whitcomb Riley. And so did Browning and Lanier and other great masters of art. But in expressing a truth through art, it should be borne in mind that *selection* is an important principle. If a disagreeable truth is not also an essential, it should not be used in art. Mr. Howells has the art of selection in a remarkable degree. Mr. Enneking says: "The Ideal is the choicest expression of the Real." Truth is an essential of all art. I do not well see how there can be art without some truth. I hold it to be the duty of the true artist to state his truth as subtly as may be. In other words: if he has a truth to manifest and he can present it without giving offense and still retain its power, he should so present it, but if he must choose between giving offense and receding from his position, he should stand by his principle and state his truth fearlessly.

In all art, ancient and modern, that which is in touch with contemporaneous life adheres closest to truth, because it is produced through some peculiar social condition. The romancer finds but little to inspire him in typical life, he therefore deals with the exceptional life, and draws largely upon his imagination and upon the romancers who have gone before. He loves the "lady of romance with her falcon," "the sleeping troubadour," "the knight and his squire." He loves the blare of the trumpets and the clang of the arms of romance; and while, if he be an artist, he must start with truth for the basis of his theme, he cannot adhere to it, for if he does his heroes and heroines, knights and ladies, will speedily become mere men and women, and his romance reality.

Perhaps I can best further illustrate my subject by talking of that about which I know the most, my own work.

My experience has taught me that there has always been some truth in the drama—a grain it may be, but nevertheless some.

During the first twenty years of my career as an actor the literature of the stage was limited. We had any quantity of plays, but not much literature, and absolutely no differentiation or characterization. It is true that we had the plays of Shakespeare, Goethe, Schiller, Goldsmith, Sheridan, Knowles, and other great dramatists. These plays were of course exceptional in quality, and were known as "the *legitimate drama*." But in the main we relied upon what was called "the *standard drama*," containing any number of miscellaneous plays of more or less merit, by any number of miscellaneous authors of more or less merit. We had tragedy, melodrama, domestic drama, spectacle, and farce. The standard drama of that day was a drama of plot rather than of purpose. The dramatist was concerned first of all with his plot. A play without a plot could not have obtained a hearing twenty years ago. In fact it is pretty hard work today to get a hearing for a play based upon theme and character, and depending upon treatment and not upon plot; but twenty years ago such a thing would have been impossible. And so, while it is true that we had some excellent plays, they each had a plot, a hero, and a villain, and always ended with virtue triumphant. The hero always married the heroine, and the villain was always foiled before the final curtain fell. The characters in these plays were of a necessity more or less artificial.

The system then in vogue was the "star system," that is, a star actor traveled from city to city and presented the plays of his repertoire with the assistance of the local stock company, instead of with his own company, as is the custom now. We had some marvelous actors in those days, when you consider the material they had to work with. In many instances they actually made those artificial characters human, and those plotty plays real.

The stage sword-combat was one of the essentials of the standard melodrama, the authors having no less an authority than Shakespeare for precedent. We used to gather in the wings to watch two tragedians fight the combat in the last act of Shakespeare's *Richard III* or *Macbeth*, a very laughable affair to me now, but very real to me then; and those actors, although they had studied and rehearsed every blow, and knew just when and where to strike, thrust, parry, and guard, were very much in earnest when night came and the battle was on.

The grandest actor I ever saw was Edwin Forrest, but he was a grievous disappointment to me in the combats at the end of the tragedies; he said they had no value, and he dismissed them with a few simple blows. Edwin Booth cared little for the combats, except for the duel between Hamlet and Laertes. He was an expert in the use of the foil, and was very particular that his Laertes should be worthy of his steel; but as a whole he expressed the poetry and philosophy of Shakespeare's plays intellectually, in his own marvelous personality, and suppressed or simplified that in them which was obvious or theatric. It is told of him that being asked what in Shakespeare impressed him most, he replied "The level lines."

On the other hand, we had tragedians who felt that Shakespeare, like some of the authors who came after him, wrote his tragedies having in view the sole idea of the stage combats in the last act; and they acted them after that fashion. One I have in mind who, whenever he played Richard III or Macbeth, used to place extra swords at both wings of the stage, in order that the fight might not be curtailed through the breaking of a sword. With him an actor might omit some of Shakespeare's lines, but he must not miss a blow of the combat. Imagine Macbeth and Macduff coming together in Birnam Wood or in some other wood, to fight to the death, having previously hidden extra swords in all the trees.

Personally I never cared much for the heroic drama. I have appeared in the entire round of its leading characters. Strange as it may now seem, I have played the Romeos, the Claude Melnottes, the Armand Duvals, the Charles Surfaces, the Benedicks, the Cliffords, the Petruchios, and all the rest of the fascinating heroes of the legitimate and standard drama, and I was never such a *very* handsome man, either. I was pretty bad in most of them, I guess. They never appealed to me seriously.

The domestic drama, on the contrary, always appealed to me; the simpler the play the better for me. The more direct the talk, the more earnest I became. When I had a sailor, such as William in *Black Eyed Susan*, or as Ben Bolt, to play, or a peasant like Martin Haywood in the *Rent Day*, or like Tom Bobolink in *Temptation*, I was at home. In characters like these I never failed to impress my audience.

Then came the Dickens drama, and I played Ham Peggoty in *Little Em'ly* and made the actors cry. And why? Because the author was human, and the character real, and I did not act it from the conventional actor standpoint, but from the Charles Dickens standpoint. Later on I traveled as supporting star with the famous Boston actress, Lucille Western, and I played Bill Sikes to her Nancy Sikes. A little girl once stopped Miss Western on Broadway, New York, and said: "Miss Western, I hate that Mr. Herne, he's such a brute; he always makes *you* cry." After a while I commenced to travel alone, and I played a repertoire which included several Dickens characters—Caleb Plummer, Dan'l Peggoty, Capt'n Cuttle, and others. Charles Dickens was a great man. His characters are not always typical, and some of them are grotesque, but, oh! so representative, so full of humanity, so full of the great personality of the man, so positively art for truth's sake. I feel that I owe much to Charles Dickens. I feel that reading his books, and loving them, and acting some of his characters, have helped materially in my dramatic development.

Then came Dion Boucicault, a very exceptional actor as well as a very remarkable dramatist, with his beautiful pictures of Irish peasant life. *The Colleen Bawn, Arrah-na-Pogue, The Shaughraun,* every one with a plot, every one with its stage hero and its stage villain, but ah! so charged with Irish atmosphere, so fragrant with the breath of the shamrock that you might shut your eyes and listen, and imagine you were in Ireland. And then such a plea for humanity (for humanity, like truth, is universal), for the common things of life, and for the common people of Ireland!

And at length it came to pass that I wrote a play myself, and Mrs. Herne called it *Hearts of Oak. Hearts of Oak* was a new departure in playwriting, in that it contained neither a hero nor a villain. It had a plot, but it had no hero and no villain, and one of the chief characters in the play was a one-year-old baby. It was a simple story of Marblehead folk in its whaling days. It was a bit of crude construction, but it touched a sympathetic chord somewhere and it was a great success. I next wrote *The Minute Men,* a story of colonial times, taking in Paul Revere's ride to Lexington, the battle of Lexington, and the stand at Concord Bridge. Mrs. Herne had a glorious character, Dorothy Foxglove. Unquestionably *The Minute Men* was a step nearer being true than was *Hearts of Oak,* but it was not nearly so successful. In fact it was a financial failure.

My next exertion resulted in a play called *Drifting Apart,* a story of Gloucester fisherman life, and it was another step forward. Its weakest point was its comedy element—a stage soubrette and a stage funny man. I never could write stage comedy; I can write humor—the humor born of the intensity of life—but I cannot write stage comedy. This play failed financially, chiefly, I now believe, through lack of good management and my inability to get a proper placement for it. Nevertheless it proved to be a tremendous potentiality let loose. Mrs. Herne's Mary Miller in that play was flesh and blood and bone, and those who have seen her in that wonderful impersonation will never forget the humanity in *Drifting Apart,* nor the art for truth's sake in Mrs. Herne's Mary Miller. As I said, "it was a potentiality," an unconscious potentiality which attracted to us a sympathetic man, now an esteemed friend, who in turn brought others, and our lives were broadened and bettered, for through these friends we learned that we had been unconsciously working along the lines of thought held by some of the great modern masters of art.

Again "the muse labored," and it brought forth a very imperfect drama-child, which we called *The Hawthornes*. But before *The Hawthornes* matured, *Margaret Fleming* was born, full-fledged, the epitome of a powerful but savage truth. Every theater door was slammed shut against this play, and we took the little Chickering Hall on Tremont Street in this city of Boston and gave a *Margaret Fleming* season of two weeks, for the few who were ready to receive it. The play was faulty, didactic in places, but there has been nothing *just* like it given to the stage, before nor since. Mr. Howells called it an epoch-*marking* play. Not an epoch-*making* play, remember, but an epoch-*marking* play.

In the character of Margaret Fleming, Mrs. Herne made the supreme effort of her life and reached the crowning point in dramatic art, but neither the writing nor her work was understood, except by a few persons, and so *Margaret Fleming* was reverently laid away to await the unfolding of a more general appreciation of all such work. It stood the test of dignified approbation and the jeers of scoffers. It has no apology to offer for daring to live, for live it will; its silent potentiality is working slowly and surely. Mrs. Herne can afford to rest upon that masterpiece; certainly there can be no higher ideal of art than she aimed to reach in *Margaret Fleming*. Form, color, love, maternity, truth—she gave her highest expression of all of them in that play.

Disheartened but not altogether discouraged, I turned again to *The Hawthornes*. Mrs. Herne had gone with two of our daughters to spend a few weeks of the summer at Lemoine on Frenchman's Bay in Maine, and she insisted that I should come there and work on the play, and get the benefit of true color and Maine atmosphere—and I went. What an exalted idea of God one gets down in that old pine state! One must recognize the sublimity which constantly manifests itself there. It is worth something to live for two summer months at Lemoine on Frenchman's Bay— that beautiful, inconstant bay, one minute white with rage, the next all smiles, and gently lapping the foothills of old Mount Desert, with the purple mist on the Blue Hills in the distance on the one hand, the Schoodac range on the other, the perfume of the pine trees in every breath you inhale, the roar of the ocean eight miles away, and the bluest of blue skies overarching all. In such a spot a man must realize, if he never has realized it before, that he and this planet are one, a part of the universal whole.

Under the influence of such spiritual surroundings *The*

Hawthornes struggled to adapt itself to a new environment. It sloughed off its old skin and took on new form and color. Its stage people began by degrees to assume the character and affect the speech of the typical men and women of Maine, imbued with all the spirituality and intensity of coexistent life. Stage traditions vanished. *The Hawthornes* lost its identity and emerged a survival of the fittest, and Mrs. Herne called it *Shore Acres*.

I have been autobiographical because I wanted to show how persistent a force truth is, and how it compels the unconscious medium to express it. I did not set myself the task of writing *Shore Acres* as it now stands; it grew, and I grew with it; and while I did not realize all its spirituality until its stage presentation set that spirituality free, still it must have had possession of me while writing, or I could not so have written.

When I sat down to write *Hearts of Oak*, I did not say to myself, "I'm going to write a play in which there shall be neither the traditional stage hero nor the stage villain." They are not true and therefore did not assert themselves, did not persist—that's all. Such characters do not exist in life, nor do they appear in any of my plays.

Art is a personal expression of life. The finer the form and color and the larger the truth, the higher the art.

Hamilton Wright Mabie, in his *Short Studies in Literature*, gives one a very broad and yet a very comprehensive insight into the world of art. "Genius," says Mr. Mabie, "is personality, but not individuality. The greatest genius is he who infuses the largest personality and the least individuality into his work. He will never express himself, nor exploit his idiosyncrasies, but his work will radiate his personality, which is his soul."

Art is universal. It can be claimed by no man, creed, race, or time; and all *art* is good. It serves its time and place, and fertilizes the art to come. The artist of today is the medium for the expression of the art of today, fertilized by race memories of past ages of art—more perfect by reason of the struggles, the failures, the inferiority, and the sublimity of ages of art.

Art for art's sake and art for truth's sake, in the last analysis, it seems to me, are identical.

Art for truth's sake is the higher art, because it contains a larger degree of the vital principles of fertilization. Its race quality is its supreme quality, and therefore it will better serve the race and the art to come. Mr. Mabie says:

To express some part or aspect of absolute truth in the speech of the day is the task of all who express themselves *powerfully*, through art. The truth does not belong to the time, for truth is for all time; but for the form which that truth shall take, the greatest artist must depend upon the age in which he lives.

But before a man can impart a truth he must himself be of the truth, and before a man can receive a truth he must have the consciousness of truth within his own being.

Artists are products of the time. The exceptional singers, poets, painters, sculptors, novelists, actors, and others are being constantly impelled to strive for excellence by the potentiality of all the artists, great and small, who have gone before. Goethe saw this, when he said:

People are always talking about originality—but what do they mean? As soon as we are born the world begins to work upon us, and this goes on to the end. And after all, what can we call our own, except energy, strength, and will? If I could give an account of all that I owe to great predecessors and contemporaries, there would be but a small balance in my favor.

The race is the mother of the artist.

"Art," says Mr. Mabie, "is the expression of a man's whole nature and life, something that grows *out* of *him*, and not something which he puts together with mechanical dexterity."

I stand for art for truth's sake because it perpetuates the everyday life of its time, because it develops the latent beauty of the so-called commonplaces of life, because it dignifies labor and reveals the divinity of the common man.

It is generally held that the province of the drama is to amuse. I claim that it has a higher purpose—that its mission is to interest and to instruct. It should not *preach* objectively, but it should teach subjectively; and so I stand for truth in the drama, because it is elemental, it gets to the bottom of a question. It strikes at unequal standards and unjust systems. It is as unyielding as it is honest. It is as tender as it is inflexible. It has supreme faith in man. It believes that that which was good in the beginning cannot be bad at the end. It sets forth clearly that the concern of one is the concern of all. It stands for the higher development and thus the individual liberty of the human race.

II

WILLIAM DEAN HOWELLS

Some New American Plays

A certain range of American and English plays which I have lately been seeing seem to divide themselves, broadly, into two sorts quite according to their nationality: the domestic sort and the society sort. The distinction applies both to such realistic and fantastic satires as *The Admirable Crichton*, *Whitewashing Julia*, and *Candida*, and to such widely differing pictures of our own life as *The County Chairman*, *Her Own Way*, *Glad of It*, *Our New Minister*, and *The Other Girl*. The English plays have to do with man as a society man, both in the narrower and the wider sense, and the American plays have to do with man as a family man; and I hope that a little thought about them will confirm the reader in any impression he may have that with us the main human interest is the home, and that with the English the main human interest is society. But lest we should be unduly proud of our difference from the English in this point, I hasten to suggest that this is because in the narrower English sense we have no society, and if we have a great deal of home, it is because we are still almost entirely rustic in origin, and preponderantly simple in our conceptions of happiness. In the wider sense we certainly have society; and it is a defect of our playwrighting that it does not carry over from the home to humanity. Its interest does not live from man to man, but from men to women, and from women to men; it has no implications; its meanings are for the given time and place only. When it comes to artistic merit in the plays, we have still less reason for national pride. Few of the American plays will compare with the English, in dramatic art, though I think one or two of Mr. Clyde Fitch's recent plays will compare well with the best of them.

I was especially interested in *Her Own Way* because it added the final touch of proof which convinced me of the truth of what I have been saying, and turned my latent theory into an opinion

Reprinted from *Harper's Weekly*, January 16, 1904, pp. 89–90.

which I was at once eager to urge upon others. Here was, if ever there was, an American society play, and the motives were those which animate the sex which has such society as we have in its keeping. The ambition to get on and up was in the foreground with the thoughtless and restless young wife, and her delightfully ridiculous mother, and the desire to give her the means darkled in the background in the disastrous speculations of the husband and son-in-law. Of course there was the fine girl who, being already up and on, could afford to respire an atmosphere of womanly dignity, to wish to give herself in unselfish love to the man of her heart, and to give all she has to her wretched brother when he has ruined himself to gratify his wife's senseless aspirations. But when it comes to the operation of the motives, one perceives that the real interest of the play is domestic, and that the interest does not pass the instance. The family ideal pervades it, and the whole family insists on getting itself represented. At any rate I prefer to believe that Mr. Fitch was instinctively yielding to this insistence, and not merely indulging his desire to do the scene, when he did that admirable little scene of the children's birthday dinner which opens the play. It is not the less admirable because the children are mostly spoiled brats, but perhaps the more so, and they are such natural children that the children who do them have no difficulty in doing them perfectly. Their mother is a spoiled brat, too, and when opportunity comes in the crying and scolding and screaming scene with the husband who owns that he has muddled her money away, she too is so natural that the actress has no difficulty in doing her perfectly. In her and her mother, and her cousin who serves as the villain of the piece (a very frank scoundrel), the obvious pretence is that the question is social, but the fact is always that it is domestic. It scarcely transcends in its suggestion the four walls of the house where the action passes, and it reaches the spectator only through the domestic atmosphere which so thoroughly involves American life. The villain himself practices his darkest misdeeds that he may win the fine girl for his wife, and make a home for her which shall be her kingdom, and in this he is morally of the same fiber as the gallant captain who goes out to the Philippines, and in a process of our benevolent assimilation has both his arms shot through and has to let her take him in hers when he comes back.

It was almost the only moment in the play when I could have accused the author of excess, or not have owned that he was giving me evidence of his growth as a dramatist and a student of human nature. I thought he went far in *The Girl with the Green Eyes*, but in *Her Own Way*, he goes farther and always on the right road. I am not saying that he does so consciously; perhaps no one gets on consciously; and I am still vexed with a suspicion, which may be unworthy, that he does not much mind doing a bad thing aesthetically, if he thinks he has to do it. But all through this play I realized that I was witnessing the work of a man who was more and more sensible of the two kinds of conscience which a man must almost equally have if he will go to the end of the right road. Mr. Fitch's errors, indeed, are of a sort that can be promptly put behind him and forgotten; they have the property of displeasing the public so entirely that they are not even remembered against him. The rule of his production seems to be now a good play and now a bad play, and they follow each other in such swift succession that the good ones instantly blot out the sense of the bad ones. I am not of those who would make his fertile invention a reproach to him. Rather, I think it is something for us to be glad of, for in a way his rapidity supplies our numerical defect of dramatists. Besides, fertility is hardly a fault in a dramatist. Lope de Vega wrote plays all but without number; Goldoni wrote them by scores; Scribe did them by hundreds; and the dramatists who live in a few plays are apt to be the dramatists whose other plays have been lost. Mr. Fitch seems to have the gift of getting New York, or the spirit of New York, not only recognizably but unmistakably upon the stage. Some how, he has this gift, and I think it a great one, for of all the world's capitals, New York is the most difficult to seize in that essence by which she differs from the others. This is so impalpable that it seems almost aerial, it seems almost ethereal. It is a glancing light, a flying odor, but Mr. Fitch knows how to capture it and imprison it in a volatile moment. The light may be lurid and the odor offensive, but that is beside the question.

He has caught it again and again in his very newest piece, *Glad of It*, which I found still more convincing of his growing power and skill. It was certainly no slight feat to grasp all those fugitive details of a certain order, or disorder, of New York life, and reduce them to a unity which had form and life. But this was what Mr. Fitch had done in his comedy, which with all its farcical excesses had still the complexion of comedy, and with all its extravagance was not unnatural. There were times when it seemed to splay helplessly about, but it arrived individual and shapely, and in the retrospect it showed like a work of art. If its vulgarities made the flesh creep, they were vulgarities of the author's observation and not of his invention, and he was no more trammelled in the immoralities than in the vulgarities of his material: his shoppers and shopgirls, his actresses and their "angels," his floorwalker and stage manager, and the frightful squabbles of their loves and hates. It was as if he had said to himself, that if he were going to do this thing, he would do it unsparingly; he would not put a pretty face on it; these mean and ugly passions should not even wear tights, but should show themselves naked in his scene. It was his sole duty, if he regarded their representation as a duty at all, not in any wise to tell flattering lies about them; and he has told the truth to the extreme of letting his shopgirls and chorus girls scold and scream and even swear, when it is their nature to. He has sufficiently defined the fact that others whose nature it is not to, do not indulge these violences; just as in *Her Own Way*, he distinguishes society women according to their temperaments and ambitions. The play imparts an extraordinary sense of vitality, of life crude and raw, but most potently gifted in getting there, whatever the destination may be. It is as naïvely pretty and sweet in certain rather spare moments as it is naïvely coarse and selfish in certain other moments which are rather lavish. It is full of the riot of the competition which is the motive of our commercial and political life, and such social and professional life as it shows is seen distinctly as *business*. From first to last it is business which rules the aspirations and intentions, not less in the heart of the good girl who will do any good thing for her lover, than in the heart of the bad girl who will do any bad thing for herself, and will even "marry temporarily" the man she is betrothed to, in order to marry finally the man she really wants. A multitude of things are got into the scheme of a shopgirl blazing into a theatrical star, and then quenching her own light with the fool wilfulness of a wanton; but I do not feel that too many things were got in. There was a vivid and incessant play of invention, but there was no sense of repetition except in the rehearsal scene, though perhaps the love-material was rather eked out at the last. Mr. Fitch's last acts, indeed, are so apt to give way under him that I wish he could invent some means of not having any last acts; I think the dramatic effect would be better, notwithstanding the generally accepted convention of their necessity. What one can more seriously say of the piece, even with its last act, is that it is vastly amusing, and even if sadly amusing, still amusing. Of all its amusing passages, it seems to me that those embodying the shopping scene, with the shabby motives of the shoppers worked, as it were, by the rising and falling elevator, were the most amusing; or there, at least, the pang of regret was faintest. It was such a scene as Miss Beatrice Herford might have imagined and presented, but being adapted to the stage, and not to the ends of her more delicate art, it was so finely done. Much the same might be said of the twilight scene on the veranda of the seaside boardinghouse, with the mosquitoes stealing upon the gossip, and inarticulately recognized by the slapping long before their presence was acknowledged by a word.

I hope Mr. Fitch will go on giving us more and more plays, since he seems apt to work free of his faults in that way; and I wish Mr. George Ade would make haste to get *The County Chairman* behind something truer as quickly as Mr. Fitch wipes out a bad thing with a good one. The figure of the chairman himself is what redeems the play, but, excellent as he is, he is not sufficient to do all the work. The chairman is a genuine product of our political conditions, and as Harold Frederic discovered, now a good many years ago, he is where he is more for power than for spoil. Mr. Ade imparts the Midwestern quality of his chairman in characteristic crises, and he does not altogether disable our belief in him by attributing to the whole-souled, cynical politician, in a certain exigency, the moldy motive of an unaging young love for the wife of the bad deacon whom he is trying to beat for prosecuting attorney. But all the same the motive is too moldy for use by any but a theatrical playwright. I was troubled in several events of the piece, by the fear that the stage had prevailed too much with the caustic wit, the unerring realist of *Fables in Slang*, of *Pink Marsh*, of *Doc Horne*, of *Artie*; and that he had done what it wished him to do, rather than what he wished himself to do. There was a whistling and a too opportune boy who had come out of the property room, and there was a troop of Indiana villagers who had been translated from a comic-opera chorus for the purpose they were put to. The purpose was such as sopranos and contraltos are never put to in the Middle West, as I recall it; for women take no part in politics there, though they sometimes do so in the East in emulation of Englishwomen politicians. In democracies, women stay at home during political campaigns, quite as much as if the campaigns were military, and the Middle West is distinctly a democracy in this respect. There is indeed one fine instant in which the youth of both sexes mingle in Mr. Ade's play, not only probably, but inevitably, and all flock to see the five-ten express come in, and enjoy the one excitment of their forty-eight-hour day. That is like a touch in some of the *Fables*, and there is a preciously worthless darky in the piece, who is like a vision of the real thing from *Pink Marsh*. There is also an admirable sage in butternut who

> Obeys at eve the voice obeyed at prime

when it calls to the saloon, and who otherwise spends his un-broken leisure on a bench under a tree. He is beautiful because true, but the rest, except the county chairman himself, are not true, even when they are beautiful. Of course all this is not say-ing that there are not many laughs in the piece, or that in spite of the structural unnaturalness there is not much naturalness in it; but it was as if, being perplexed in the extreme by the theater's insistence as to what a play was, the author had yielded, and let it make something out of his material which, if it was a play, was hard work for the enlightened imagination, and with all its cheer must be a grief for the judicious.

There were really some things in it that no one but Mr. Ade himself could fitly characterize, and I should like especially to have him try his trenchant hand on that boy who has whistled his way through so much rural drama, to such unmerited per-manence that my expectation ached for him throughout *Our New Minister*, though it ached in vain. Many other things that I could have expected were there, and I think the audience liked them when it got them, largely because it had been looking for them. It was a very simple-hearted audience, which one could easily love, and it filled the popular theater where the piece was given fairly well. It roared throughout at the Yankee village types represented, and stood a lot of preaching with the interest which the average American still feels in preaching, especially when it assails the old theologies and quotes scripture against them. Charity for the erring was the theme of these generous homilies, so unsparing of bigotry, hypocrisy, and villainy; and the love interest which is supposed to play so main a part in win-ning the popular favor was of the slightest. The piece, though perhaps new in New York, was not new, and I was lured to see it in spite of a feeling that I had already seen it somewhere, by the attribution of the authorship to Mr. Denman Thompson, an artist to whom I was willing to make the offering of almost any risk. Without him we should not have had *The Old Homestead*, sweetest and simplest of the dramas which are native to us, or in their generations *Shore Acres* and *The County Chairman*; and to an author-actor of his rare quality one must be willing to sacrifice much. I do not say that seeing *Our New Minister* was not too much; but I knew that all about me were people who would have been willing to repeat the sacrifice almost indefinitely. I heard them telling one another what was coming next, and apparently finding great comfort in their foreknowledge. For their sakes, one could wish something better than they were having in *Our New Minister*, and something truer than they would have got in *The County Chairman*. They seem to me quite worthwhile, those simple hearts, and I believe their heads are not unworthy of the best the drama can do for them.

One was as far from them as one could well get, both in the action and the audience at the house which witnessed the representation of Mr. Augustus Thomas's play of *The Other Girl*, and still remain within the reach of the same dramatic art. Mr. Thomas has come home in this charming comedy from Arizona, Alabama, Missouri, Kentucky, and wherever else he has been in Greater America to still Greater New York, and has given us a society play in which passionate girlhood, Philadelphia propriety, self-sacrificing friendship, athletic religion, and physical manhood are the motives that mingle for an effect purely comic. The piece brims with actuality; it is all here and now; and it has a frankness in the operation of its motives, which is in itself very wholesome and refreshing. It is in obedience to the same law which rules in the heart of Natasha in *War and Peace*, when she is mad to elope with Anatole Kuragin, and in the heart of the society girl who marries the pugilist Cashel Byron in Mr. Bernard Shaw's novel, that Catherine Fulton tries to run away from her betrothed with Kid Garvin the prizefighter; and in this she is no less natural than mystical. But her friend Estelle Kitteridge, who smuggles herself into Catherine's place in the Kid's automobile, and "saves" her, as women are saved in the theater, is neither mystical nor natural, but a fake of the novelist's, long past its first youth. It is a pity, for this is almost the sole blemish of a piece, which within the limits of the supposed case, is delightfully possible, and has many moments of delicious veracity. It sparkles with wit and abounds in humorous satire, which if it never implies a meaning beyond the given instance, is hearty, genuine, and unforced. It is full of laughs, for which one need not afterwards be ashamed, and by this negative praise, I mean almost the highest praise. I could not well give a due sense of the perfection with which each of the persons is characterized, without giving an undue sense of it; but in the case of Kid Garvin, I should say that I do not see how he could be better suggested than in the lying frankness, the manly meanness, the strictly limited magnanimity, and businesslike chivalry of which his strange mixture is compact. He is to my thinking the great triumph of the piece, which has its chief defect in the fake I have mentioned. Among its minor triumphs I should like to mention the Philadelphia father of Catherine, and the absolutely New York actuality of Waterman and his wife. It is easy to mention these persons, but to do them as Mr. Thomas does them could have been by no means easy, even for Mr. Thomas, who has taught us to expect such good work from him.

His comedy pours no such swelling tide of life, life wilful, powerful, forceful, as Mr. Fitch's satire pours upon the scene, but in its one moment of passion, smilingly yet thrillingly recognized, it touches a corner of the heart unreached by the brilliant audacities of the brother dramatist. But here I have confronted two playwrights whom I have been all along saying to myself I would not compare, because that would be useless and senseless, since their qualities are as positive as the defects of their qualities, and a comparison of them could only involve injustice to both. I should like to put the blame on them, as they finally face each other in spite of me, for my intention has been so good. What I can say without regret and without censure is that I am glad to have them both on the New York ground, and to get a notion of how they view it. It is the American ground, with all the American interests densely grouped and vividly foreshortened. I wish they could see above it and beyond it to those wider human interests to which the English dramatists are now inviting our gaze.

III

WALTER PRICHARD EATON

Our Infant Industry

I once asked James Huneker what the new book he was then writing was about. "About the drama," he replied. "American?" I inquired. "I said about the drama," Mr. Huneker retorted, with a Monalisacal smile. Yet he has always been among the first to encourage American effort towards self-expression in all the arts, writing with equal facility and always breast forward about drama, music, and painting; he has a right to his somewhat bitter jest. It is only those of us who have played the Jeremiah; who have raised our voices in loud lamentation over the lost art of acting as exemplified by Booth and Barrett, Warren and Gilbert; who have sighed for the grandeur that was the Boston Museum stock company and the glory that was Augustin Daly; who scorn Clyde Fitch because he isn't Pinero and George Ade because he isn't Ibsen—it is those of us who have not the right to elevate our noses at that struggling little provincial, the American drama. Philip Hale has said that Emma Eames sings "Who is Sylvia?" as if Sylvia were not on her calling list. That is the attitude of some of us toward American plays, the attitude, too, in high places. It is not the attitude to foster a native art.

And it is not justified by the facts.

In years not remote there was, to be sure, no such thing as American drama. In the theater the good men do lives after them; the evil is fortunately oft interred with their bones. The winnowing winds of time separate the chaff, and if there is any wheat it lies finally plain to the sight. But the floor of our theater in past generations lay bare. What did our great actors of the past play, in what roles did they make their mighty reputations, which the graybeards of today use like clubs to whack the head of each aspiring actor of the present who tries to push himself up? Shakespeare, Sheridan, Goldsmith, Robertson, Morton (he of *Box and*

Reprinted from *The American Stage of To-day* (Boston, 1908), pp. 6–26, by permission of Mrs. Elise Underhill Eaton.

Cox), Buckstone, Scribe, Dumas—these are typical names of the dramatists who furnished the dramatic fare for our fathers in the theater. The less said about the native drama, perhaps, the better.

Mrs. Mowatt's *Fashion*, produced in New York in 1845, was perhaps the first native drama of any considerable merit. Epes Sargent furnished a prologue which contained these significant lines:

> Bah! homemade calicoes are well enough,
> But homemade dramas *must* be stupid stuff:
> Had it the *London* stamp 'twould do; but then,
> For plays we lack the manners and the men!

Edgar Allan Poe said the play resembled *The School for Scandal* "as the shell resembles the living locust." But the play had a great success, even in England. It must have contained some truth of observation in its satire of New York society. But even the memory of it has passed away; nor did it even then stem the tide of importations or inspire native successors. Twenty-two years later Augustin Daly wrote *Under the Gaslight*, and shortly after, *A Flash of Lightning*, supposedly realistic dramas of the day. Apparently their realism was all of the "real pump" variety, not much above the level of present-day melodrama. The rescue of the hero who had been bound to the railroad track by the heroine who had been locked in the station was the feature of *Under the Gaslight!* Bronson Howard's farce, *Saratoga*, produced in 1870, somewhat more deserved Mr. Daly's catch phrase for his new theater, "contemporaneous human interest." But even that play was antiquated in a few years. Mr. Daly's own play, *Divorce*, remotely based on a novel by Trollope, produced in 1871, was described as a "satire on the raw, pretentious, and wealth-worshiping society of the young republic." It was very popular, running for almost a season. But it led to nothing—at least it led Mr. Daly to nothing. For twenty years the stage at his theater continued to show the same endless list of adaptations from the French or German, the classic comedies, Shakespeare (rudely mutilated in text and clumsily encumbered with scenery), with now and then a new play from London. *Rip van Winkle* and *Uncle Tom's Cabin* were the only American plays that endured, for reasons other than their dramatic merit, though Frank Mayo's *Davy Crockett* was picturesque and sentimentally effective. Twenty-five or thirty years ago Janauschek was playing

Meg Merrilies, Booth was playing Hamlet and his "classic" repertoire, Sothern was playing Dundreary, John T. Raymond was amusing audiences as Micawber, for dramatizations of Dickens were then the vogue. It was all quite innocent and edifying, no doubt, and almighty artistic, but just what it was accomplishing toward the development of an American drama, or how in its endless repetitions of the same old thing it was leading the theater toward anything new or better, is rather hard to see. When the old folks say to us youngsters, "Alas, the actors are all dead now!" let us reply, "Yes? Well, so are most of their plays. There has been some gain, anyhow. You gloried in your actors then? Of course you did; you had to have something of your own to glory in!"

But, curiously coincident with the rise of Pinero and Jones in England and keeping step with the sudden spread of continental influence, especially the influence of Ibsen, over the English-speaking stage, a native American drama began to struggle up that was not mere sentimental treacle or feeble apings of outworn models, but something like an adult art, something with the tingle of reality about it. American writers began to seize hold of American subjects with more than an infantile grip. Along the path blazed by the comedies of Bronson Howard and his *Shenandoah* came Gillette's *Held by the Enemy*, and then his splendid *Secret Service*, and finally James A. Herne's two pieces of pioneer realism, *Shore Acres* and *Griffith Davenport*, the latter produced not quite ten years ago. Clyde Fitch, meanwhile, had laid hold on Nathan Hale for a dramatic hero and lanced contemporaneous frivolous society, and Augustus Thomas had dramatized various states of the union. With the exception of *Griffith Davenport* (which was very uneven in quality) these plays were accepted by the public; and, having accepted them, the public could not retreat into the past, nor could the playwright. When a child has learned that he can walk, he refuses to crawl. The American playwright had found his legs.

And the problem now is, what use is he making of his legs, whither is he walking? For the road that the American dramatist took when his work was serious work, work that strove for, if it did not always attain, dignity and truth, was the road of realism. And there are many who always wonder, a little needlessly, perhaps, where realism will lead, what beauty or satisfaction it can give to us when its "photographic fidelity" has ceased to be a novelty.

Very few of us, I fancy, who saw James A. Herne play *Shore Acres* fifteen years ago have forgotten the final moments of that play. Old Nathan'el Berry, his troubles laid, his heart at rest, sent every one to bed, walked to the kitchen window and, scratching off a little frost, peered out into the winter night a moment, then made fast the doors, banked the fire, blew out the lamps, and, his candle held high, climbed with slow, aged steps up the stairs to his chamber. At the landing he turned and paused for a last look at the room below, quite dim save for the glow from the fire and the faint flicker of his candle flame. Everything in the old New England kitchen where so much of joy and tragedy had come to fruition, where his life had been lived and his heart almost broken, rested peaceful and still in the red glow, under the benediction of his eye. Then he passed across the bedroom threshold and the stage grew still darker. Through a mist of cleansing tears you beheld for a hushed moment the deserted kitchen and knew the power of silence, the still soul of an empty room. Then the curtain sank. It was pantomime raised to poetry, it was the realism of fact doing the work of language, and doing it for once quite as well. The play is still presented every season, though it was written fifteen years ago. How much deeper or more poetically, you ask, have our playwrights wrought since? How far has the prose drama of contemporary life advanced beyond the point where Herne left it? How much nearer is it to the ideal goal of literature? For surely a domestic pantomime, depending for its effect absolutely on a stage and actors, cannot be considered as literature, for it cannot be printed.

And the answer is to be found, of course, in the native dramas which have been written since. Side by side with an increasing readiness on the part of the American public to patronize and enjoy the more advanced drama of Europe, especially the plays of Ibsen, there has come over the native writers an increasing desire to comment on contemporary life as well as to reflect it; we are beginning to find ideas in our drama. And ideas breed style, for they cannot be expressed without language and form, and language cannot express intellectual processes unless it is carefully chosen or form unless it is nicely adjusted.

But what is an idea? Heine's coachman said, "An idea? Nu, nu, an idea's an idea! An idea's any damn nonsense a man gets in his head!" It is in this sense that critics are supposed to use the word when they speak of the drama of ideas, especially by those people who "know what they like." (Incidentally, the trouble with

such people is that they very seldom *do* know what they like.)
An idea in the drama may be defined as rather more a matter of
purpose than content. It is a thesis, to be sure, an appeal to the
head as well as to the emotions. But in the best dramas it is rather
felt than seen, fused, as it should be, with the dramatic action;
it tells as dignity, giving a weight and purpose to the play beyond
the moment's amusement. It is the author's symbol in his play
that a stage story has its meanings and its problems, too, no less
than life; for the modern author regards his story as a piece of
life. So the idea in *Hamlet* is the tragedy, not of accident and
bodily death, but of the irresolute will, of the mind "sicklied
o'er with the pale cast of thought"; and *Hamlet* can be fully
enjoyed only by stern, intellectual effort. The idea in *The School
for Scandal* is plain enough, and it is not expounded in the screen
scene, which is all some later playwrights have copied from the
play. The idea in Sudermann's *Magda* is individualism. The idea
in each and every one of Ibsen's plays shapes the story, is inter-
woven in the action, rises like strange vapor into symbols. Yet
Hamlet, The School for Scandal, Magda, A Doll's House, are
generally accepted, even by those who know what they like, as
absorbing stage stories. Perhaps an idea in a drama is after all but
a sign that the author has brains.

Well, our American playwrights, since the twentieth century
put on its baby shoes and began to toddle toward boyhood,
have been acquiring brains. And if there have been but one or
two native dramas written since *Shore Acres* with so much of
real poetic value, there have been many written with equal naturalness of detail and greater naturalness of plot and deeper intellectual appeal. Without forsaking that truth to contemporary
life, that realism of speech and character and incident which was
blazed as the path the new American drama should take, our
authors have shown undoubted signs of a growing desire and
ability to go farther, to reflect on what they portray, to make
the facts of life illustrate some truth of conduct, to fashion their
dramas, not with the outworn blocks of stage story, but with the
living problems of the hour. We too, in our modest little way,
are beginning to have a drama of ideas. And, in one instance at
least, a playwright has gone farther still down the rich road of
realism and has found poetry at the end. William Vaughn
Moody has written *The Great Divide*.

Since the century began we have had three plays from Clyde

Fitch that have illustrated not only his femininely facile observation of the surface aspects of fashionable life, but a preoccupation with an idea as well. *The Climbers, The Girl with the Green Eyes,* and *The Truth,* all had a sincerity of purpose and more than a passing interest as mere stage stories. Unfortunately, Mr. Fitch seems destined never quite to keep a play on a consistent level, if that level is high or serious. Theatricalness marred one play, lack of inevitableness the second, and a gross intrusion of buffoonery the third. For two acts *The Truth* is written with a naturalness of dialogue, a quiet, economic, inevitable development, a grasp of character that rival the best prose drama of modern France. Then farce intrudes; or, if Mr. Fitch objects, as he is said to do, that the characters of the father and the Baltimore boardinghouse lady are drawn from life, something so like farce that the effect is the same. The atmosphere of reality is gone, at any rate, the unity of the play is shattered. Yet, with every shortcoming allowed for, these three plays by Mr. Fitch mark an advance in American drama along the road of realism toward literature, toward the drama that can be printed and read, because behind the actors and the painted scene is the idea, the appeal to the intelligence, the firm basis of dignity and purpose.

William Gillette has produced nothing of consequence since *Sherlock Holmes,* a wildly improbable melodrama made marvelously probable in the theater, not alone by the ingenuity of its construction, but by the naturalness of its method in the writing and the acting. James A. Herne is dead. Bronson Howard is also dead. Besides Mr. Fitch, Augustus Thomas is alone of the important men of the nineties still contributing to our stage along the lines then laid down, and his latest achievement, *The Witching Hour,* . . . is at once the most natural, the most thoughtful, and the most interesting of all his works. It is, in fact, one of the best plays yet produced in America. But chiefly it is to the new writers who have arisen that we must look for our native drama in the immediate future. Of them all—alas, not too numerous a band!—William Vaughn Moody seems easily the leader; a judgment one does not hesitate to make, though it is based on a single play. Mr. Moody sprang full-armed out of the University of Chicago, where he was a professor of English, like Minerva from the brow of Jove; and *The Great Divide,* which Margaret Anglin and Henry Miller had brought East from Chi-

cago without attracting any attention by the way, swam into
our ken at the Princess Theater, New York, on October 3, 1906,
like a new planet. Its success was instantaneous with critics and
public. Written in a nervous, highly wrought, imaginative prose
that flashed out similes worthy of Shelley and yet did no violence
to dramatic propriety, the new play gave the beholder a sense
of style and literary distinction as rare as it was refreshing. Discussion waged, and will no doubt wage as long as the play is
given, regarding the probability of the incident on which the
scheme of the action is based,—the continued acceptance of
Stephen, a rough miner, who had come to her cabin bent on
rape, by Ruth, a girl of puritan New England. But, this premise
once granted, the action moves with utter naturalness, with
speed, directness, and a fine economy of method to the end.
Personally, I find no difficulty in granting Mr. Moody his premise; I am willing to grant nearly anything as possible in the ways
of a woman with a man. But if I did find difficulty, that would
not affect the value of the play, which is a drama of two souls
clashing each on each. The external means used to bring them
into conflict does not matter much, for the interest is not there.
As a painter falsifies the light on his landscape to throw some
salient object, the soul of it, into high relief, and thus wins
perhaps a deeper truth, so Mr. Moody might forgivably have
been more careless about probability than he was—if he *was*
careless at all, which I do not for a moment admit.

A drama of two souls, that is *The Great Divide*, a struggle between the old puritan formalism of conscience and pragmatism,
between what William James would call the tender-minded and
the tough-minded temperaments. In certain moods Ruth and
Stephen seem to me very real human beings; in other moods they
are but abstractions transcending the personal, symbols of those
inborn tendencies of soul that underlie all our emotions, all our
reasonings, that are the deepest, the most powerful forces in
human life. No other American play has ever gone so deep, has
ever seized hold of so powerful an idea; and no other American
play has ever wrought an idea into a dramatic story with such
dignity and grace of language, such poetry of image and emotion. One is almost tempted to say that no other American play
has ever found the soul. From a drunken impule to rape, Stephen
rises step by step to nobility, because for him the rightness of
an action is in its result, moral truth is found in his own nature's

shrinking or expansion. Sin may be a steppingstone to salvation, not because of any evangelistic "repentance," but because it shows him the good which he takes, letting the rest go forgotten. Ruth, on the other hand, though a dim, primitive impulse urged her at first to Stephen,—an impulse so deep that by most of us, perhaps, it is never felt, lying far down in our souls, and we say Ruth's action is "grossly improbable,"—was fettered by conscience, that composite of a thousand years of religious and social formalism. The chain of nuggets Stephen paid to the other ruffian to buy her for himself was to her a burning badge of shame, and with true New England chop-logic she felt that she had in some way atoned when by her own toil she had bought it back. It was her scarlet letter, no less scarlet for the formality of a marriage ceremony. It is surprising, in an American play, how little the marriage ceremony figures in *The Great Divide*. Mr. Moody has gone behind it. In this soul-drama externals are burned away, and primal things, becoming naked, become decent, become wonderful. Ruth finally left Stephen for her staid New England home, not able to see the new Stephen who had risen from the old, not able to forget the drunken ruffian who had burst into her cabin bent on rape, not able to win out of error the precious good, but demanding a truth perfect from the beginning, an absolute perfection. And thus she would have wrecked two lives for a tradition and violated the mystic impulse deep in her heart that drove her still toward Stephen. But he would not have it so. He followed her East. He won her fully for himself at last. The soul that faces morning and the rising sun, that sees good and evil, sin and righteousness, as alike but rungs on the ladder of happiness, was finally triumphant. And the poet who wrote this play, his first, is still a young man, promising many new dramas for our stage. He is the most thoughtful, imaginative, and cultured playwright we now boast, and his substantial success should encourage more men of literary training and high ideals to write for the theater. There is plenty of room for them.

Two plays that in the seasons just past have had tremendous vogue are *The Lion and the Mouse*, by Charles Klein, and *The Man of the Hour*, by George Broadhurst. Neither play can take high rank as a finished drama, and neither author is a newcomer to our theater, but both plays illustrate the increasing intellectual drift of the stage. In the former the overshadowing problem of the trusts finds a steady, if feeble and distorted, reflection; in the latter, graft in municipal politics is the theme. In the former Mr. Klein defeats a billionaire magnate by a woman's wit; in the latter Mr. Broadhurst combats graft by finding an honest candidate and electing him. Neither solution, perhaps, is wholly convincing! But fifteen years ago no manager would have dared to set either problem on the stage, nor would it have occurred to Mr. Klein or Mr. Broadhurst to ask him to do so. Realism is pulling even our weaker writers into line with life and stirring up their mental machinery.

To speak of *Ben Hur* or *The Music Master*, the two most popular plays, if the number of performances be taken as a standard, that have gone forth from Broadway in the last decade, as examples of American or any other kind of realism would be to laugh. Why *Ben Hur* has been so enormously patronized, a thing of bombastic rhetoric, inflated scenery, pasteboard piety, and mechanical excitement, one cannot explain without being branded a hopeless cynic. *The Music Master*, a piece of mid-Victorian sentimentality for all the external truthfulness of its setting, of course won its way into all hearts by virtue of the exquisite and compelling art of David Warfield. Public discernment in the theater is a slow growth and starts at the top. Down through each layer of the public you come upon other layers still, to revel in the pasteboard piety of *Ben Hur* or to hail *Way Down East* as a masterpiece in the same breath with *Shore Acres*. The success of such plays at any period is not significant. The critic of the theater, on the watch for new tendencies, for signs of growth, will find significant the success of those plays written by men who have something new to say. Among such writers, besides Mr. Moody, the seasons immediately past have produced Miss Rachel Crothers and Eugene Walter. The former, in *The Three of Us*, displayed a rare feeling for quiet, significant naturalism, even though her third-act scene was the inevitable bachelor's apartment, her villain the inevitable woman's villain who never drew the breath of life. It is Miss Crother's promise some day, perhaps, in stage stories to bring a woman's tact and insight to bear on our vexed domestic problems. Mr. Walter's talent is essentially, almost scornfully, masculine. Sometimes one very nearly accuses him of belonging to the "good red blood" school. His merits are a strong, if untutored, grasp on dramatic effects, and apparently a desire, not always controlled as yet, to tear the fourth wall out of every room, to get life upon the stage even if he has to be rude about it. He has shown us two plays, both in the season of 1907–8, *The Wolf* and *Paid in Full*. The former is a stilted melodrama of the Canadian north woods, but with something of the forest gloom so haunting it that you feel the author's intention to have been greater than his achievement. The latter . . . comes near to being a social study of New York life, realistic, dramatic, informed with a valuable idea.

Other playwrights we have also, and one of them, at least, George Ade, has reflected certain phases of American life as truthfully as could be asked. *The College Widow* was a genre picture of triumphant skill, executed with exuberant yet loving humor. But Mr. Ade has no power of dramatic development. He cannot penetrate the surface. Percy MacKaye, a young playwright of unusual scholarship and unbending idealism, is the only one of our newer dramatic authors to write in verse for the practical theater. Two of his plays, *The Canterbury Pilgrims*, a poetic comedy with Chaucer and the Wife of Bath as the leading characters, and *Fenris the Wolf*, a Wagnerian libretto, have not been produced, but Miss Marlowe has played his *Jeanne d'Arc* both here and in London, and Bertha Kalisch produced his *Sappho and Phaon*, a tragedy. Neither was successful enough to warrant the assertion that Mr. MacKaye is the dramatic poet to lead the wandering tribes of the twentieth century into the promised land of blank verse. Mr. MacKaye's prose drama, *The Scarecrow*, based on Hawthorne's *Feathertop*, seems at present his most effective work, though it has not yet been shown save between covers. Its demands on the scenic artist and on the leading actor are severe, but there is an uncanny suggestion of the supernatural in it and a pathos cross-shot with the grim humor of Hawthorne which ought to place it on the stage. It is the least conventional in theme and treatment of its author's plays, and the most directly wrought. Mr. MacKaye has also written a prose comedy of character, *Mater*, which will be produced by Henry Miller. Here, with light and graceful touch, the author has a little fun with the unbending socialists and political reformers, and in the person of Mater herself, a lyrical child-woman who impersonates her own daughter to aid her son, to the disgust of the daughter and the rage of the son, but who in reality is the most sensible and efficient person in the play, he has created a character of charm and originality. The moral of *Mater* is not, perhaps, quite clear—if that is a fault. The satire is too gentle to point a purpose, save the purpose to show a curious type of New England woman. Mr. MacKaye as dramatist lacks a certain clarity and incisiveness. His plays do not quite *bite*. But no one can spend an hour in his presence without feeling the tonic of his fine spirit, of his sincerity and idealism. Like Mr. Moody, he has the grace of culture and of lyric speech. He will surely find his honorable place on our stage, though it will hardly be by fleeing to Greek or Norse mythology.

These authors, then, who are bringing to bear on the problem of creating an American drama the largest amount of dramatic skill, truthful observation, intelligent reflection, and passion for reality are the ones who are keeping our drama connected with life, who are leading our stage on toward better things by making it a vital force in the community. Only two of them, it will be noted, are poets. They alone have the sense of literary style to strike out beautiful language. *The Great Divide* and Mr. MacKaye's dramas alone perhaps fully bear the test of print. We need not worry, however. Our stage is not yet so flooded with reality that we need alarm ourselves about the drift of realism. We shall need more of it before we need less, and it is not by fleeing reality but by plunging through it that, for the modern mind, the deeper truth is found. Already the intellectual thesis is creeping into our plays of contemporary life. The mere scenic fidelity of Belasco seems tame, old-fashioned. Already Mr. Moody has broken through into spiritual poetry, and Mr. Thomas has brought the occult home to daily life. The realists may very well be left to themselves. They will work out their own dramatic salvation—and ours. They are on the one inevitable road today. Let us leave them with the words of T. E. Brown, the Manx poet, who, in one of those wonderful letters of his, wrote:

> You comfort me much by kind words of sympathy. I hope you don't often find me in a melancholic mood. But now and then I dare say I'm rather like an old cat; "slickin' meeself with mee own slaver." You've seen the like? You stroke them a bit, and they're pleased enough with that for a change. But they go on, slick, slick, slick, till the melancholy is gone, and behould ye! they're out in the bushes after them blackbirds, "as bowl' as bowl'."

There still are blackbirds and there still is blank verse. But just now we must slick, slick, slick.

IV

JAMES GIBBONS HUNEKER

David Belasco

"David Belasco presents Mrs. Leslie Carter!" I read no more. The faded playbill on my desk set whirring the subtle mechanism of memory, and presently I was launched on a little excursion into the past. Psychologists tell us that we live forward, think backward; a formula that neatly divides the past from the future; two aspects of one and the same thing. So the old-time announcement that headed this theater program served the purpose of liberating from my frozen subconsciousness a cloud of recollections which swarmed like moths about a summer lamp. David Belasco was the lamp, and my memories of him the incessant moths; a mere piece of paper that became as potent as some antique and muttered conjuration whose magic evokes the wraiths of vanished years. I saw, crystal-clear, a young man with raven-black hair, eyes so large and luminous that their irises had no defined color, the thick lashes and eyebrows a color-note for the face; the delicate aquiline nose that seemed less Syrian than Assyrian, and a profile that had something archaic and Eastern. You may see such sharp silhouettes on Babylonian or Egyptian tablets and tombs in the British Museum. Exotic, yes; but the vitality that burned in the eyes of the man and his few, significant gestures revealed an intense, concentrated nature, one that could be stopped by nothing short of extinction. And the personality of David Belasco today is not a whit altered—if anything it is intensified; not mellowed, because he was born without angles. He is as much a riddle as he was three decades ago. Personality is an eternal enigma.

This young man was given to wandering about the streets at night. Hard-working in the daytime, after he saw the curtain fall he loved to walk, not alone for the fresh air, but to commune with his thoughts. He was always a mighty wrestler with his ideas. The logic of life implanted in his brain, and filtered

Reprinted from *The Outlook*, CXXVII (1921), 418–22.

through the sieve of heredity, was importunate. Why? it asked, and he had to furnish an answer or feel defeated. Nor were the questions that assailed his maturing brain only those of the theater. He had asked, Why? from the time he began to run away from his mother's apron strings on those "wandering feet," as she satirically yet tenderly described his propensity to disappear daily from the hearth. All of us pretend to some philosophy of life, and the little David began early to construct one. When I first met him, he had definite ideas of art and life, though the crystallizing process was at its commencement. Notwithstanding the simplicity of his speech and bearing, David Belasco is a complex personality.

The paradoxes are many. He was, luckily for him, born a "Sunday child," as the old German saying hath it; and there is in him a generous admixture of feminine sensitivity and intuition, a temperament that feels before it reasons; in a word, he "resembles his mother," the Irish phrase it. Now this responsive and sensitive nature of his—one that has caused him much sorrow as well as joy—presents a masculine surface of so resistent a fiber that it has been as a coat of mail his life long. Many are the battles in which it has protected him. He is an idealist, but his idealism would have proved his undoing if it had not been served by a volition that could never be swerved. It seems strange to relate that such a dreamer possessed pugnacious prowess. This man with a sense of the beautiful could hold his own when necessary. There was once a famous English pugilist among the Belascos. In searching for the salient traits in the personality of David Belasco this little fact must not be forgotten. It is a paradox all the same.

As there is a reason for everything, a peep at his forebears may aid us in the search for the characteristics. There is Jewish blood in his veins, more than enough to furnish the "precious quintessence" of which George du Maurier wrote. This, allied to the Portuguese strain, has, no doubt, lent to his fancy its rich coloring. But it is unsafe to generalize in these matters. There is Arthur Pinero, for example, who is of the same origin—both Portuguese and Jewish. He is all logic and realism; imagination seldom rules in his work. His beaver-like brow betokens the builder, not the dreamer. He is, while eminently the master of contemporary British drama, its least imaginative creator. Of course I mean what is commonly accepted as poetic, fanciful, whimsical, such as the productions of Barrie, Shaw, and the wonderful John

Synge. Dramatic characterization and invention Pinero has in abundance. No one but a playboy of the Western world could have conceived two such masterpieces as *Iris* and *The Second Mrs. Tanqueray*. Nevertheless his Pegasus does not often climb starwards.

The foreign strains in David Belasco have made him true to type. Originally Portuguese, his parents hailed from England. Well known in the theatrical world, a restless race of beings, their gypsy strain has peeped out more than once in their son. He had an actor father, versatile to the point of destructiveness —for versatility is a good servant and bad master; and a mother, the homemaker about whom rallied these diverging units, a central point that gave the inquisitive lad some sense of stability. But always the quest after new fortunes; the far West, the Northwest, large cities and little, the bare hills beneath the few stars, the noisy mining towns and their crudeness. Like his Semitic ancestors, David was a wanderer on the face of the earth before he was out of short clothes. However, there were modifying influences. He came early under the mild and beneficent influence of the Roman Catholic priesthood. California was still semi-Spanish. With his inherited love of all that is mystic, exotic, of rich and ordered ceremonial, of the luxury appertaining to the Lord in the ritual that recalls the Hebrew, even more ancient faiths, it is not surprising that the lad should fall in love with a strange religion. He loves it today. I have heard him speak with reverence and enthusiasm of the mysteries of Catholicism. They soothed and made captive his too centrifugal temperament at the hour when he was most given to flying off at a tangent. He is ever grateful to the sympathetic priest who saw so clearly into his youthful soul. But David Belasco has an older racial pull in him, and it has been the prime factor in his remarkable performances; for a virtuoso in several arts he is, a much greater actor than some he fathered artistically.

Yet I suppose if you asked him what he is, he would promptly reply: "I am an American." It is true. Race manifests itself principally in his aesthetic predilections. For religious dogma he has never cared beyond putting into practice the Golden Rule. But he is a patriot, and from the moment he began to feel his vocation he has never ceased considering the problem of our native drama. And always optimistically. Not a propagandist with drums and trumpets, it will be found after the roll call has been

sounded that David Belasco's contribution to the American theater, both as producer and dramatist, has been of historical importance. He began with a Crummles and pump realism, as was
the fashion of his day, but he is far from all that now. David
Belasco had to submit to the law of growing organisms, he had
to develop, and in his particular case it was either progress or a
perishing of soul and body. He was cast out early on his own
resources. A roving spirit, he was curious of life at all hazards,
and this curiosity sometimes led him into dubious places. He
knew the seamy side of San Francisco. There were moments
when his mother despaired of him. But he was never dissipated.
He frequented barrooms and did not fear other aspects of the
underworld. In his juvenile way he tried to see life steadily and
as a whole, but what he saw sometimes confused his reason.

He loved mankind because he had the semidivine gift of pity.
This transposition of his mobile personality was no adroit sentimental play-acting. David, the would-be slayer of the Goliath
of sin and sluggishness, has never lost his profound sympathy for
his fellowman. At times it amounts to sheer divination. It is his
feminine side in operation. Sometimes it slips into mere sentimentality, and his art suffers thereby. And it is also the keystone
to his success in training his artists; a sixth sense, that serves him
infallibly as an agent of clairvoyance. In his art Belasco is clair-
voyant. He has been called a wizard, but his wizardry deals with
externals; his genuine distinction lies in his ability to comprehend
character.

Consider the inevitable current of his career. "I, too, am an
actor," he could have said, without parodying Correggio, after
he saw Charles Kean. Though the road was obscure, he boldly
ventured forth on its tortuous thoroughfares, and whether as
clown, bareback rider, peddler, newspaperman, callboy, "super,"
actor in small parts, or prompter, he assumed his devious tasks
with a vim that singled him out as one of the foreordained. No
doubt it was a will-o'-the-wisp, this mad pursuit of an impossible
ideal, but striving after the highest is the best intellectual gym-
nastic for a future artist. Nowadays, thanks to the debased ideal
of the theater, the very mention of discipline revolts the soul of
the beginner. Where, indeed, are the glorious examples of yes-
teryear? The only prize to be run for and wrested from an indifferent public is pecuniary success. Let art go hang!

In the days of Belasco's youth the American stage shone like a constellation. There were not only stock companies everywhere, but there were such men and women as Edwin Booth, Charlotte Cushman, Mrs. D. P. Bowers, Mr. and Mrs. John Drew, Barrett, McCullough, Modjeska, Lotta, John T. Raymond, the elder Sothern (most incomparable of comedians), James A. Herne, Clara Morris, Genevieve Ward, Jeffreys Lewis, E. J. Buckley, Maud Granger, Harry Montague, Frederick Warde, Charles Coghlan, Rose Coghlan, Charles Thorne, F. F. Mackay, the two Western sisters, the lovely Adelaide Neilson—the list might be prolonged for many pages. Young Belasco saw these people at close range. He studied them. He worked with that prodigal of talents, Dion Boucicault. He became acquainted with the classics of the drama. He heard Shakespeare where Shakespeare is best heard—on the stage. He was a student at first hand, and, not having the time, he did not trouble himself about the aesthetics of playwriting, but kept that task for his leisure later years, after he had learned more in the fire of the footlights than the professors of the drama can ever tell him. He has always been catholic in his tastes, always receptive to new influences, never rejecting novelty because it wore a repellent mask, instinctively knowing that practice comes before theory, that creation is the parent of criticism.

Let it be said, and it cannot be said too often: The theater is the theater; and if this is a platitude, then engrave it on your memory, for it is a golden platitude. In derision as well as sorrow, some Frenchman said that over the portal of every playhouse should be inscribed this legend: All Reality abandon ye who enter here! Precisely. Though it was meant in a subversive sense, this warning embodies the first law and last of the theater. It must not be real, for reality is a slayer of illusion. It may be divorced from life, divorced from literature, yet remain invincibly itself. The frame is quite rigid. There it is, that bald, cold, empty space which during the traffic of two hours you must fill with what seems like life, else fall by the wayside with those who cannot unravel the secret of the sphinx. It is all so inviting, so hospitable to every form of literary talent; but the laws of the Medes and Persians were not more immutable than are the drastic limitations of the theater. Zola went further when he declared: The theater of the future will be naturalistic or it will be nothing. It is not yet and never will be naturalistic. You may reel off at the tip of your tongue the Three Unities and the

Thirty-six Situations, but the knowledge of these and a thousand axioms besides cannot make of a sow's ear a silken purse. "How to Write a Play" lectures have never taught any one the art of play-making.

During our nocturnal promenades Mr. Belasco opened his heart to me concerning his artistic aspirations. He had not been in New York long, though already recognized as a man of promise. Necessity pinched, for he had a family to support, and in him the domestic virtues had early blossomed. He was then at the Madison Square Theater; it was during the Mallory regime. He worked unremittingly. And not always in congenial surroundings. Theaterland is hardly territory where altruism is indigenous. The struggle for life therein takes on the ugliest semblance; at times buccaneering, with its concomitants, cutting throats, walking the plank, and plundering, seems more merciful. To be sure, there were some noteworthy managers—Lester Wallack, A. M. Palmer, Augustin Daly, Daniel Frohman, J. M. Hill, and a few others—who upheld standards, but then, as now, the rank and file were the same. Charles Frohman, a gentleman by the grace of God, was a close friend of David Belasco even during the time when divided by business interests, and the living manager speaks of his dead associate with unmistakable affection.

As a stage director he always achieved success. There was no disputing his mastery of his material. Years of adapting, rewriting, translating, had endowed him, coupled with his enormous experience, with swiftness in attacking any problem that presented itself and an inevitable tact in the handling of his forces. The principal reason why he has been successful in his fashioning of raw material is that, apart from his technical training, he is an untiring student of human nature. The procrustean theory of training he discards. That way lies the arbitrary, the machine-made. He, if I may be allowed a slight exaggeration, fits his play to his actors. This simply means that he studies the instrument from the keys of which he extorts music. No two humans are alike. Belasco spies on souls. He makes his inferences; sometimes he goes on a wrong tack; not, however, often. He finds what he wants. A touch or two and the organism plays its own tune. He literally educes from his woman or man what is already in both of them. When he encounters a great natural mimetic gift like David Warfield's, he is happy. A hint to such an intelligence suffices. With lesser people he seldom fails, for he varies his procedure with each person.

My personal belief is that he hypnotizes his players—let us call it that for want of a better word—else how account for the many instances of actors and actresses who won success, artistic and otherwise, and have faded into mediocrity when they passed from under his personal domination? I know this has a Svengali flavor, but I am willing to let the statement stand for what it is worth—that under the intellectual supervision of this keen critic artists give out what is best in them. This much may be said without fear of contradiction: There is no precise Belasco method, no particular school; no actor or actress has ever lost his or her individuality; rather has that individuality been accentuated and defined. Mrs. Carter's case is a signal instance, as well as that of Blanche Bates. I have sat through rehearsals at the Belasco Theater when a full-dress rehearsal was as long and torturesome as an initial rehearsal. I have seen this impresario of accents, gestures, and attitudes go through an entire night, till morning found his guests pallid, nervous, irritable, while he was as fresh as his company; his enthusiasm kept everyone vital, everyone save the curious students in the stalls. David Belasco is the last of that old line of stage managers who teaches by personal precept. And I don't mind telling you that I suspect there is concealed in him somewhere an autocrat.

I once wrote of him that if Richard Wagner had collaborated with him in stage management it would have been to the lasting benefit of Bayreuth. The first garish school of stage decoration was an ugly dissonance in Wagner's attempt at a synthesis of the seven arts. Primarily David Belasco is a painter. He wields a big brush and paints broadly, but he can produce miniature effects; effects that charm, atmospheric effects. Nothing so exotically beautiful has ever been shown as the *décor* of *The Darling of the Gods*. Never mind the verisimilitude of the story. The scenic surroundings were more Japanese than the play itself—an attenuated echo of Pierre Loti's exquisite *Madame Chrysanthème*. But the stage was a marvel of evocation. *The River of Souls* brought into the theater a vision almost as mystical and melancholy as a page from Dante's *Inferno*. Truly a moving picture. A proof before all letters! One that since has been paraded abroad as a triumphant discovery of the New Art. In all the theaters I visited at London and on the Continent I saw nothing that had not been forestalled by the genius of Belasco; not the startling lighting effects of Gordon Craig, nor the atmospheric innovations of Reinhardt, nor the resonant decorations of Bakst were novel to me, for I had watched the experiments at the several Belasco theaters, had heard the discoverer himself discourse his theme.

His fastidious taste in music he demonstrated by abolishing music during the *entr'actes*. The double stage, an invention of the fertile Steele Mackaye, anticipated the Munich revolving stage by years and was utilized by Belasco when at the Madison Square Theater. But credit for his innumerable devices, artistic and mechanical, has yet to be given him in many quarters; though the tendency to overemphasize his abilities as a manager at the expense of his dramatic triumphs is deplorable. Mr. Belasco is not a theatrical upholsterer. He is more interested in the play than its setting. That he provides an adequate frame for his picture testifies to his disinterested love of perfection. If a period is to be illustrated, he illustrates it. The exact milieu is his motto. The sumptuous Du Barry epoch, the gorgeous exoticism of the Japanese, the American interiors in *The Easiest Way*, the austere simplicity of *Marie Odile*—four walls, a table, a few chairs, an image of the Madonna, a painting, two or three pigeons, and a small cast—to mention a few of his productions, testify to his sense of the eternal fitness of atmosphere. Nothing ever smacked of certain American scenes more than *The Girl I Left Behind Me*, *The Heart of Maryland*, *Peter Grimm*, or *The Music Master*.

His art has grown in *finesse*. He has become more impressionistic. He suggests rather than states. The contemporary stage, thanks to the rather bleak decorative scheme of Ibsen and his followers, has become simpler in accessories. Despite the color extravagances of the Russian ballet, the furnishings of the drama are more sober than, say, a decade ago. The picture itself has become simplified; formerly one couldn't see the forest because of the trees therein or follow the piece because of its *mise-en-scène*. I have watched plays in fear and trembling because of the cart loads of things on the stage, among which the actors painfully threaded their way. And that, too, was a passing fashion. Everything changes in the theater except the theater itself. George Moore in a recent preface tells a story about Granville

Barker. That ingenious manager, actor, and playwright was explaining to a friend the "mentality of his characters" in a projected play of his, when he was thus interrupted: "Get on with the story; it's the story that counts." In this anecdote is compressed the wisdom of ages as seen through the spectacles of practical Mr. Everyman. For David Belasco the story's the thing.

He has written and collaborated in the writing of many plays. He has had his failures. I recall his *Younger Son*, an adaptation from the German, put on, if I remember right, at the Empire Theater. Something went wrong, though it had several fine episodes. The adapter was implacable; he it was who insisted that the piece be taken off. He was always his sternest critic. For nowadays this play would be a masterpiece. I remember, too, *La Belle Russe*. It was merely sensational in the violent style of its day, and Gallic to the core. However, this is not a record of Mr. Belasco's achievements as a dramatist. He fought hard for recognition and won his way slowly and not ungrudgingly. In his naïve and candid autobiography you may read the unique record of his climb to fortune. He is not without a touch of mysticism; was there ever any one connected with the theater who was altogether free from its harmless superstitions? He believes in his star. Why not? It has hung there on the firmament of his consciousness since he can remember. He won't admit the fact that he hung it himself. But there it is. And, call it his ideal or what you will, he has followed this glowing symbol from the wilderness into the promised land. Nor has it ceased to shine for him. He is as full of artistic projects as he was forty years ago. Happy man to grow younger in his heart though his head is gray! Today the vivid-appearing young man of the late eighties looks like a French abbé in some courtly scene by a pastelist of the eighteenth century. His smile has the benevolent irony of a nature that will never become cynical.

During our walks and talks in those faraway nights I often quizzed him about the Moderns. At that time, instead of writing books about Ibsen and Hauptmann, Maeterlinck and Becque, I was working in the critical trenches, throwing bombs at the uncritical old guard, which would die rather than surrender the privilege of calling Ibsen and the new dramatists "immoral, stupid, cynical, inexpert." Well, David Belasco knew all these revolutionists; he still reads them, as his library shelves show. He knows more about the practical side of Ibsen (for he admires the great Norwegian's supreme mastery of dramatic technique) than do his own faultfinders among the so-called amateur pocket playhouses. We discussed the entire movement—now a matter of history—till sometimes we were hoarse. The truth in the matter is this: David Belasco was literally born and bred in the great dramatic traditions of the golden age. Shakespeare is his god. Then the romantic French theater. And little wonder. Sentiments more than ideas are the pabulum of his plays. He is unafraid of old conventions. He is an abnormally normal man. The New Movement is less a dramatic revolution than a filtration of modern motives into the theater. The Ibsen technique dates back to the inexhaustible Scribe; while the Norwegian leans heavily in the matter of the thesis play on Dumas *fils*. Characterization is his trump card.

Now, problems of a certain sort do not intrigue the fancy of Mr. Belasco. He dislikes the pulpit in the theater. While he willingly admits that in the domain of drama there are many mansions, he is principally interested in what the psychologists call the primary emotions; the setting is of secondary interest. A piece full of black class hatred and lust, like the extraordinary *Miss Julie* of Strindberg, does not appeal to his sensibilities. Why? Question of temperament. Its "modernity" has nothing to do with the matter. It is, with all its shuddering power, too frank, too brutal, for him. He demands the consoling veils of illusion to cover the nakedness of the human soul. If a man loves the classic English school of portraiture and landscape, the suave mellow tones of Sir Joshua Reynolds, the fragile grace and delicious melting hues of Gainsborough, the humid glory of the clouds in a Constable country scene, shall we quarrel with him for not preferring Manet or Degas? Mr. Belasco admires Ibsen, and he appreciates the skill and sincerity of Degas and Manet. But he sticks to his Reynolds and Constable and Gainsborough. Other days, other ways.

He has said: "The true realism is not to reproduce material things; . . . it is to reproduce the realities of inner life." The theater, despite its obvious exteriority, has its inner life. I don't think that Mr. Belasco has cared to explore certain crannies of that "inner life," because the dwellers on the threshold are rather disquieting to behold. Ibsen still speaks in an unknown tongue to the majority. This is not an apology but an explanation. For me the popular play of the day is no better, no worse, than it was years ago. It is for public consumption, and in the theater we Americans like to sip sweets, not to think. In the meantime let us rejoice in the possession of Belasco's rare artistic personality, for he has done so much for our native theater. And on this note I must end these halting impressions summoned from the past by the sight of an old play bill: "David Belasco presents Lenore Ulric in *The Son-Daughter*."

V

ROBERT BENCHLEY

The Musical Theater

The Apollo and the Times Square Theaters, with their adjoining lobbies, are so close together that when you go out in front of one between the acts, you are quite likely to saunter back into the other. In fact, your correspondent did.

It so happened that *Love Birds* opened at the Apollo on the same night that *The Right Girl* opened at the Times Square. *Love Birds* was chosen as the lucky production to be reviewed first in this department because the name of the theater begins with "A."

So much time was spent in front of the two houses before the performance watching theater parties lose themselves that the opening chorus was missed. A great deal of enjoyment may be had simply by standing on the sidewalk and watching the sudden disintegration of theater parties. An automobile draws up at the curb and the two men who have been sitting all cramped up on the little seats pop out at the opening of the door. They each extract a lady and start for the entrance. One couple goes into the Apollo; the other into the Times Square. In the meantime, Father and Mother have been tumbling out of the limousine, and while Father is telling Potter what time to come back for them, Mother is scurrying after Spencer and Evelyn into the Apollo. Father then unerringly picks the Times Square.

There is a brief period while tickets are being presented at the door. Then the ones who chose the wrong entrance appear, looking very sheepish after a bitter argument with the doorman. Great anger is expressed at the rest of the party for not waiting for them. Sometimes they call the whole thing off and go home.

And then another automobile draws up to the curb.

Reprinted from *Life* and *The New Yorker* by permission of the publishers and Mrs. Robert Benchley.

But one can't stand out on the sidewalk during the entire performance, even if one is a critic. And the first act of *Love Birds* was on.

The first act of *Love Birds* is just about what you would expect the first act of a musical comedy named *Love Birds* to be. It always has been. There is a song in which the hero complains that girls aren't like they used to be when Grandma was a girl, during the second chorus of which a young lady comes on dressed as—what do you think? Grandma! Yes, sir, that's what she comes on dressed as, crinoline, parasol and all. It is a riot. On this particular night, the parasol refused to open at the crucial point in the song, a feature which lent just the right touch of novelty to the thing.

There is also a charming scene in which a large lady in red becomes intoxicated.

The stars of the performance are Pat Rooney and Marion Bent, of vaudeville fame, and if you like Pat Rooney and Marion Bent there is no reason why you shouldn't enjoy them here. Otherwise the chief pleasure of the performance will be derived from looking at and listening to Miss Elizabeth Hines and in experiencing some songs sung by Elizabeth Murray.

Something better may have come in the second act, but it was during the intermission that the big transfer scene was staged. By a peculiar coincidence (it seems now as if there must almost have been some mysterious force at work in the affair) the audience from *The Right Girl* were standing in excited groups in front of the Times Square Theater just as the inmates of the Apollo came out to get a breath of sea air right off the Forty-second Street meadows. One thing led to another and your correspondent ambled a little too far to the left, with the result that when the doorman to the Times Square cried "Curtain!" we dashed impetuously in there.

It was decided that it would be better to stand up back during this act, near an exit, in case the drunken lady took it into her head to come on again. This did away with whatever scene there might have been had we attempted to occupy by force seat M-2.

Aside from the fact that there wasn't so much of Rooney and Bent, there was really no way of telling that this was not the second act of the same show we had started out with. It might have been the second act of any musical show. They sang a song about an oriental serenade, and one in which Love was graphically shown as a steam engine, with the chorus men taking hold of hands and giving a lovely imitation of a piston rod. You could half shut your eyes and almost kid yourself into believing that it was a real engine right there on the stage. You could entirely shut your eyes and almost kid yourself into believing that all men were created free and equal.

It semed rather odd that Rooney and Bent didn't come on, and once in a while there was something that sounded just a trifle out of keeping with the plot of *Love Birds* as it had been unfolded in the first act. But, on the whole, the thing hung together as well as most musical shows, and what few suspicious moments there were could easily be laid to first-night nervousness.

So it really doesn't make much difference whether you see *Love Birds* and *The Right Girl* on the same night or on separate nights—or at all.

—*Life*, March 31, 1921, pp. 464–65.

Mr. Ziegfeld—Meet Mr. White!

It was bound to happen sooner or later that Mr. George White, by the simple process of improving his *Scandals* each year, would overtake and pass the comparatively static *Ziegfeld Follies*. This is Mr. White's year. He has turned out a show which is better than the *Follies* in almost every department. Its only point of inferiority is that it isn't named the *Ziegfeld Follies*.

There was a time when Mr. White felt that he had to hand out a little lesson in civics along with his fun making, and consequently was accustomed to introduce strange pageants and satiric thrusts aimed at such *res publicae* as the Panama Canal Tolls Repeal or the Sundry Appropriations Bill. This year he has let the country go to the dogs and has devoted himself almost entirely to entertainment, at which he succeeds remarkably well.

True, there is one number which takes upon itself the task of holding censorship up to ridicule and which succeeds, as most attempts of this sort do, in making censorship seem almost a virtue. The best way in dealing with things like censorship is to let them hold themselves up to ridicule, which they will do ably in about three days if left alone. Somehow our revue authors lack something of the subtlety necessary to the delicate task of gilding the lily.

But, on the whole, the *Scandals* are a great credit to Mr. White.

He has taken a tip from John Murray Anderson in the matter of black and white as an effective combination for settings, and has also observed the simple Charlot folk in their comedy sketches and noted that one good idea as a basis for a comedy sketch is worth more than one bad idea.

An especially smart trick is the elimination of the opening chorus entirely, and the substitution of a little song, with an excellent lyric, sung by two young ladies named Williams (sisters, according to a lobby rumor). The burden of the song is that you (the audience) have come in so late that you have missed the opening chorus, and then they proceed to tell you some of the delectable features which your tardiness has cost you. The only trouble is that most of the audience will really believe that they *have* missed the opening, as most of the audience *will* have come in late.

We are now willing to admit that Lester Allen is funny, this marking the end of a six-year struggle on our part. One reason may be that this year he has been given some funny material. A performer is practically helpless with bad material, and Mr. Allen has served more than his fair amount of time at hard labor with heavy jokes. We have never had any struggle to enjoy the work of Tom Patricola, and it is easier in this show than ever before.

There is also a super burlesque of a mammy song, done with great feeling by Mr. Will Mahoney in partial blackface. This number, with its devastating kidding of the "goin' back" school of melodic hoke, brings back the original function of the American revue as founded by the Great Master Cohan in his two revues of dear memory (*reverent bowing and genuflection*). If there were any justice in the world at all, our revues would devote themselves almost entirely to kidding the truck of the previous legitimate season, instead of laying themselves open to kidding by taking themselves so seriously. Perhaps, after Mr. Cohan stops being cross, he will come back and do a Cohan revue burlesquing the *Follies*, the *Music Box*, the *Scandals* and the rest.

An interesting psychological point (if any psychological point may be called interesting) is brought out in the technique of singing the burlesque mammy song. Mr. Mahoney, by copying Mr. Jolson's hysterical frenzy, with the gradual crescendo of emotional fervor and volume of orchestral accompaniment toward the culmination of the appeal to be taken back to the dear old Mammy, impels exactly as much applause with his burlesque as Mr. Jolson does with his earnest effort. There is something about that crescendo which brings an audience to its feet even though it knows that the thing is being spoofed. Proving that it makes no difference at all what you say or sing, so long as you gradually increase the volume of sound and emotion toward the end. This is a trick known to all successful public speakers, especially to Mayor James Curley of Boston, who could make a hall-ful of 100 per cent white Nordic Protestants applaud wildly at a papist speech, simply by building up to his climax in the manner of Mr. Jolson singing a mammy song. There is nothing else for you to do but applaud when the thing is finished in that manner.

We might try ENDING A PAGE LIKE THAT!

—Life, July 31, 1924, p. 18.

AVOIDING THE ISSUE

The first review we ever wrote for this paper we devoted to a lengthy and highly literary attempt to explain why Ed Wynn was funny. And here we are, after eight years, trying to do it again.

Mr. Wynn is a great temptation to writers about the theater, because he presents what seems at first to be a subject which can be handled with ease and yet with a certain amount of analytical and academic impressiveness. He is the kind of comedian that people write about for the *Yale Review* or the *Dial*, because he offers a cosmic aspect together with the chance to quote a few good gags.

But all the writing in the world never seems quite to explain the phenomenon. When you have written all you have to say, there still remains something to be brought out. You may isolate the germ plasm which makes you laugh at him, but you can't explain the feeling you have inside you while you are laughing.

And if that isn't a perfect example of the kind of ineffectual Ed Wynn analysis we mean, we have never read any. We did a better job in the first article we wrote on the subject.

The current Ed Wynn vehicle is called *Manhattan Mary*, and is Mr. George White's latest taunt to Mr. Ziegfeld. It is another great big show, not so scandalizing as his *Scandals* but containing much the same sort of entertainment value. It has a plot which centers around the adventures of the personable Miss Ona Munson in getting a job in—of all shows— the George White *Scandals*.

Lou Holtz is there and performs the difficult task of getting laughs in a show with Mr. Wynn. On one occasion he even does his specialty alone on the stage with Mr. Wynn, while the latter merely stands by, shaking his head with polite interest in the proceedings. It is a brave thing for Mr. Holtz to do, but he makes the grade.

George White himself appears at one point in the show and demonstrates his new heel-and-toe maneuver—the "five-step." It was Mr. White who introduced the Black Bottom a season or two ago, but nothing seems to have frightened him out of the idea of going ahead with his missionary work.

The five-step seems a little complicated for country-club dancing. We are certain that we could never have mastered it, not even before we threw our knee out last summer. But Mr. White seems to do it very well himself and to have taught lots of people in his show to do it. It does, however, appear to be a step which is going to call for a lot more swinging space than is afforded by the average nightclub dance floor. The carnage is likely to be frightful if more than two couples start doing it. Perhaps a good carnage might not be a bad thing in the average nightclub.

We are discussing all these features of *Manhattan Mary* at such length because we feel that, if we don't, we shall get on an analysis of Ed Wynn. It is, we feel, that detached, wistful acceptance of the world and its burdens which shines through those spectacles which is—

And then there are the melodious McCarthy Sisters and Mr. Paul Frawley, who has probably misunderstood more heroines and later forgiven them in the finale than any other juvenile on the American stage. You wouldn't believe that a young man *could* misunderstand a girl like Ona Munson as blindly as Mr. Frawley does, but it doesn't seem to make any difference to her. She is right back under his window the next night. Mr. Wynn is there helping her, with that inexorable sangfroid even in the face of what must be intense personal excitement, that understanding of the ages, that—

—*Life*, October 27, 1927, p. 19.

MR. WHITE'S NINTH

The new season may not open technically until some time in August, but to theater-goers who have fidgeted through the

shoestring ventures of May and June Mr. George White's
Scandals early in July mark the gala take-off. Just to see a show
in which the curtain works correctly is excitement enough.

And Mr. White's curtains all work to perfection, and very
pretty curtains they are, too. Several other things were probably
fixed before the second night; so there wouldn't be much use in
listing them here. If Mr. White was sitting out front with a pad
and pencil he caught them. And we regret to say that Mr. White
must have been sitting out front, as he didn't appear in the show
at all, not even in a spot which seemed to have been built for him
—"The Origin of the Tap-Dance."

And while we are on the subject of building up spots and
entrances, no young lady ever had an entrance built up for her
more elaborately than Miss Pennington's, when the entire orchestra, with megaphones, arose and sang a song about "Pennie"
to bring her on. And, speaking entirely from our own personal
taste, what followed was something less than a sensation. The
older we grow as a reviewer of revues, the less inclined we are
to go on giving Miss Pennington's knees a good notice. Pretty
knees are all right, but the world moves and we have been spoiled
by dancers who spend their vacations working up something
new for their next show. If we sound like a cross old bear in
saying this it is because we have wanted to say it for several seasons and have, through our repression, grown slightly peevish
about it. The whole thing probably boils down to the fact that
the beast in us has never been aroused during one of Miss Pennington's numbers.

Most of Mr. White's principals, however, we could stand
seeing year after year, even if they never changed their stuff
(and we certainly have been put to the test). We have been following Harry Richman around ever since he began singing
"There was an old man about ninety" at the old "Wigwam,"
and if we were going to tire of him, we should have done so
long ago. We would follow Miss Frances Williams around just
as long if it weren't for what people would say. Miss Williams
and Mr. Richman have several of their regulation numbers together and succeed in making a great deal out of not much. Their
duet, "What D'ya Say?" is the one this year to be done in front
of the rose-bower. It is to their credit that they do not yield to
the temptation to appear during the second chorus framed in the
little oval above the bower. But there is the oval, just crying out

for two heads to appear through it. It would be pretty terrible if this notice gave them the idea.

And, while we are on the song hits, it seemed that the usually worthy De Sylva-Brown-Henderson trio have not quite come up to their standard this year, although probably in two months we shall be unable to believe that we didn't see the virtues of such established successes as "On the Crest of a Wave" and "Pickin' Cotton." Our chief objection to the score is its synthetic quality, at least three numbers containing passages to which words of earlier song hits could be sung in unison. (If you must know, "On the Crest of a Wave" brings back the verse of "Tea for Two" in its opening bars, "Origin of the Tap-Dance" even more of "Miss Annabelle Lee," and "What D'ya Say?" in effect at least, is a sister ship to "Give Us a Little Kiss.") Needless to say, all of the songs go over big.

The sketches, practically all of which end with the customary revolver blackout, are funnier than usual, although a couple of them have been done before in other shows—the one on "Credits" being practically identical with one done in the *Garrick Gaieties*, and "Chicago," a combination of one from *Americana* and Mr. White's own *The Feud* of last year.

The sketches which *are* original, however, are very original, such as the burlesque on *Strange Interlude*, in which the characters *act* what they are really thinking as they read their lines, and the "Vocafilm" act between Harry Richmond and Willie Howard.

As most of the sketches contain the Phoenician personality of Mr. Willie Howard they would be funny anyway. It seems to us that Mr. Howard grows more and more comic as the years go by, or else we grow easier and easier to amuse. And Tom Patricola's tremendous vitality and varied talents constitute another feature of which we never weary. Mr. Patricola has that same friendly personal quality which is Will Rogers' great asset on the stage, making it possible for him to please you even when he is doing nothing particularly pleasing in itself.

For those to whom excursions into the more animal forms of comedy are distasteful, we issue the warning that there are several sketches, as there usually are in the *Scandals*, which will offend, but if Mr. White was out front counting the laughs on the opening night he will already have omitted one or two of them as not worth the risk.

If we seem to have been a bit carping toward a show which is, almost from beginning to end, a good show, it is because we have had more space at our command for this one and because we have set out during the coming season, to spot as definitely as possible any features which have been lifted from the past. This habit among revue and musical comedy writers of appropriating things they have heard in other shows is becoming so taken for granted and so almost universal that it constitutes one of the main defects of our native output and, wholly aside from the professional ethics of the thing, it makes for duller evenings among those of us who have to see every show every year.

But, even with those reprises which we have listed, the *Scandals* are never dull and they fill a long-felt want in the summer schedule. Mr. White has done it again and is in line for congratulations.

Although it is not in our field, we should also like to compliment whoever is responsible for changing the type-face in the programs. It makes it a pleasure to look up names, especially when they are such names as have been here assembled.

—Life, July 19, 1928, p. 16.

THE MESSRS. MINSKY, MORAL AGENTS

Those who feel that our drama has come upon evil days, and that there is no health in us, should take a trip down to Houston Street and Second Avenue, where the National Winter Garden (*né* Minsky's Burlesque) upholds the standard of highly moral entertainment. Summer is perhaps not the ideal season for burlesque shows, what with one thing and another, but when it is a question of spiritual refreshment, a little democratic crowding and tobacco smoke don't seem very important.

Over the proscenium at the National Winter Garden is the following (in quotation marks): "The Show's the Thing," with credit given to "Wm. Shakespeare." Nothing could be fairer than that. Within these precincts "the show" certainly *is* the thing. And no funny business about it, either. There are none of your imported doo-dabs from Paris, no trick curtains or big electrical effects. There are the "National Winter Garden Rosebuds," a little group of earnest comedians, and the "National Winter Garden Rosebuds" again.

The "Rosebuds" strike the dominant academic note of the whole affair when they appear in the opening chorus representing several of our more advanced institutions of learning. Columbia, carrying the symbolism through, is the largest of the "Rosebuds," but Princeton's sweater fits a little more precisely. Owing probably to some last-minute disagreement with the rules committee, Harvard is not represented, but Yale is there in what might be termed "full force," and very fine and handsome she is, too. Lobby gossip had it that she was the original model for the Yale Bowl.

But it is not so much what the Rosebuds do that gives the show its touch of distinction; it is how they do it. The Rosebuds are not the puppets of any one director. Each Rosebud is for herself. She has individuality. If she wants to do a tap dance while her neighbor is doing the rhythmic knee dip, she does a tap dance. Somebody else in the line is doing a tap dance, anyway.

And there is none of this forced smiling that choruses in the uptown shows are under contract to display while dancing. If a Rosebud feels like smiling, she may, but if, in her mind, her work is more important, if the particular steps which she has chosen to execute at that particular moment call for her undivided attention, she sets her lips, watches her feet and leaves the artificial smile for the dilettante dancers whose hearts are not in their work.

From a hasty survey of those who did smile, however, we should say that, compared with burlesque choruses of five years ago, the gold-teeth vogue for milady is on the wane.

But the moral tone of the National Winter Garden strikes full and clear in the big spectacular number, entitled "His Satanic Majesty." Here, instead of the shameless pageants of the uptown revues, where the progress of Butterfly from tadpole to cocoon, or Famous Cut-Flowers of History, can be transformed into a gorgeous parade of sinful stimuli—here we find the theme almost evangelical, the Wages of Sin and the Nobility of Honest Labor.

In this parade we see the Selfish Banker, the Gilded Youth, the Scarlet Woman, all passing in revue before the Master Sinner himself, and all reaping the harvest of Death immediately on reaching the wings. But the Working Man, with dinner-pail and pipe, is deaf to the whisperings of the Fiend, and he alone passes on to his reward, confounding the Forces of Evil amid thunderous applause.

It is either very moral, or else U.S. Steel Corporation anti-Bolshevik propaganda. We can't make out which.

ɪ A sample of how facts are faced at the National Winter Garden may be found in one of the song hits of the show. Where Mr. Berlin would give us "At Peace with the World," and Mr. White, "This Is My Lucky Day," the realists at Houston Street and Second Avenue make Art imitate Life with "I Had You, I Lost You, I Found You, Only to Lose You Again." No compromise here, my masters!

—*Life*, August 5, 1926, p. 21.

THE VANITIES

No matter what you like, or what you don't like, in a revue, you are pretty sure to find both in Earl Carroll's new *Vanities*. Unfortunately, all the good stuff doesn't come in one act and all the bad stuff in another, otherwise you could get home, or somewhere, by 10:30, after an hysterically pleasant evening. As it is, there are some moments which are pretty trying.

If I were rearranging the show according to my personal taste, I would group all the unpleasant features in the first act and all the good ones in the second, thereby allowing time for an argument over the dinner check and a leisurely bicycle ride to the theatre, arriving just in time to be vastly amused. In order to hold your attention, I will make up the bad act first.

I would let the opening stand just about as it is and thereby miss the chorus which chants in unison those credit lines which are usually reserved for program-worms to peruse between acts. Very early in the act I was not going to see would come a window-dressing sketch in which, of all inoffensive people, Mr. Jimmie Savo is made to play scavenger for some of the less bearable refuse in which the show abounds. A number called "Hittin' the Bottle" is irritating simply because it tries to do something dirty without actually laying itself open to police action, a subterfuge never resorted to by a good, honest dirt-show; and several ancient sotto voce gags, such as "I don't know; he had his hat on," which have been dignified with dialogue as blackouts, could easily be crowded into this first and worse act.

Much of the stuff by which Mr. Carroll has evidently set great store would, under my present plan, go on just about one hour before I arrived. A great deal of the gold and silver curtain-sliding (and, until revue-producers can fix a curtain so that it does not slide in jerks, I will refuse to be impressed), a great deal of the dancing, and especially the Big Punch finale to the first act by which Mr. Carroll possibly thought to get himself nominated for the Presidency—all of this would go on while I was eating dinner.

The Big Punch finale to the first act really deserves a word by itself. It is the sort of thing that Mr. George White outgrew five years ago, the sort of thing that Broadway does when it goes serious. Mr. White reached the peak of his political satire when he showed the Spirit of Muscle Shoals either defying or comforting Uncle Sam—I forget which. Mr. Carroll has taken up the torch and now comes out with a smashing denunciation of prohibition which would convert the most confirmed wet to the Anti-Saloon League. There is a series of rousing *tableaux vivants*, showing first Mr. Jack Benny as one of the signers of the Declaration of Independence; then as Lincoln (fortunately without a beard) delivering excerpts from his Gettysburg address on a field which would seem to indicate that Pennsylvania was, at that time, cut through by the Mississippi River, with the old Gettysburg levee in the background; then as an evangelical congressman of 1930 enunciating, in ringing tones, the principle of Light Ryes and Gins, preceded by a tableau, naturally called "Over There," in which the boys are seen going over the top in knee-length burberries. Throughout all of this stirring appeal there runs the lyric sung by young ladies in nothing much colored red and blue, "Is This the Law?" On the whole, I do not very well see how prohibition can stand up another day under this assault.

Then there is an elaborate and mysterious arrangement, whereby several naked young ladies and one what might better be a naked young man are suspended, at great expense, in some medium resembling water, where they make odd rotary movements probably designed to give the effect of swimming. The illusion was not quite strong enough to move me to anything more spirited than a mild curiosity as to just what it was they were doing. I would put them in the first act, along with the rest.

So far I am afraid this has sounded as if I didn't enjoy myself at the *Vanities*. I did, however, and it was because of the quantity of good things which I have saved for the act immediately to follow my entrance into the theater. No show which has Jimmy Savo, Jack Benny, Herb Williams, and Patsy Kelly can fail to amuse. Mr. Savo is at his best in wistful pantomime; mercurial in mood, now running very fast back and forth, now drooping in shy inferiority until it seems as if he is about to disappear entirely into his trousers. His sadly sweet face, as he tries to conceal the fact that he is about to violate the code of good manners by dropping a burnt match on the floor, will break your heart. I have a feeling that Mr. Savo would become the idol of France and Germany if we were ever fools enough to let him go.

Mr. Benny has long been a weakness of this department's. Probably the straightest player of all our revue comedians, he can, by drawing in his cheeks ever so slightly or changing the angle of his hat a fraction, or even simply by pausing before reading a line, give an invaluable grace to the clumsiest witticism, and he has plenty of chance to work this miracle in some of the sketches in which Mr. Carroll has placed him. There is a vague resemblance to a combined Phil Baker and Ben Bernie about him, but it is Mr. Benny and his own individual art which make him the ingratiating comedian that he is.

I need only to recall Herb Williams to your mind as the former member of the team of Williams and Wolfus, the man with the yellow button shoes on the wrong feet who was constantly calling for "Spot*light*!," to indicate why he is another superb member of Mr. Carroll's comedy backfield. He goes in for dangerous pianos as his specialty, although his scene with Patsy Kelly, in which an obtrusive Angelus and an equally obtrusive orchestra-leader with an unbreakable head almost call a complete halt to the proceedings, is something which you must be sure to catch, the first really good number in the show.

I am already on record as having made over my entire estate to Miss Kelly whenever she shall have need of it. Fed up with the show, even on the opening night, she ambles through scene after scene, throwing away lines which, through her indifference to them, suddenly become worth keeping. Among Society's debts to Mr. Frank Fay is that for his inviting Miss Kelly up on the stage to afternoon tea several seasons ago.

With these four comedians at work, even in those sketches which open with a bellboy carrying bags and saying "Right this way!", Mr. Carroll need not worry about his show's being a success. As is his wont, he has been prodigal in good comics, the only revue-producer who knows a good comic when he sees one. He has also been prodigal in his costuming and settings, and, although I had almost overlooked them, in ravishing young ladies. I have not my files at hand, but I venture to say that this year's *Vanities* is practically top in pulchritude.

So, even with one whole act made up of leavings, there ought to be enough entertainment here to make a valuable summer's evening for anyone who doesn't mind taking his peck of dirt all in one meal.

—*The New Yorker*, July 12, 1930, pp. 26, 28, 30.

The Cossacks who raided Mr. Carroll's *Vanities* showed excellent taste in concentrating their complaints on the window-dressing scene. It was easily the most offensive one in the show and Mr. Savo himself ought to be a lot happier with it in its present form. There is dirt and dirt. The window-dressing scene was one kind; Mr. Benny's traveling-salesman act, with the cow and the milkmaid, is another. Just where the difference comes would be difficult to analyze, especially with the postal authorities as snoopy as they are, but there is a difference. Perhaps some of it lies in the fact that Mr. Benny handles a situation like that with considerable tact. Then, too, the cow lends a wholesome, rustic air to the scene which relieves it of some of the "sophistication" of which Mr. Carroll is so proud. With the window-dressing scene fixed up and several of the more naked people out of the show, the *Vanities* is now just *one* of the rawest performances on record instead of *the* rawest. It speaks very well for the ingenuousness of the police examiners that they saw nothing censorable in the "Hittin' the Bottle" number. They must lead very sheltered lives themselves.

—*The New Yorker*, July 19, 1930, p. 28.

Dawn

The summer theatrical season, up until now on a par with the summer elk season for excitement, has suddenly burst forth into something distinctly resembling splendor, as nearly as we can remember splendor in the summer theatre. It may all be due to seeing a lot of bright lights again, but I have a feeling that things are going to be a lot better from now on, thanks to Max Gordon and Dwight Wiman and their two shows. At any rate, things are going to *seem* better.

Of course, the chief impression of splendor comes from Mr. Gordon's *The Band Wagon*. Here is a production! I do not know whether it cost a lot of money or not, but it could have cost a million dollars and not have been any better. And furthermore, even on the opening night everything worked. We used to have a lot of fun with Hassard Short because of his elevators and teetering tableaux, but that was evidently just a phase, like whistling through the teeth or playing the mandolin. Mr. Short, backed up by Albert Johnson's backdrops and Howard Dietz' imagination, has emerged from under the old-time piles of gold brocade, bearing with him the practically perfect production.

Lest you get the impression that *The Band Wagon* is nothing but a trip through the Petit Trianon, let us hasten to add that it enlists the services of any number of sterling performers. I have had occasion before, or perhaps I have gone out of my way to take occasion, to toss the old forage cap high in the air over the dancing of Mr. Fred Astaire. So far as I am concerned it is still up in the air, relieving me of the necessity of tossing it again at this point. But it is as a comic that Mr. Astaire blossoms forth in *The Band Wagon*, and a comic worthy to play alongside his comical little sister Adele, which is no faint praise, as she is at her best here. As the backward Southern boy commenting without emotion on the mighty fine "baudy o' wauter" or the German lieutenant singing "I love Louisa" (and I defy anybody to witness that gay merry-go-round finale to the first act and still worry about Russian wheat-dumping), Mr. Astaire becomes one of the most valuable pieces of theatrical property in the business. He also plays the accordion.

Another surprise for those of us who have followed Frank Morgan from his early sneering villainies through his high comedy in *The Firebrand* into the paths of his Topaze is the tonal quality of the singing voice in such rich, fruity numbers as "Nanette" (in full quartet) or his lament with Miss Astaire on being miserable together (hey-hey). Is there no limit to this man's powers?

Helen Broderick has already gone down on the records as being one of my weaknesses. She does not always have the best material in a show, but she always has the best way of handling it. Which is probably the reason she is given most of the suggestive lines to read. You may take them or leave them; as for Miss Broderick, she leaves them. And she can make a tall man look smaller than any woman in the world.

The weak part of *The Band Wagon*, if any show so obviously in the prime of health can be said to have weak parts, is the sketches. In the opening of the show (which you must under no circumstances miss) there is a burlesque of the ordinary revue so devastating as to make the ordinary revue producer shoot himself if he had any sense. In it a great deal of justifiable kidding is leveled at the conventional blackout. But the blackout, banal as it has become, has its advantages. It at least brings the sketch to a close, a trick which seems to have eluded Mr. Kaufman and Mr. Dietz (of all people!). The sketches themselves have as funny lines in them as have ever been heard in revue sketches, but, like the tell-tale wineglass in the murder-mystery sketch they have false bottoms. And, while we are on this subject, if I did not know both authors personally, I would have suspected that one or both had some very definite skatological complex, so concerned are they, in a boyish fashion with matters which hitherto have concerned the J. L. Mott Company alone. They are not particularly offensive, unless you happen to feel them so, but it is certain that the two best satirists that our theatre has today must have more mature ideas to kid about. However, Messrs. Kaufman and Dietz (and, according to the program, the entire production was under Mr. Dietz' supervision, which should elect him President easily) have done enough to mark them as wondermen in the theatre.

We have space enough only to mention the other features of *The Band Wagon*, such as Tilly Losch's lovely dancing (the opera-house ballet with Mr. Astaire being sensational, thanks also to Mr. Johnson's setting), the very nice music by Arthur Schwartz, who is at his best in the simple peasant tunes such as "Hoops" and "I Love Louisa," the protean versatility of Philip Loeb and the hundred and one other items which go to make *The Band Wagon* the year's top.

The *Third Little Show* does not compete in any way with *The Band Wagon*. It sticks to its original intention of being an intimate, genteel, and at all times pleasant revue. In this it succeeds as well as its grandfather, the first *Little Show*, and that is saying a great, great deal.

In the first place, it has Beatrice Lillie, which is also saying a great, great deal. Miss Lillie has never been better. In fact, she has a new power, impossible (fortunately for my readers) to analyze, which will give her imitators something new to work on for quite a while and something which I doubt if they ever quite catch. If Miss Lillie were the only one in the *Third Little Show* it would be imperative that you see it.

But there is Ernest Truex, alternating between moods of high excitement and Lilliputian depression, rushing back and forth in a mad thing by S. J. Perelman (who ought to write more sketches, with the sketch market what it is) and globe-trotting from Grand Central to 125th Street in Marc Connelly's travel epic. There is Walter O'Keefe, who not only appears "in one" but adds his personality to the sketches and sings one of the best numbers in the show. The music is good, serviceable revue music (but, incidentally, was "I've Got a Crush on You, Sweetie-Pie" such a good number in its day that it should have been perpetuated through the years, first with "Fine and Dandy" and now, in fainter echo, with "Falling in Love"?) and Noel Coward's "Mad Dogs and Englishmen," as sung by Miss Lillie and a chorus of British subjects, is the best satirical single number in town. Then there is Carl Randall, who has been away too long with his easy dancing, to carry that important end of the business. Needless to say, Jo Mielziner's settings are just exactly right and even more than that.

In other words, you can see the *Third Little Show* on one night and *The Band Wagon* on the next and have a swell time at both. Which is pretty good for one summer.

—*The New Yorker*, June 13, 1931, pp. 28, 30.

"THEY'RE OFF!"

One of the most plaintive accusations leveled at dramatic critics by producers (usually made to the critic's boss) runs something like this:

"Here I go and make an investment of two hundred and fifty thousand dollars in a show, and, with a couple of smart cracks, some whippersnapper comes along and can kick it right out the window. It's all wrong, Joe."

Now, in the first place, no critic is influential enough to kick even six dollars out of any window if the producer has a good show, or even if he hasn't. And, in the second and important place, that proposed amendment to the Constitution making it *obligatory* for a producer every year to sink a certain amount of money in a production, whether or not he has something that is worth it to begin with, was defeated in Congress by an overwhelming majority last year. Some producers haven't heard about that yet. It is the producer's business what he does with his, or his sucker's, two hundred and fifty thousand dollars, but, once he has decided that the material on hand justifies his throwing it into a show, it is the critic's business to write about that show as he sees it. The imperiling of the original investment came when the producer called the first rehearsal.

Mr. Earl Carroll has invested a great deal more than two hundred and fifty thousand dollars of somebody's money in his new theater and his new *Vanities*. Rumor, usually slightly drunk, places the whole check at four millions. As far as the theater goes, a stunning job has been done, in the very best modern tradition, and its spacious reaches will, it is to be hoped, accommodate in the future many thousands of patrons grateful to Mr. Carroll for his return to the so-called "three-dollar top."

As for the present *Vanities*, I can not see where the amount of Mr. Carroll's investment should have anything to do with a paid reviewer's proclaiming it very, very bad to the few readers who take his word in such matters. Such a proclamation is herewith made.

In former *Vanities*, Mr. Carroll's definitely Negroid taste in matters of color and stage effects has been more than made up for by his lavish supply of good, red-nosed clowning. Where two comics would have served an ordinary producer, Mr. Carroll has given us five, and we have been grateful. Most of the really funny clowns in our theater have, at one time or another, crashed headlong across the stage of the Earl Carroll, usually in a group. This year, however, Will Mahoney and William Demarest have been given the brunt (and "brunt" is just the word) of the comedy to carry, and, while they are both expert comedians in their own lines, they have here been sunk so close to the hips in the clam-flats of the world's dirtiest sketches (and when I say "dirty," I mean "dirty," for I am an old public-school boy with a strong stomach) that they never have a chance to show what everybody knows they possess. Mr. Mahoney extricates himself for an all-too-brief interlude while he executes a really original dance on a giant xylophone, and once Mr. Demarest gets the cello of beloved memory between his knees for a futile excursion into the comedy of an elder day, but the only real laughs in the show come when Mitchell and Durant completely destroy each other in an epic exhibition of hurtling and whamming. They also participate in the only clean, and the only funny, blackout of the show, something called "So you won't talk!" This, unfortunately, lasts only one minute.

The lack of laughable comedy brings into full relief Mr. Carroll's little weaknesses in the field of aesthetics. Never has so much money been spent on such violently unpleasant effects. Leaving aside the tendency to pastel everything in pinks and greens and, when other colors are used, to hit upon just the most ham combinations or shades, and also allowing for the boyish craving to have things like shoe buckles light up with electricity (always good for a big hand with an American audience), there still remain to be explained the two-ton dinosaur which, after dropping a naked lady from its maw in order to give her opportunity to dance, proceeds to emit periodic gushes of water from the corners of its jaws in what is presumably an excess of *Sehnsucht*; the horrible enlargement on a screen of what were possibly once the lovely faces of the chorus; and that monstrosity of bad taste and bad coloring which, to the rather faulty accompaniment of dozens of tom-toms, is supposed in some way to be related to Ravel's *Bolero*. I find that I am very nearly alone in cringing at this massive finale to the first act, for it is considered to be a masterpiece of pagan splendor by many who ought to know better, but my jaded senses refuse to thrill to three stages full of assorted loincloths and scimitars (really a very good dance, if we could be permitted to see it) with rising platforms disgorging dozens more at every beat of the drums, and a strange, unaccountable set-piece of some sort, studded with naked ladies who do not fit into any picture except that of a *carte postale*, moving slowly up and down and up and down against the backdrop, like one of those undulating horizons in a shooting gallery from which one is supposed to pop off ducks and clay pipes. In fact, if the concessionaires at Coney Island had the money to work with which Mr. Carroll has had, we might expect Surf Avenue to be lined with replicas of this startling *Bolero* number. I have an idea that M. Ravel himself might join me in my lonely wincing at this sight if he were to see it, for, although I am not privy to his moods, I can not believe that this was exactly what he had in mind. In fact, the only person who *could* have had it in mind before Mr. Carroll was the manufacturer of those decalcomania which we, as children, used to transfer to the backs of our hands with spit.

On the credit side, such as it is, of Mr. Carroll's expensive entertainment comes first the "Mask and Hands" dance, created and staged by Gluck Sandor, which opens the second act with a beauty quite out of keeping with the rest of the exhibition; the interesting and slightly spooky demonstration of Professor Theremin's method of producing music from the air (instead, as Mr. John Anderson says, of producing it from some other songwriter's studio); the dancing of the Slate Brothers and Al Norman; and the singing of Miss Lillian Roth whenever she could get herself out of bed long enough to sing.

Mr. Carroll may be helping his beloved Theater and his slightly less-beloved Road by bringing back the three-dollar seat in these Hard Times, and in this we wish him and his smart theater all the luck in the world, but he is also offering a frightening example of how *not* to spend money at a time when any money at all is hard enough to get. Revolutions have been started with less provocation.

—The New Yorker, September 5, 1931, pp. 26, 28.

Top and Bottom

It is usually a mistake to see an old favorite revived, especially if it be a musical comedy. You may have been going about for years mooning reminiscently to less experienced friends, letting a sad look come into your eyes when excerpts from the dear score are played, and muttering "They don't write 'em like that nowadays," until you actually believe yourself that *The Prince of Pilsen* or *The Yankee Consul* were the best shows you ever saw or ever expect to see.

And then, during a slow stretch, some manager revives your Old Favorite. The least that you can do is to take a theater party including everyone to whom you have been touting it for fifteen or twenty years, and this you do with every confidence in the world. Then begin the explanations. It isn't done as well as it was originally—these shoddy revivals, you know. Something has been left out, presumably about two-thirds of the book. (What ever became of those laughs which followed on each other's heels, as you remember it?) The orchestra isn't big enough and they are not using the same orchestrations. And, above all, the people, those wonderful people of the original cast, are gone. Obviously *some*thing has happened.

Show Boat is just about the first Old Favorite to hold up in revival. Perhaps this is because it is not so old. Four and a half years would seem to be the ideal time to allow a musical-comedy hit to mellow. Possibly it is because Mr. Ziegfeld has revived it with just as much care as he first produced it, and with the original cast (with two exceptions which make it even better). Even though the prices are lower, there has been no perceptible scrimping on Mr. Ziegfeld's part. But probably it is because in *Show Boat* Jerome Kern and Oscar Hammerstein II wrote the best all-around musical comedy of modern times. Certainly the combination of these three factors makes it the best musical-comedy revival.

It seems even better in revival than it did on that opening night in Christmas Week of 1927, because Mr. Kern's lovely melodies have made just enough of a nook for themselves in our minds to fit in comfortably the first second we hear the opening bars. We also know, when Mr. Winninger crouches low and says "Hap—," that it is eventually to be followed by "—py New Year!" and we get that much longer laugh. We enjoy the opening scene on the levee all the more because we know that it is to be followed by an even better scene on the stage of the Cotton Blossom and that they both are to be followed by the scenes at the World's Fair and the Trocadero Music Hall. And when we look at our programs and see that the cast still includes Edna May Oliver (we hope that Miss Oliver realized, from the stirring greeting accorded to her on the opening night, that there are some things the theater can give an actress that the movies can't, including the personal contact of a loving audience), Charles Winninger, Eva Puck and Sammy White, Helen Morgan, and Norma Terris, then we know exactly what to expect—and what is even more grateful, we get it. Dennis King, one of the two substitutions, although his speech is not so much that of one of the old Ravenals of Tennessee as one of the old Ravenals of Stoke Poges, is an added asset to the ensemble and it is hardly necessary to say that Paul Robeson makes "Old Man River" an even more thrilling experience than it was at first—which is saying just about as much as could be said without bursting a blood vessel.

Incidentally, we ought to know enough by now to remember that the first singing of "Old Man River" comes fairly early in the show and that no dinner party in the world is worth lingering over long enough to miss it. In fact, it would be a good idea to postpone dinner until midnight and get into the theater for the rise of the curtain, for in 1928 a great many people never heard "Only Make Believe" at all until they heard it played around town or in Paris. Not since *Iolanthe* has there been a score which started off with so many prescribed numbers—and also finished with them. It would be an impertinence to list all the ones that you must hear, for you know them already, but in revival we also find that several of the songs accorded to Miss Puck and Mr. White, although never featured, have smart enough lyrics by Mr. Hammerstein to make them stand out in any ordinary show, especially as sung by Miss Puck and Mr. White. (Oh, let's drop all this pretence and call them "the Whites." Everybody knows about it by now.) And, once again, let us call attention to young Mr. Hammerstein's not-enough-recognized claim to distinction as a lyricist and librettist. Working with the original rich sentiment of Miss Ferber's novel, he has fashioned words in such a manner as not only to bear analysis but also to dig pretty deeply into the heartstrings for a succession of good ripe chords.

Perhaps some of the nostalgic quality of *Show Boat*, unusual in a show which is not five years old, comes from the fact that when we first heard it we were having an awfully good time. (Remember 1928?) Public psychology being what it is, stranger things have happened than people going out of the present production of *Show Boat* sufficiently inspired to have an awfully good time again. Just as we used to wear the same green tie to examinations for good luck, it may be that what we needed was the sound of "Old Man River" to keep things going.

Jumping down from *Show Boat*, we find something called *There You Are*. *There You Are* is a revival without having ever been produced before. It is a revival of practically everything that we never wanted to see again, from the opening chorus of "then drink-drink-drink" (pointing to cherry-colored glasses) outside the Inn of the Blue Dove, with the comic landlord in a green apron rushing on and off, to the closing chorus, which I am fortunately unable to report on. It has not only "ze best dam caballero in all Mehi-ho," but "ze most dangerous bandit" and "ze most beautiful señorita." It has not only a number called "Safe in Your Arms" and one called "Love Lives On," but also "Just a Little Pent-House and You" and a "Legend of the Mission Bells." Hyman Adler thought it worth producing, doubtless because it gave him a chance to burn up his tenor and soprano leads by holding the stage for a big personal finale to the first act. Miss Ilse Marvenga might well be, and has been, in a better show, although we must renew our old protest against sopranos' being comical. It was a tough break for *There You Are* to open during the same week as *Show Boat*. I think it was a tough break for it to open at all.

—The New Yorker, May 28, 1932, pp. 26, 28.

JUST ROBERTA

In order to get the full emotional value out of one of Jerome Kern's lovely scores, it really should be taken in a large, blue bowl of Oscar Hammerstein's special brew of sentimental ambrosia, as in *Music in the Air* or *Show Boat*. It does not tear you down so much in a setting of gowns and gags like *Roberta*. Sweet as the strains are when they strike the ear, the heart remains practically untouched.

Roberta (out of Alice Duer Miller's novel, *Gowns by Roberta*) is a colorful and expensive pageant, with several other things aside from Mr. Kern's music to recommend it, including an agreeable cast. But it must also be said that it contains volley after volley of some of the most immature gags ever conceived by an adult mind. (I take it for granted that they are the product of an adult mind. No child could have had the stamina to stay up as late at rehearsals as must have been necessary in the fight to keep them in.)

This is too bad, because one is tempted, in reporting on the show to inquiring friends, to quote freely from the book before saying anything about the music, the settings, or the people concerned. Word-of-mouth advertising being what it is, the news value of *Roberta* does not seem to lie so much in the fact that Lyda Roberti is swell (or perhaps this has ceased to be news), that Fay Templeton steals the first scene, or that a new quipster of the Baker-Bernie school has been introduced in the person of Bob Hope, as that someone says: "She has given me the air," and someone else says: "Oh, I thought you said she had given you *an heir!*," or that another unfortunate says: "Underneath, she has a heart that's gold" (you have to say "*that's* gold" in order to get the full value out of the comeback), and someone comes back with: "Did you say 'gold' or 'cold'?" It is news like that that hurts a show.

It is especially unfortunate that *Roberta* is loaded to the gunwales with this type of freight, for there are several people in the cast who might very well do wonders with a really good crack.

A comparative newcomer to Broadway, the aforementioned Bob Hope, has a slick, humorous style of delivery which ought to put him in the front rank of talking bandmasters as soon as he gets something to say which does not bring the blush of shame to his cheeks. George Murphy, besides dancing nicely, can make you think that his lines are almost good until you stop to mull them over. And, of course, Lyda Roberti *makes* her lines good, whether they are or not.

We might as well face the fact that Miss Roberti is what is known in scientific circles as an "irresistible force." It is practically impossible not to give in to her in the face of that disarming Polish grin. It is she who puts an end, for all time, to the dignity of silks and satins, when, following an elaborate fashion parade of Kiviette creations, she descends the steps dressed in royal bride's array, followed by train-bearers and bridesmaids, and destroys both the God of Love and the God of Fashion with a song called "I'll Be Hard to Handle," of which two lines are: "I'll say with a shrug, I think you're a mugg—to marry me." After this, we may expect no more bridal numbers.

It was a stroke of genius on someone's part to engage Miss Fay Templeton for the role of Roberta, for while she is on, the natural sentimentality surrounding her return to the musical-comedy stage supplies the missing heartbeats to Mr. Kern's music. During the offstage rendition of Russell Bennett's delicate arrangement of "The Touch of Your Hand," while Tamara and William Hain were wrapping her shawl about the old lady for her last nap, the best of the sweetness of "Music in the Air" was recaptured.

Tamara and Mr. Hain sing well together, and Tamara herself makes as nice a heroine as Mr. Kern could ask. A pretty tribute to the newly recognized Soviet Republic came in the last act when she, as an expatriate Russian princess, stood in full regalia and sang the Czarist national hymn. If Mr. Litvinoff happened to be celebrating the evening of his diplomatic *coup* by attending the opening of *Roberta*, were his ears red!

Of the remaining principals, Mr. Raymond Middleton had the dual disadvantage of having to play a moronic fullback turned dressmaker and of not being asked to sing oftener.

Thus we see that *Roberta* has plenty of good points and that it is only because its bad points are so distracting that it turns out to be one of those praiseworthy musical comedies during which one is constantly looking at one's program to see how much more of it there is going to be.

—The New Yorker, November 25, 1933, pp. 30, 32.

Two Big Ones

Two very widely touted pieces of property came into town last week, laboring under the disadvantage that all widely touted shows labor under, especially when they are pieces of property. As far as this department goes (and you have no idea what a short distance that is), *Porgy and Bess* did not live up to its touting, and *Jubilee!* did.

The best way to explain about *Porgy and Bess,* as far as I am concerned, is to descend into what is known as plain English. I do not happen to like the operatic form of singing a story, and the older I grow, the less ashamed I am to admit it. I liked the original *Porgy* much better, because the people didn't sing when they should have been talking. Is that awful to say?

In the second place, although I am a Negrophile from way back, I am no longer as much stirred as I once was by Negro rhythms and Negro choral formations. Mr. Gershwin has captured everything that he set out to capture, and has put an enormous amount of work into its assembling, but since the original *Porgy* we have had so many imitations, and so many excellent Negro choruses have marched under the bridge, that the fine excitement of them has worn off. This is unfortunate, for Mr. Gershwin has devised some fine excitement in his score, but, as far as I am concerned (understood), it comes about eight years too late. (This is *definitely* awful to say.)

In Mr. Mamoulian's production, and Mr. Soudeikine's settings, there is the same thrill that there was in the original *Porgy,* and that is saying a great deal. In the exigency of finding people who could sing, instead of act, I think that something has been sacrificed in the way of authority, and until a woman came in, in the middle of the second act, and sang one word—"Strawberries" —I did not feel that anyone was really alive. (Her name is, I find by looking it up, Helen Dowdy.) This comes, I am sure, from the necessity of engaging singers instead of actors, and exemplifies what is wrong with *Porgy and Bess* from the point of view of the layman who feels that opera is a bastard art.

Having thus placed myself in the despicable minority, I will withdraw, advising everyone to see (or hear) *Porgy and Bess* in order to judge for himself. If you didn't see the original *Porgy*, you will get a great kick out of it. If you did, you may get another. I just happened not to.

Oddly enough, the chief virtue of *Jubilee!*, which sets out so doggedly to be sophisticated, is its simple naïveté. The lyrics which Mr. Cole Porter has devised, with an eye to pleasing perhaps eighteen people, are negligible in market value. His music is, I have a feeling, better than he knows, because he has hidden his most valuable tunes in incidental choruses, such as the entrance of the ladies-in-waiting at the beginning of the last act. (Really something.)

But in Joe Mielziner's settings and Irene Sharaff's and Connie DePinna's costumes there is a freshness and almost heartbreaking simplicity which makes *Jubilee!* an experience comparable to *Mary Rose* for those who are easily moved by sheer loveliness, and such numbers as "What a Nice Municipal Park" could bring ready tears to susceptible eyes at any moment. Even the dance steps (Miss Rasch's) are nostalgic in their simplicity and make one glad that people can still hop and skip and jump.

Miss Mary Boland's technique is too well known to call for comment here. She is definitely an asset to any show as far as popular acclaim goes. Mr. Melville Cooper, whose performance in red slippers in *Laburnum Grove* threw his department into tantrums of delight, is still infallible as far as we are concerned. The rest of the cast, which includes May Boley, June Knight, Derek Williams, and Charles Walters, do everything that Mr. Woolley, who directed the dialogue, could have wished (I haven't checked with Mr. Woolley on this).

The main point is that Messrs. Moss Hart, Cole Porter, Hassard Short, Max Gordon, and (everybody's sweetheart) Sam Harris have a show in *Jubilee!* which is heart-warming and beautiful, and I hope that it runs forever, because it is so nice.

—*The New Yorker*, October 19, 1935, pp. 32, 34.

PRO FLESH AND BLOOD

Stage productions involving rocky crags and storms at sea may look pretty sleazy in comparison with movies of their type, and now and then a drawing-room scene in the theater seems strangely old-fashioned and unreal after some of the expert trickeries of the Silver Screen.

But, boy, when you sit in a theater and see a stage full of real girls, in real colors, performing chorus numbers in real flesh and blood, and can sit back in your seat (or forward) and take it in all at once with your own eyes, without having to be panned from left to right on a camera, then you realize that all the movie millions in the world can't create a spectacle even to approximate it for all-round satisfaction of the senses.

In the first place, no matter how gorgeous the settings and costumes may be for a Hollywood extravaganza when they are being photographed, and no matter how intricate the dance routines may be at the hands of the country's best directors and the feet of the country's best dancers, in the movie theater they all boil down to a screen the size of an air-mail stamp, where you either get a black-and-white long shot in which you couldn't recognize your own mother, even if you knew her place in the chorus, or a series of rotating closeups showing two-thirds of a body in some sort of individual action, or another series of medium shots, giving you an inkling of what two or three of the people are doing and thinking at that particular moment. That's no way to look at a chorus in action.

Of course, when color photography becomes common, the drab slate-gray note will be relieved and the magnificent colors in which movie musicals are actually made will not be wasted, as they are now, but even then, how are you going to look along a whole line of girls, with one *coup d'oeil*, without having to wait for the whim of the cameraman? How are you going to pick out the one you like best, and look at her exclusively if you happen to want to? How are you, in other words going to enjoy a musical show to your heart's content? The movies have taken all Romance out of musicals.

These possibly lecherous remarks have been brought on by the satisfaction of watching the chorus in *Red, Hot, and Blue!*, one of the too-few real musical shows on Broadway right now. The girls are pretty and have style, Constance Ripley has designed some lovely costumes, and we see them in the colors in which they were designed, not Eastman gray. George Hale has arranged some excellent dances, and we see them being danced all at once and in the same theater with us, not on a mirrored floor half a mile away. Donald Oenslager's settings are bright and cheerful, and the whole thing makes you feel very warm and gay, and glad that Mr. Vinton Freedley still believes that there should be some excitement about watching a musical comedy.

In the matter of stars, we have Jimmy Durante, Ethel Merman, and Bob Hope. I shall have to control myself in speaking of Mr. Durante, as I sometimes seem prone to overdo my enthusiasm for him and his charms. All that I will say is that I have never seen him better, and let it go at that. Miss Merman is her usual dynamic self, and I have an idea that one or two of Mr. Cole Porter's songs benefit greatly by her powers of projection, although, on a second visit to the show, I was convinced that Mr. Porter's score is much better than I thought it the first time. Certainly "It's De-Lovely," "A Little Skipper from Heaven Above," and "Hymn to Hymen" are first grade, and if he wanted to make "Down in the Depths, on the 90th Floor" another version of "Night and Day," he had a perfect right to. His lyrics are, as usual, in a class by themselves.

In the matter of the book of Messrs. Lindsay and Crouse, I feel that they rather underestimated their own taste when they settled on the mark of a hot waffle iron on a young lady's *derrière* as their theme and then proceeded to pun their way ahead in the same vein, but as far as I am concerned, Mr. Hope can carry quite a lot of corny dialogue without giving offence (Heaven knows he has had to in the past) and he helps Miss Polly Walters in her even more difficult assignment. The Hartmans, as incidental comedy of their own devising, are also an addition.

Of course, it is probably unfair to say that the book is under par and then say that Mr. Durante has never been funnier, for the authors presumably were in the same building when his material was being devised. If he is at his best, and Miss Merman sings Mr. Porter's music, and the chorus is beautiful to look at, what is there really to cavil at?

And, to get back to our thesis, there is a new musical comedy in town which makes any million-dollar Hollywood production look like just what it is—a moving picture on a screen.

—*The New Yorker*, November 7, 1936, pp. 28, 32.

VI

STARK YOUNG

The Apron String in Our Theater

If you talk about an outside influence on an art, you must first
be clear about the fundamentals of that art. To go very far into
the relation of our theater to the English, we must know first of
all that the art of the theater is an art to itself. It differs from
every other art. We must know the sources from which it springs
and the means—drama, setting, costume, acting, music—that
make it up and that contribute to its ends, which are the expression of human living. We must know that in entering into this
art every element, such as drama, costumes, action, becomes
something that it was not before; drama is not literature, architecture is no longer architecture but translated into another art,
and so with everything involved. The importance of a country
in the theater depends on how far it is endowed with means and
methods and resources by which the art of the theater as an expression of life is furthered.

The necessity for such an understanding at the very outset was
borne sharply in upon me last spring. In a discussion of the season in New York, in an article in *The North American Review*,
I touched in passing on a subject that needs talking about at more
length, the importance of our theater's getting away from the
influence of the English theater. This statement, with a very
brief indication of the reasons for it, brought from Mr. St. John
Ervine a delightful reply and an invitation through *The London
Observer* for me to discuss the matter in greater detail at some
future time. In his article Mr. St. John Ervine says that in his
judgment I am on safe ground when I ask America to discover a
drama of its own. To that one can only say, obviously, we should
hope so. Mr. Ervine wonders if I am merely repeating the anti–
Anglo-Saxon theories of Mr. Mencken; to which I reply that
even if I had such a prejudice I should not indulge it at the ex-

Reprinted from *The North American Review*, CCXVI (1922), 833–42,
by permission of the Executor of Stark Young's estate.

pense of art. Well, that point being settled, then, Mr. Ervine would like to know just what there can be in the theaters of other countries rather than the English that I want our theater, if it turns to any foreign stage, to follow. Mr. Young, he says, finds the drama in England valueless in comparison with Russia, Germany, Italy, or Spain. He wishes me to stoop to particulars from the heights of airy generalities and oblige him by naming the drama in all those countries which reduce English drama to the level of the negligible. Shakespeare and Shaw, he says, are being played in many places on the Continent; what is there better in the drama of Italy or Spain or Russia? And Mr. Ervine makes some American comparisons.

Well, to that I might say I know nothing better in those countries than Shakespeare and Shaw. But that is not the point at all. When he talks like that Mr. Ervine is doing exactly what nearly every other writer on the subject does. He does not talk of the art of the theater and seems unaware that there is such an art. He gets off on to drama, which is only one element of this art; and for all that what he says about drama comes to, he might as well be talking of literature. And when I talk of the influence of one country's theater on another I have no competitive interest in whether these theaters are better or not than our own. That sort of contest can reach no decisions except on the grounds of mere personal taste and prejudice. And I am not exactly talking about the occurrence of admirable instances of plays. I talk of qualities, resources. A country that is significant for our theater will be one where there is manifestly a talent for and an abundance of one or more of these essential qualities. The whole discussion turns on that. How much resource has the English theater for the expression of English living, of all living if you like? In England how much of the abundance of life wells up and speaks through the forms of the theater? As for dramas, I mean not separate plays so much as the gift or possibility of expressing life in terms of the theater. I mean not so much single instances of acting, but the possession of those attributes that go to make acting a complete and significant art. I mean not the mere occurrence of excellent settings, but the gift for expressing our visual experience in terms of the theater and for making that expression significant.

The relation of our theater to the English is an important subject. We have in America now no small impulse toward a theater of our own. From many lands and peoples we have brought magnificent stores of characteristics to draw upon and infinitely diverse dreams and ways of living. We have natural conditions unlike those to be found anywhere else in the world, we have our own kind of energy, our own development of society, our own hopes of the future and judgment of the past, waiting to be expressed in an art of the theater. For influences, if we choose, we have the whole world to turn to. How far our turning in the theater to England is profitable or cramping, a profound need or a mere hangover of colonialism, is a question to think upon.

In the first place there is no absolute necessity, of course, that the theater of a country borrow anywhere. The primary need is that it develop out of its own kind. Soul is form and doth the body make, as Spenser said; the form of our art of the theater will necessarily come out of what we have to express. In the end we shall have to find our own feet to stand upon. But the history of art is full of influences always; for that is the natural tendency of human art as of human beings. Influences, then, we have and shall have; and influences at their best may very well be our participation in the accumulated riches of the world. But an influence in order to count must come from a source dictated by our profoundest needs. It must not be a mere parental accident. We have leaned on the English theater more because we chanced to be an English colony than because of any deep need of it.

Moreover, it does not follow that, because a race is gifted in one direction, it is necessarily gifted in another. The powers of a race, like a man's, may culminate in a complete expression of itself in one art and in another art may only stammer. The English race has, obviously, a talent for governing and for colonization, demonstrated the world over, and for developing a governing class. It has a talent for sports; and, I think, a talent for poetry, though I am aware that in saying so I should have to defend the racial conception of what the poetic is. But the English are not gifted to anything like the same extent in the theater. And even if there were an adequate theatrical expression of English life, it does not follow that it would suffice for us. We are not pure English but many races, and we live under very different conditions. We may need England in many ways, commercially, culturally—and even for the Anglo-Saxon domination of the world, if one likes to cherish that rather self-complacent dream of things—and from the English we can learn much. But from their theater we can get little. If it is better than ours that is because the culture, the social life, the literary elements that go to make it up are better, and not because of any essentially theatrical elements in it.

I know the objection that comes up immediately. It is exactly the kind of thing that one expects to come up in the discussion of any art by people who bring little thought or understanding to the fundamentals of it; just as a man may see the harmony of tone or the painstaking in a picture without in the least knowing what painting is. The objection is this: How much better the diction of English actors is than ours! How much better the manners of a company of English actors than of one of our companies! And that is very true. But the answer is simple. First of all, the diction and manner that people are talking about in these English companies is largely a negative thing. The excellence of it consists not so much in anything done as in what is not done; it is not so crude as ours, not so loud, not so vulgar. Second, diction and manners in any important sense are not mere pleasing reservations and harmonious discretions; they are things that contain in themselves a constructive abundance, they are elements of style, they have in them their own passionate intention and their revelation of proportion and meaning. The English theater, unlike the French or the Tuscan, cannot be said to show any real talent for diction and manners as creative elements in the art of the theater. Diction and manners, as we find them on the English stage, are scarcely art at all; they are only parts of the ordinary life of England and, as everyone knows, far from being standards of perfection, are actually below the level of the best social tradition. We may copy all this but there is little in it for us beyond mere imitation. And the imitation of English speaking would make a fool of the American stage insofar as that speech is unlike our own. But in Rome or Paris we have at least a chance of finding a theater in which diction and manner are seen as creative elements in an art. We need the influence of the theaters with a sense of the possibilities of words and manner as revelations of life, and a conviction of the necessity of cultivating them as means toward high and complete theatrical expression.

In the most lasting element of the art of the theater, the drama, the English theater, compared to that of other countries has nowadays little to teach us. Shakespeare, of course, belongs not only to the English but to all English-speaking theaters, since Shakespeare's England no longer exists. And even Shakespeare handed on no dramatic form that later dramatists have been able to use.

There seems to be a darkness and chaos at the very heart of his art that remains more or less unmanageable. But granting everything to Shakespeare, if you like, the fact remains that England is almost the last place to see him played. The renowned schools of Irving and Tree only botched him up; they prettified Shakespeare's magnificent intelligence and ungovernable current of life; and Forbes Robertson, for all his fine moments, played that favorite and stupid English trick where the classics are concerned, of turning everything into the Bible, which, whatever its virtues may be, is scarcely the Shakespeare of the seventeenth century. Leaving Shakespeare out of it, then, very much as we might leave out Spenser or Milton or Aristophanes, we turn to the English drama of later times. Meantime we must remember that we do not look just now at a drama for its special and unique merits. We look to it as a possible influence for our own; and such a possibility depends on the gift it shows for expressing its matter in terms of the theater, and on its gift for form that is significant as a dramatic vehicle. In this sense there is always on the Continent a dramatist who is better than his English competitor in the same kind. Congreve, for all his fine ear and literary gift, is far inferior as theater to Molière, as are Sheridan, Goldsmith, and their like. Pinero in the same field of thought and life and method is nothing to Ibsen. Galsworthy, for all his poise and ease and his equable cricket, is a mild form of a dozen Continentals; by the side of Chekhov his realism is like an invitation to tea; by the side of Strindberg Galsworthy is like playing cribbage with the beadle. For a glowing and sensuous rendering of the rich and tragic splendor of men and passions and cities, D'Annunzio has found the dramatic expression. The remarkable work of John Synge follows him at a distance. For the macabre and heroic and wilful and witty and romantic there is Benavente. Compared to what the Russians can say of life's warmth and grayness and depths of suffering, Stanley Houghton and the rest of the Manchester School of dramatists are like milking cows on a field of battle. These boasted Manchester realists have developed a kind of problem method of their own, no doubt; but they remain sterile in their monotony. They are like provincials arguing self-consciously before a Sunday School superintendent a question which the larger world has long since located and more or less settled and which can be treated now, if at all, only in terms of vigorous creation. Barrie is a delightful and adorable personage who can encourage us to be sweet and droll when we can and as we can; but Barrie is an influence better for our souls than for our theater. Shaw has no respect for the theater or for any other art in itself. He abounds in fine passages; he encourages us to talk and to put ideas into drama—from him we might learn how to let our drama have a little more brains and how to make what thoughts we have more lively and provocative. But with Shaw the theater is more of a reformer's outlet and a theorist's mouthpiece than an artist's medium. His success is in talk and theory rather than in imaginative creation. Gilbert and Sullivan are English essentially. Their quality of humor is not ours, though we like it for a season now and then. In their direction we have already on the way to something of value our musical comedies and reviews, our jazz and follies; which, good or bad, are representative, in their spirits, their extravagant quantities and their accentuations, of a definite element in American life. Out of English drama nowadays there are numerous plays that we might enjoy if played in our theater. But except for the literary element in the art of the theater, about which Shaw and John Synge could teach us a good deal, there is little English drama that could bring us any dilation of our powers of expression or any revelation of new regions of living to be expressed.

An Englishman who starts out to be an actor struggles with certain racial traits that are handicaps to the art. He has first of all a body that is not expressive; whereas an expressive and eloquent and magnetic body and gesture is the main focus of the art of acting. He distrusts the exhibition of feeling and prefers talking about emotion to showing it; whereas the ideal in acting is the achievement of a medium by which the life going on within can be exhibited, as a delicate scientific experiment is shown through glass. He dislikes the effect of calculation in anything, of premediated craft. He prefers to think that things are sincere in the limited sense of being not thought out, though he knows how unlikely that must be; in a word the Englishman is afraid of conscious art. Whereas, in acting, the supreme style—as well as all secure technique—derives from a combination of sensibility and calculation, and moves toward an ideal of distinction with a touch in it of conscious elaboration.

The voice of the English actor compared to ours is a fine one. It is more even, a better tone, a better precision. But compared to the French or the Russian or Italian voice, the English is a very limited instrument. It is apt to be dry, to be cramped in the throat, and too self-conscious for the greatest effects, in tragedy especially. It suits admirably the one thing in which English actors do really excel, their social comedy. But the English voice in general, though it can give us points, has nothing for us compared to almost any theater on the Continent, where the use of the voice is more studied, where the tone has more range, the breathing more freedom, and the vowels more purity.

The acting of social comedy is the best thing about the English theater. But what it gains in charm and humor and psychology, it often lacks in style; it is rarely smart or elegant or vivid. And it takes its quality not so much out of any talent for acting as out of the gently ordered social sense, the introspection, whimsy, individualism, the cranks, the droll egoists, of the life it portrays. Outside this single field of their comedy, English acting is poor compared to almost any of the Continental. It has no style compared to the French; no realism compared to the Russian; no warmth or translucent actuality, no beautiful fluidity, no magnetism, compared to the Italian; no lyrical fervor, romantic flexibility, and swift clarity of results compared to the Spanish. For our actors the English theater has a few pleasing and personal and more or less negative benefits; but from it we can acquire little that is fundamental in the art of acting. In any fundamental sense we have already what the English have. The English actor has very little of the vitality, the physical and mental animation, the style, the magnetism, the free and flowing rhythm, and a kind of poignant impulse and passionate eloquence of humanity, that are the sources of a great art of acting.

In the directing of plays the English achieve more unity, a better ensemble, than we do; but in this the Russians or the Germans are infinitely superior. In décor the English theater has, of course, Gordon Craig, though it remains to be seen just how important and inclusive Gordon Craig's ideas will come to be regarded in the theater of the next fifty years. But however that may be, there is no need to go to England to learn from him. One might as well go to Corsica to study military tactics. For Gordon Craig we go to Russia or Berlin or Vienna, and even at home we have more of him than in London.

For the English their theater is not, in any profound sense, racially expressive. Among them the developments of government, of morals, of sports and of private religion and sects, command a great and absorbing interest. The arts of poetry and of social living have also for a chosen few a deep and old interest. And all these have found means for the expression of themselves. But it cannot be said that the English theater covers or includes English life to any wide and deep extent. And what is more, far from finding itself expressed there, the English nature mistrusts the theater. There is something still in the mass of Anglo-Saxons that is hostile to the very stage itself. This hostility and mistrust began long before the days of the Puritans but it came to a head under them, and it has never quite died out. It feels that at best the theater is a place for mere amusement, that it is wicked and flippant or inconsequent. This prejudice the settlers of America brought with them to our shores. For it is a significant fact that in a country that was so exciting, so adventurous, so dramatic and so free as ours, there should have been even up to this time so little real expression in dramatic form of our life. Other more artistically gifted races have helped us past this limitation somewhat. But so far as the art of the theater is concerned, the strain of our Anglo-Saxon forefathers in us is more inhibitive than otherwise; the "Mayflower" harbored no Muse among her passengers, and such brave barks as touched Virginia's sands brought with them gods of pleasure and eloquence but not of the theater. The teaching of our brave and pious forefathers turns us away from what might be one of the greatest means of expression for American life.

And with this mistrust of the theater, which persists to such a degree in England and—in the provinces especially—among us, goes another fact. The English do not take the theater seriously. The most interesting and distinguished people in England have not often been devotees of the theater. London does not take the theater seriously as Moscow does, where the fervor and warmth and speculative intensity of the Russian life are carried to the play and where the activity of the soul is continued in terms of a living art. London does not, like Madrid and Rome and Milan, take the theater seriously by taking it naturally, taking it as a part of the day, a thing like love, food, daylight, that one accepts as a matter of course, a place where whole families sit together, children grow up out of their nurses' arms, and the day's life is renewed in an easy and vivid and moving embodiment of it. These countries, and not England, will influence us, if any can, to give the theater a more genuine and necessary place in our life.

And, finally, there is only one kind of influence of one art on another that has any significance, that makes sense when we talk of it. It is an exact parallel of the influence that one man has on another. If one man merely tries to imitate another, copies his walk, his clothes, his personal mannerisms, he ends by being very silly and negligible. But if he discovers in another man qualities that he admires and a way of taking life that seems to him admirable, he may with advantage cultivate in himself these qualities and these modes of approach to experience; and through what he learns thereby he may be enabled to express his own life with more beauty and success. An influence in art works in precisely the same way. The influence of any theater on ours will depend for its health on one thing, the extent to which there is an understanding that our theater seeks for its uses certain qualities and modes of expression that will enlarge its significance. An influence that appears in the shape of borrowed names and plots and novelties is of small importance. On the Continent there may be qualities—the exact and vibrant realism of the Russian temperament, for example—that we might possibly learn to recognize in ourselves and to bring into our drama. There may be certain modes of treatment—German expressionism for example—that may seem to dilate for us the region of dramatic expression. There may be directions of mentality—say the French ability to create a character that is at once the type and the individual—that may show us new ways of observation. There may be habits—such as the Spanish way of passing at will from prose to verse and back again—that may help our theater toward relaxation and flexibility of mood. Or there may be physical endowments—the Italians, for instance, whose bodies are such lucid and vigorous mediums for their ideas—that may remind us of the importance of muscular co-ordination and gesture and magnetism. But the English theater affords us opportunity for little beyond colonial tradition and imitation.

But leaving aside any particular theater or country, the one main issue, obviously, in the American theater is that it develops a medium of expression that can embody American life. The important thing is that we find for ourselves in the art of the theater a real dialect. To perfect this dialect our theater may borrow from any in the world. But when, through its own labor and evolution and through the contributions of other theaters, the American theater has developed this medium adequate to its ends, nothing else can be done for it. Nothing further of any significance can be added to it. Except superficially, through mere imitation or theft, there is no influence that can help beyond this point of acquiring a medium of expression. After that the quality of our theater will depend on the quality of the life that it expresses.

VII

GEORGE JEAN NATHAN

Eugene O'Neill

Although O'Neill's *All God's Chillun Got Wings* has not yet been produced as I write—it is scheduled for presentation within the next few weeks—I may be forgiven for venturing a few words on it in view of the copious flood of ga-ga that followed its publication in these pages. Participants in the emission of this drool have included everyone from Prof. Dr. Arthur Brisbane, of the Bibliothèque Hearst, to Colonel Billy Mayfield, of the Benevolent Protective Order of the Ku Klux Klan, Texas Lodge, from the dramatic critic of the Windgap, Pennsylvania, *International News-Herald* to the shepherd of the Baptist flock at Horsecough, Virginia, and from a member of the faculty of Princeton University to the owners, publishers, editors, and editorial writers of half of the Southern newspapers. Black men have protested in the press that the play is a libel on their race, since it shows an educated Negro taking for wife a drab of the streets. White men have protested in turn that it is an insult to their race, since it shows a white woman, no matter what her morals, taking unto her bosom a coon. The heroic Colonel Mayfield, in an editorial in the *Fiery Cross*, demands the immediate dispatch of the author on the ground that he is a Catholic and hence doubtless trying to stir up the Negroes to arm, march on Washington, and burn down the Nordic White House. The always passionately sincere Brisbane, in an editorial in the Hearst journals, says "Look Out! There Will Be Race Riots!" The New York moralmorons are hot with indignation because O'Neill shows a white woman kissing a Negro's hand. Dramatic critics, all but one of whom confess they haven't read the play, denounce it vehemently on the ground that they have heard from someone who read an article by someone in some one of the papers that it is going to be played by a real Negro and a white actress, which is awful. The

Reprinted from *The American Mercury* by permission of Mrs. Julie Haydon Nathan.

American Legion, through certain of its mediums of expression published in the Middle West, announces flamingly that it considers the play subversive of 100 per cent American patriotism in that it seeks to undo all the good that was accomplished by the Legion's winning of the late war. The lucid argument of the Legion is that a piece of writing that deals with miscegenation and that is supposed to be authentically American is sure to alienate certain of our late allies in arms. It is the further belief of the Legion's spokesmen in the Middle West that there may be German propaganda concealed somewhere in the enterprise. In all probability, observe the Legion's spokesmen, the producers of the play will be found to be either German or of German descent. The names of these producers, whom the Texas Chapter of the Ku Klux on the other hand insists must be Jews, are clearly of a German-Yiddish flavor, to wit, Macgowan, O'Neill, and Jones.

It has been some time since a play has succeeded in causing so much commotion. Why this particular play has caused it, I can't make out, unless it is that the number of half-wits in America is increasing much faster than any of us has believed. There is absolutely nothing in the play that is in the slightest degree offensive to any human being above the mental level of an apple dumpling. The initial thread of theme is simply *Abie's Irish Rose* with Abie blacked up. And the final turn of theme is simply that of Wilson Barrett's *The Sign of the Cross* with the off-stage howling of lions left out. *Uncle Tom's Cabin* has been played at different times by six companies with real Negroes in the role of Uncle Tom—two black prizefighters (the famous Peter Jackson was one of them) are among those who have played the part—and no one, even south of the Mason-Dixon line, has so much as let out a whisper when these real Negroes have fondled and kissed the white Little Evas. The late Bert Williams not only played in many sketches with white women, but cavorted gayly for years with white feminine flesh on our music show stage. In *All God's Chillun Got Wings*, there is no physical contact between the Negro and the white woman save in the matter of their hands. Once, true enough, after a scene of frenzied mental aberration, the white actress is called upon to kiss the Negro's hands "as a child might, tenderly and gratefully," but the intrinsic feeling and impression here are not far removed from the Uncle Tom—Little Eva kind of thing.

To object to the play because it treats of miscegenation is to object to the drama *Othello* ("Othello is made by Shakespeare in every respect a Negro."—August Wilhelm Schlegel), or to the opera *L'Africaine*, or to the Kipling story of "Georgie Porgie." To object to it because it shows a man and a woman of different color and of antagonistic race in the attitude of lovers is to object to Sheldon's *The Nigger*, De Mille's *Strongheart*, Selwyn's *The Arab*, and the current *White Cargo*, to mention but four out of any number of popular theater plays that have gone their way unmolested, to say nothing of *Madame Butterfly*, *Lakmé* and *Aïda*. To argue against it that, since it shows a white woman marrying a Negro it therefore *ipso facto* places its mark of approval on such marriages is to argue that since *Tosca* shows a woman stabbing a chief of police to death it therefore *ipso facto* places its mark of approval on the universal murdering of policemen. The O'Neill play, it is quite true, shows a certain white woman and a certain Negro in the married relation, but it obviously has no more intention of generalizing from this single and isolated case than has such a play as *The Bowery After Dark* which, following the line of profound logic that has been exercised in the case of the O'Neill play, would seek to prove that all Chinamen are bent upon getting white women into dark cellars for purposes of anatomical dirty work. *All God's Chillun Got Wings* is simply O'Neill's attempt to show what *would* happen psychologically *if* a white woman, whatever her station, *were* to marry a Negro. Plainly enough, in order to show what *would* happen, he has theatrically and dramatically to deduce his findings from the visualized situation. Otherwise, save he wished to resort to the idiotic dream formula—which doubtless would pacify the dolts who are currently so much worked up—he would have no play. How far he has succeeded in achieving his intention, the readers of the play may judge for themselves. It is my own belief that he has achieved the end he had in view. His play is unquestionably enfeebled by its sketchiness, by its perhaps too great economy of means, but it nonetheless presents its theme sincerely, intelligently, sympathetically, and, it seems to me, dramatically. There is a measure of cloudiness in its final passages, yet this cloudiness is doubtless inherent in the very nature of the theme. The hoopdedoodle that has been raised over that theme and over the planned theatrical presentation of the play expounding it must make any halfway intelligent Pullman porter shake his head sadly in pity for the mentality of a certain portion of the race that, by the grace of God, sits in the plush chairs.

In the case of *Welded*, O'Neill has tried on Strindberg's whiskers with the same unfortunate result as in the instance of an earlier play called *The First Man*. Following the technic of the late lamented August, he has set himself so to intensify and even hyperbolize a theme as to evoke the dramatic effect from the theme's overtones rather than, as is the more general manner, from its undertones. The attempt, in a word, is to duplicate the technic of such a drama as *The Father*, the power of which is derived not by suggestion and implication, but from the sparks that fly upward from a prodigious and deafening pounding on the anvil. The attempt, as I have said, is a failure, for all one gets in O'Neill's play is the prodigious and deafening pounding. The sparks simply will not come out. Now and again one discerns something that looks vaguely like a spark, but on closer inspection it turns out to be only an imitation lightning-bug that has been cunningly concealed in the actors' sleeves.

What O'Neill had in mind in the writing of *Welded* was, unquestionably, a realistic analysis of love after the manner of Strindberg's *Dance of Death*. What he planned to show was that a deep love is but hate in silks and satin, that suspicion, cruelty, torture, self-flagellation and voluptuous misery and torment are part and parcel of it, that it constantly murders itself and that its corpse comes to life again after each murder with an increased vitality, and that once a man and a woman have become sealed in this bond of hateful love they are, for all their tugging and pulling, caught irrevocably in the trap of their exalted degradation. What he actually shows, however, is only vaguely what he set out to show. His intent and achievement are miles apart. He goes aground on the rocks of exaggeration. His philosophical melodrama is so full of psychological revolver shots, jumps off the Brooklyn Bridge, incendiary Chinamen, galloping hose carts, forest fires, wild locomotives, sawmills, dynamite kegs, time fuses, mechanical infernal machines, battles under the sea, mine explosions, Italian blackhanders, last minute pardons, sinking ocean liners, and fights to the death on rafts that the effect is akin to trying to read a treatise on the theme on a bump-the-bumps. O'Neill rolls up his sleeves and piles on the agony with the as-siduity of a longshoreman. He has misjudged, it seems to me com-pletely, the Strindberg method. That method is the intensifica-tion of a theme from within. O'Neill has intensified his theme from without. He has piled psychological and physical situation on situation until the structure topples over with a burlesque clatter. Strindberg magnified the psyche of his characters. O'Neill magnifies their actions.

Welded has already been written by another dramatist who made of it one of the masterpieces of modern drama. I refer, of course, to Porto-Riche and *Amoureuse*, perhaps the finest play on the subject ever written. Porto-Riche wrote his play simply, unaffectedly. There is no three-alarm dramaturgy in it, as there is in O'Neill's. It moves quietly, convincingly, devastatingly, on its even and temperate course. *Welded*, on the other hand, has a terrible time with itself. It is forever climbing up the sides of steep mountains with ear-rending grunts and groans and with excruciating pains in its middle when all the while there lies a smooth, easy valley path to the other side of the mountain in plain view. It is constantly bawling at the top of its lungs when there is need for nothing but a whisper. It is always sitting down on its own hat.

The simple truth about the play is that its characters are intrinsically nothing but hams. O'Neill has intensified his human beings to the point where they are no longer human beings, or symbols of human beings, but just actors. And to pile Pelion on Ossa, he has made one of these characters an actress and another a Broadway theatrical manager! Further to add to the joviality of the occasion, the producers engaged Ben-Ami, an actor who would play Huckleberry Finn in the manner of Ermete Novelli making a gala address at a Lambs' Club banquet in honor of Robert B. Mantell, for the role of the idealistic playwright. This Ben-Ami, an actor intensified to such a degree that he seems al-ways in danger of biting himself, brought to the already highly actorized role an artillery of histrionic nonsense that made it doubly unreal and absurd. (If you wish to gain an idea of the way Ben-Ami acts, imagine Eddie Cantor and Morris Gest in a free-for-all fight.) Miss Doris Keane managed the woman's role with a fair share of skill. The staging of the manuscript by Stark Young was satisfactory save in the matter of lighting. Unless my eyes deceived me on the opening night, it was high noon outside the window of the room in Act II although the time was two o'clock in the morning. Again, the dawn of the last act was of a peculiar pea-green shade, as of Maeterlinck full of Chartreuse. Still again, although the room of Act I was illuminated only by a small and arty table lamp at the extreme left of the stage, the center of the stage—the battleground of the actors—was whimsically bathed in a dazzling radiance by a powerful balcony spotlight. After all, one can at times forgive Belasco many things, even his Catholic collar, Presbyterian coat, and Methodist breeches.

—May, 1924.

Under the recent delusion that he made a dramatization of Coleridge's *The Rime of the Ancient Mariner*, what Eugene O'Neill actually made was a moving picture. What drama lies in the poem, he extracted, and in its place put a series of cutbacks and fade-outs that needed only a few additional scenes showing the Bride running through a daisy field, the Third Wedding Guest standing in meditation beside a high waterfall and the Ancient Mariner silhouetted at the close against the evening sky to convert the whole thing into a film of the popular order. O'Neill's theory of dramatizing the Coleridge ululation reposed in the typical cinema notion of leaving nothing to the imagination. While an actor with a voice full of cramps and a face full of whiskers, thus depicting the Ancient Mariner, stood at stage right and declaimed the lines, the electrician periodically turned on and off a green light which illuminated the center of the stage and revealed a group of sailors engaged in retailing a pantomimic accompaniment. Thus, when the interlocutor recited that portion of the poem which has to do with the blight that fell upon the ship, the green light came on and showed the sailors lying flat on the floor, and when the recitation recalled the passing of the blight, the light came on again and showed them getting slowly to their feet. It was all as literal as the late Charlie Bigelow's Weber and Fields recitation of *The Midnight Ride of Paul Revere*, with its off-stage accompaniment of hollow cocoanut shells and its shaking of a cowbell to indicate the heroic messenger's frantic ringing of the countryside's front-door bells.

The weakness of the Provincetown Theater group, as with the majority of semiamateur organizations, lies in its preoccupation with lighting and scenery at the expense of drama. Thus, as a forepiece to the O'Neill contribution, a production was made of Molière's *George Dandin, or the Husband Confounded* apparently for ño other reason save that it offered the Messrs. Macgowan and Jones an opportunity to frame it in the kind of Redoutensaal setting so enthusiastically set forth by them in their last year's eminently readable volume on Continental stagecraft. The O'Neill offering, too, was doubtless welcomed chiefly as an occasion to experiment with masks and shadow lighting. All such experiments, of course, are valuable in their way, and many of them turn out to be possessed of much beauty and theatrical effectiveness, but the cornerstone of every theater in the world is a typewritten manuscript, not a new kind of bunchlight or a new way of draping curtains. A barn with a burlap backdrop and a row of oil lamps is a great theater if a Rostand writes its plays. A palace with scenes by Michelangelo and lighting by the German government itself is something less than a theater if it fails to realize that the play is ever and alone the thing.

—June, 1924.

The influences presently bearing down most heavily upon Eugene O'Neill are Strindberg and the German expressionists. Much of his most recent dramatic writing reflects a synthesis of the two. His earlier work, which was free from these influences, was as meritorious as his later work has been relatively weak. Strindberg is in his grave, and the German expressionists are already on their way to the cemetery. O'Neill should give up buying tin wreaths and following funeral processions. His path lies in the other direction.

—September, 1924.

A finely imagined and dignified piece of dramatic writing, Eugene O'Neill's *Desire Under the Elms* moves along engrossingly for about half its distance and then gradually loses its quality of theatrical interest. I have read the play and seen it acted. It reads extremely well and holds the attention unwaveringly from start to finish. But it does not play so well. Behind the footlights, after a vigorous hour or so, it slowly peters out. I have tried to figure out the reason for this, but my deductions do not entirely satisfy me. It may be that in this drama O'Neill has seen human emotions too greatly in the altogether and has been too uncompromising in the surgery he has performed upon them. It may be that these eminently admirable and praiseworthy qualities of his have been the very things that have removed the necessary theatrical effect from his play. For the stage, after all, as I have observed in the past, is not the place for consistent and resolute analysis, but rather the place for a deceptive simulacrum of consistent and resolute analysis. What the theater calls for, in other words, is not forthright perception and intelligence so much as only those elements in forthright perception and intelligence as lend themselves to a show. The finest drama must be at bottom a show; unless it be first and foremost a show its place is less in the theater than in the library. *Desire Under the Elms* is half theater and half library.

The theme of the play may perhaps most quickly be described as a dramatization of the possessive "mine." The bitter struggle to possess—material and spiritual: gold and land and love and faith and the body—constitutes the play's essence. This theme O'Neill has related in terms of a single household in the bleak New England of 1850; and his narration embraces lust, murder, seduction, theft, hate, blasphemy, illegitimacy, and almost all the other sins and crimes on the index. The dramatic intensification method of Strindberg, of which O'Neill is so ardent a disciple, is here again brought into play: emotions and actions are from moment to moment crowded together and piled atop one another into a series of constant explosions. It is a method full of danger to the playwright, as there is always the difficulty in keeping this side of the hairline that separates and distinguishes intensification from mere bald overemphasis and exaggeration. O'Neill is not always successful in differentiating between the two, and the result, when he becomes confused, runs his drama perilously near the rocks of anamorphosis. One feel this, as I have observed, much more in the acted play than in the printed play. And one feels it doubly when the play is acted as it is currently being acted in the Greenwich Village Theater.

—February, 1926.

O'NEILL'S LATEST

Four years ago, Eugene O'Neill let me read a play of his called *The Fountain*, a very beautiful play, centered in the legend of

Ponce de Leon, that told of man's eternal quest for yesterday, only to find at the end of the troubled trail that yesterday is ever in the hands and hearts of the youth of tomorrow. Four weeks ago, I saw a play by Eugene O'Neill called *The Fountain* acted on the stage of the Greenwich Village Theater, but it was not the play I had read. This other play, though much of the beauty was still in it, had become a worn and tired thing out of apparently endless rewriting. Divers producers had in the four years considered it, had even gone so far as to promise its presentation —but always with a string attached. This one had that change to recommend; that one had another. And O'Neill, oddly enough for a man who is the most independently minded writer for the American theater, had seemingly listened to each of them; and not only to each of these producers, but to the very producers who now at length have put his play on for him.

The changes that O'Neill was persuaded to make—these suggestions and hints from men who were no more competent to make meritorious suggestions to O'Neill than a beer-keg is competent to give Annette Kellerman swimming lessons—have done the play no end of damage. One can see plainly the confusion in which the dramatist found himself. Where originally there was simple loveliness and clarity, there is now a disconcerting repetitiousness and, in the concluding act of the play, an imagination become so helplessly tangled up in itself that what comes out of it, in its central vision scene, is little more than a John Murray Anderson Music Box Revue number played behind a sequin-embellished scrim. This last act of *The Fountain*, even in its original draft, was not of the quality of the preceding acts, but surely, unless my memory has gone back on me, it was in no sense or degree the flat and uninspired piece of dramatic writing that is presently being played.

Of the original play, several of the earlier episodes have been left intact, and these are as rich in a poetic imagination crossed with a biting mockery as anything our American theater has offered. In them the poet that is ever at the heart of O'Neill's bitterest goddamn takes wings. But in certain of the subsequent episodes the attempt at poetic expression takes weak refuge in golden sunsets, azure heavens, trees laden with golden fruit, dreamlands, moons, flowers, and all the similar stencils of the petty versifier. That this is to be attributed to a mind and fancy become sterile from the enervating task of ceaseless revision of the manuscript and that O'Neill simply became so worn-out that he was not himself is clearly apparent to one who has read his more recent and as yet unpresented play, *Marco Millions*. In this latter, which comes from O'Neill's hands exactly as it was originally conceived and unimpaired by helpful advice from solicitous and kindly, if blockheaded, mentors, we find all the hues and lights of imagery and invention that certain critics, unfamiliar with the tampering to which *The Fountain* was subjected, have argued the poet O'Neill incapable of.

Yet, though *The Fountain*, as it comes eventually to us in the theater, is a disappointment, it contains much to attest anew to the fact that in its author we have the first dramatist of high position that this country has produced. Against its shaky dramatic structure which ends up on a philosophic chord as banal and conventional as a Tin Pan Alley ballad's, we have that counterpoint of sentiment and irony which O'Neill alone of our American dramatists is master of. Against the leaky imagination of the concluding episodes of the play, we have such episodes as de Leon's challenge aboard the flagship of Columbus and the uncommonly lovely scene of meeting between the grown-old adventurer, his heart toughened to love, and the glamorous young daughter of the woman he forsook at Granada those years ago to follow the fortunes of a sword against Cathay. And against the periodic triteness with which the theme has been handled, we have such intermittent bravery of dramatic mind as has gone into the creation of the scene wherein the Indian Nano informs his people on the meanness of the Christian ethic and the scene wherein de Leon, now governor of Porto Rico, holds out against the Church in behalf of a great and pragmatic mercy. Faults there are in the play, and many, but what virtues it has are virtues that one encounters nowhere else in the American drama save in that part of it which O'Neill writes.

Robert Edmond Jones has designed the settings and dress of the play with much fine feeling, but he has been less successful in producing it in a manner to quicken it into theatrical life.

Among the criticisms of the play, I note a dissatisfaction with the American Indian as O'Neill has presented him. O'Neill has seen fit to give his Indians a measure of intelligible discourse. This has come as a great shock to those of my colleagues who, since their Edward S. Ellis and *The Girl I Left Behind Me* days, have been firmly convinced that the only things American Indians were capable of saying to one another were either "Ugh!" or "Big Chief Bushwah has spoken!"

—February, 1926.

. . . let us take a look at the plays recently shown in the New York theater. Here, without exception, one finds that the more authentic contributions to the art of drama are unequivocally much less ennobling, as the word goes, than the inferior ones. Thus, *Goat Song*, Franz Werfel's fine play, does nothing more than to depress man with the philosophy that the monstrous seed of revolution with its trail of devastation will never die from the world, while such a piece of balderdash as *The Love City*, by a fellow countryman of Werfel's, inspirits him with the philosophy that the forces of evil must inevitably meet with defeat. Thus again, *The Great God Brown*, Eugene O'Neill's latest and most beautifully imaginative work, bears in upon man's consciousness the rueful facts that hypocrisy triumphs in this world where truth and forthrightness fail, that noble dreams must go down to defeat before the world's prosaicism, that what the world demands is mere show and pretense and that heartache and desolation are ever the reward of great, deep, and faithful love—where, on the other hand, *The Shanghai Gesture*, a *paté* of box-office drivel, sends the spectator home with the comforting conviction that earthly lust resolves itself into tragedy, that the sinner must soon or late pay a grievous penalty and that vice is ever less profitable than virtue. Thus further, Ibsen's *Little Eyolf*, aiming to be a sermon against selfishness, actually makes mankind bitterly despairful with its demonstration that egoism, which is mortal man's one pragmatic religion and his one potential victorious battle cry, is the faith of the humiliated and defeated; *Hedda Gabler* instils a sense of the utter futility of life by showing that the bad angel of man's destiny holds ever the whip hand; and *John Gabriel Borkman* puts hope and trust to rout with its doctrine of the eternal cruel indifference and selfishness of one's offspring and with its categorical enunciation of age's chagrin and suffering. Such an unmitigated gimcrack as Capek's *The Makropoulos Secret*, to the contrary, gladdens the mortal soul with the thesis that the short span of life allotted to man by God is infinitely more desirable than a longer span would be; such a tenth-rate French boulevard play as Fauchois' *The Monkey Talks* warms the human heart and mind with a promulgation of the tenet that man's outward self, however ugly, has beneath it a true radiance and that the reward of honest love is a permanent happiness; and such commercial exhibits as *Love 'Em and Leave 'Em* and *Puppy Love* bring God nearer to earth with the eloquent assurance that self-sacrifice is the most exalted of human acts and that true affection will irresistibly find a way to the human heart.

A few words on the O'Neill and Werfel dramas. The former is in many respects the most richly imagined and brilliantly articulated work that the playwright has yet produced. In none of his previous manuscripts has O'Neill written with so deep an insight into human aspiration and defeat; in none has he achieved such moving and forceful romantic prose. His technique here is largely what it has always been: the filtering of an ironic vision of humanity through a sieve of pitiful despair and the embellishment of the residuum with the species of ejaculation customarily associated with dock laborers and vice-presidents of the United States. But there is noticeable an increasing mellowness and a paling of indignation that lift the drama into a doubled grip and power of conviction. The dialogue reaches heights of tender profundity that have seldom been equaled in the native drama. Now and again, the author's imaginative resources fail him, as, for example, in the Al Woods crook drama species of curtain line that brings to a conclusion the act wherein the police captain demands to know how "man" is spelled, but in its entirety the work has soundness, beauty, and a very real quality.

Werfel's play, like much of authentic drama, is in essence a melodrama imagined, orchestrated, and executed in terms of its overtones. I have indicated the theme. This theme the highly talented young German has set into the Slavic countryside in the period of Turkish domination. His symbol of the ugliness of revolution, however blinding and dazzling the firebrand that lights it on its way, is a monstrosity born to a man and wife in the form of a child half-human, half-goat. In the development of his motif, Werfel periodically relies more greatly upon literary means than upon dramatic, but so skilful is his employment of them that he frequently evokes a sense of drama where actually there is none. His play is one of the most meritorious that has come from the younger element in Central Europe and in its author there are gifts that are unmistakable.

—April, 1926.

The Case of O'Neill

It is a characteristic mark of the lesser level of American criticism to boost potential and still struggling talent with all the gusto at its command and then, once that talent has come into its own and is sitting pretty on top of the fence, to give it a series of kicks *à l'improviste* in the abstracted rear. Nor is the upper level of our criticism entirely free from the same antic. What is at the bottom of it is unquestionably the very human, if proportionately uncritical, impulse to help the weak and hoot the strong, to do all we can for those who need us and to dislike, out of the fonts of vanity, those who are perfectly able to take care of themselves and who no longer have any practical use for us. Since the average critic amongst us is hard put to it to submerge his *alter ego* in his judgments and appraisals, since he is unable to dissociate his mind and emotions, we are constantly entertained by the monkeyshine to which I have alluded. When a young man of promise appears on the American scene the critics invariably start out like von Suppe's *Light Cavalry*. But no sooner is the young man's promise actually realized than they take on the tone of Bizet's *Ivan the Terrible*.

Eugene O'Neill is surely not the only writer in our midst who has met with this species of criticism. In the beginning, his plays, full of promise but as yet immature, were greeted with a comprehensive and gala pounding upon drums, cymbals, and neighborhood dishpans. The racket of endorsement was deafening, and out of all proportion to the subject of celebration. But when gradually his plays began to attain to genuine solidity, imagination, and profundity, when gradually he began to settle himself squarely and securely at the very head of American dramatists, when finally he began to achieve the imprimatur of high critical praise from Europe—when this happened, the hitherto ecstatic local critical jazz and tzigane dancing stopped and in their stead the critical air became filled with Cherubini requiems, Liszt concertos pathétiques, Dvořák *opera* 89, and a whole chorus of Amnerises lifting up a despairful "Ohimè, morir mi sento." The same phenomenon has been observable in the cases of Sinclair

Lewis and Cabell, as it was observable some years back in the cases of Dreiser and Victor Herbert. At the core of the nonsense, in addition to the point I have already mentioned, is doubtless the familiar critical passion to woo esteem for its independent and flexible judgment, which latter the school of criticism in question generally seeks to demonstrate by a sudden, surprising, and intrinsically imbecile *volte face*, preceded by a certain amount of coquettish controversial detouring and by facetious animadversions on the gluey quality of such more sober critics as prefer to keep themselves in the background by repeating honest, if repetitious and hence dull, estimates of the artist under discussion instead of trying to clown themselves into notoriety and the limelight.

O'Neill, as I have said, is presently undergoing his dose of the become stereotyped rigmarole. It began to get under way when he wrote *The Great God Brown*, it got up more steam when he wrote *Marco Millions;* and it has now spread itself with a pervasive choo-choo tooting upon the appearance of his *Strange Interlude*. It is not necessary to believe that these plays constitute the finest work that he has thus far done to appreciate the absurdity of his critical leg-pinchers. It is only necessary to grant that, whatever one may happen to think of them, they are at least reputable efforts and surely, by any standard of criticism, superior to half the plays he produced in the days when all the boys and girls who are now disparaging him let themselves go full blast over her merits. One need not like *The Great God Brown*, but no one in his right senses can fail to agree that, at its worst, it is yet a better piece of work than *The Straw*. One need not think much of *Marco Millions* to allow that it is nevertheless a better job than *Welded* or *All God's Chillun*. And one may actually be convinced that *Strange Interlude* is not all that some of us think it is without believing that *Gold* or *Diff'rent* or *The First Man* or *The Fountain* is infinitely better. Yet the goose-cries shake the welkin. Arbitrarily, evidently under the impression that they have been praising O'Neill long enough, the boys and girls forget the exact quality of his plays that they hymned in the past and proceed to a loud and hollow lambasting, seeking thus to achieve their silly little day in court and to show the world what great Bismarcks they are.

What they are, I allow myself to believe, are pathetic jackasses. O'Neill certainly is susceptible of sound critical attack on a number of sides—if such attack constitutes one a jackass, then I fear that I have on occasion been a lovely one myself—but he just as certainly is not the target for the kind of squashes that are currently being projected at him. Granting that I believe his most recent work is by long odds the soundest and best that he has so far done, and duly allowing that I may be quite wrong in my opinion, it still seems to me that any critic who, having accepted his *Ile, In the Zone, Before Breakfast, The Dreamy Kid, The Long Voyage Home, Bound East for Cardiff, Where the Cross Is Made, The Rope,* and even his *Anna Christie* as admirable, can yet not find his *The Great God Brown, Marco Millions,* and *Strange Interlude* at the very least equally meritorious —that such a critic is sadly in need of a balance wheel.

Of *Marco Millions* and *Strange Interlude* I have already expressed a personal opinion in these pages, and at a time in advance of their actual stage presentation. Of the former, there is little left for me to say. Of the latter, there may be a word or two. The chief objection of the criticasters to it appears to be the author's employment of soliloquies and asides to suggest his characters' unspoken thoughts. These are declared to be unnecessary, interruptive of the action, superfluous, repetitive, and posturing. The play, already extremely long, would, it is asserted, be the more compact and better without them. Exactly the same criticism, obviously, might be made—indeed frequently has been made by the same stripe of dolts—of Schubert's *C Major Symphony,* a perfect thing, as every musician knows, despite its similar musical asides, repetitions, interruptions, and alleged superfluities. As a piece of musical writing it is relatively as long as O'Neill's play and the same arguments may be used by fools against it, but it remains none the less—to pop a platitude—a consummately beautiful work. And if it is seldom, if ever, played in its entirety, let the critics who imagine that in that fact they have found a good argument be made aware of the equally pertinent fact that *Strange Interlude* as it is currently being played on the Theater Guild's stage is also not being played in its entirety, but has been very liberally cut down.

To turn to drama, what is argued against O'Neill's asides and soliloquies may just as logically be argued against Shakespeare's. If O'Neill's might be cut out as largely superfluous and interruptive of his play's action, so might Shakespeare's. Most of the soliloquies written by the latter were simply put into his plays to please actors and the plays would move more dramatically without them. If you doubt it, read almost any one of them, even *Hamlet*, with the soliloquies and asides deleted. To contend that Shakespeare's soliloquies constitute great poetry and that O'Neill's do not is to side-step the direct issue. That issue is simply whether O'Neill's soliloquies and asides are dramaturgically valid. Poetry or lack of poetry has nothing to do with the case. In any event, the argument is based by the critical Bottoms, as so often happens, merely upon labels. The truth about soliloquies and asides as O'Neill employs them is that, while they are cunningly announced by O'Neill to represent the characters' unspoken thoughts—he is a shrewd hand at concealing the obvious and artfully masking it in a way to make the impressionables gabble—they are actually nothing more than straight dramatic speeches, as anyone can readily determine by referring, for example, to the powerful dramatic scene, say, at the conclusion of his sixth act. O'Neill has simply written his characters' thoughts in terms of straight dramatic speeches and has passed the device off on the idiotic novelty lovers by craftily insisting that they are only mute meditations.

As to the yawps over the play's considerable length—it runs for something like five hours—we engage criticism based upon the sensitiveness of the yawpers' sterns rather than upon the work of art itself. A certain critic finds that his netherland becomes weary after sitting out the play and hence confounds his netherland with his cerebrum which, in his case, is largely indistinguishable from it. Art is thus estimated not in terms of mental pleasure but of physical discomfort: the old Babbitt plaint that the Louvre is altogether too large for enjoyment and that the bathrooms at Bayreuth are awful. While it is not to be denied that a five-hour play imposes more of a strain upon one than a two and one-half-hour play, the strain surely is no reflection upon the play's quality. A Chinese drama that runs for three nights is not *ipso facto* worse than a play by Mr. Harry Delf that runs for a couple of hours. The Oberammergau *Passion Play*, that runs on and on, may still conceivably be better than one of the Rev. Dr. Charles Rann Kennedy's shorter Biblical exhibits. Shaw's two-night *Back to Methuselah* doesn't impress me as being great shakes, but the fact remains that when it was cut down to one night's playing time it was made twice as senseless and dull as it would otherwise have been.

The kind of criticism that is ladled out to our more mature artists must often reduce them to a disgusted laughter. Lewis, when he writes an *Elmer Gantry*, is met with the objection that —I quote literally from no less than thirty reviewers—"the book contains scarcely a decent character; almost all of them are hypocrites, scoundrels, and vile." The same criticism may be made of Gorki's admitted masterpiece, *Nachtasyl*. Dreiser, when he writes a novel twice as long as one of, say, Christopher Morley's, is charged with the very *embonpoint* and dispansion for which Dostoevski is acclaimed. Cabell is disparaged for doing what the Restoration writers are commended for. Sherwood Anderson is criticized for faults that in Zola are held to be virtues. And O'Neill is made mock of, in his finest and greatest play, for daring a profound and beautiful thing, far removed from the routine swamps of Broadway, instead of safely hugging the critical coasts with more of his youth confections wherein a supposed spy's secret documents turn out to be love letters, wherein a Swede is given knockout drops in a gin mill, and wherein everybody goes crazy in a green light looking for gold or ile.

—April, 1928.

THE AMERICAN PROSPECT

Until Eugene O'Neill appeared upon the scene, the American drama offered little for the mature European interest. The records, previous to his time, showed a number of writers and a number of plays of transient quality, some of them very amusing and some of them genuinely gifted in detail, but it brought to light none that bulked with body. The roll included some good melodramas that, while they departed from knavish Chinamen, heroic ensigns, and Kentucky racehorses, were hardly worth more than a three hours' audience consideration; some workmanlike but negligible farces with drolly observed national idiosyncrasies; some comedies, patterned largely after British models, that sought to be American by eliminating the butler and pronouncing such words as *secretary* and *cemetery* in four syllables instead of three; some close caricatures of American phenomena that, while very worthy in their way—Ade's, for example—were, after all, like most dramatic caricature, evanescent; and some heavily straight-faced dramas, elaborately conscious of their own pseudo-profundity, that momentarily managed to trick the pseudo-profound reviewers of the day into imagining them to be something important. But the roll included nothing, or at best very little, to persuade Europeans that our drama was anything but periodically diverting nursery play.

With O'Neill, however, the native drama has begun to take on at least a measure of the significance that it previously lacked. To argue that O'Neill, while an American, does not write strictly American drama, that is, drama that issues part and parcel out of American life but rather drama of more or less universal cast, is, of course, to beg the question. Hauptmann, Porto-Riche, Galsworthy, Pirandello, Rostand, Echegaray—for that matter, every significant dramatist from the Greeks through to Shakespeare, Molière, and Ibsen—has written drama of similar cast, for all its identification with immediate time and place. So much is the sourest kind of platitude. It is also the most superficial kind of criticism, and, in O'Neill's case, at times silly. For certain of his plays smell of America as pungently as hot dogs and the Hon. Tom Heflin. But, the one way or the other, what O'Neill has brought to the American drama, aside from his own contributions to it, is almost more than anything else precisely what Shaw brought to criticism of the drama: a gift of independence and courage to others. O'Neill has shown the aspiring American playwright that there is a place here for a wholehearted integrity in dramatic writing, and that there is a public here that is generous in its response to it. He has shown this by patient and often despairing labor, and by his uncommon personal intrepidity, and by his forthright denial of the theater as he found it, and—with convincing concreteness—by the practicability of what he dreamed and set out to accomplish and did accomplish. He has, in a few words, proved to the American playwright with potential stuff in him that he need not be fearful, as he long had been, of what is foolishly called the literary drama and of what is looked at askance as the drama of limited appeal—and that there is often a much more substantial reward, in the terms of the First National Bank, in fine and honest effort than in half-hearted or intrinsically shoddy.

The effect is already observable, not in actual achievement, perhaps, but in the direction that the native drama is going. Playwrights, having gained confidence from O'Neill's success, are beginning to apply themselves to the drama seriously. My professional duties bring me into touch with dramatic manuscripts from the four corners of the Great Democracy and the omen is plain. Most of these manuscripts are still pretty bad, but there is an intention in them that wasn't there before. They are striving for something. They are trying to dig deep, not into the souls of actors dressed up as General Sheridan, Pinero actresses dressed as Salvation Army Nells, and Supreme Court justices who believe in hypnotism, but into those of men and women out of the soil and the life that they know. They are interested not in the Solon Shingles, Mulberry Sellers, and Bardwell Slotes of vaudeville America or in the Davy Crocketts of ten-twenty-thirty melodrama America but in human beings far removed from grease-paint and close to the quivering pulse of that America unillumined by artificial light and unadorned with tinsel and false whiskers. Nor has O'Neill's influence spread merely to these rookies and the potential figures of our drama of tomorrow. The spur that he has given to playwrights already in practice, some of them long before him, is obvious to anyone who keeps an eye on the theater. Paul Green, Sidney Howard, and any number of other such newer men are plainly rowing in O'Neill's wash, as yet without much strength but surely in a direction indicated by O'Neill's compass. And even such gentlemen of earlier generations as Mr. Owen Davis, author of *Chinatown Charlie* and *Bertha, the Sewing Machine Girl*, may be observed pathetically trying to get in the swim with their *Detours* and *Icebounds*. O'Neill has sounded the new note and if there are still no dramatic musicians proficient in striking it, the desire to strike it is evident. That is something.

On a plane different from O'Neill's we find independence and courage pitching themselves no less into drama and getting rid at one swoop of all the inhibitions, chiefly of a moral nature, that American drama since its birth had been heir to. The timidity that had previously made the native drama fit fare only for Edwardian wives, sisters, and sweethearts has disappeared, and writers have ceased to be ashamed of being adults. The day when comedies like Clyde Fitch's were accepted as clinical studies of the female of the species on the ground that Fitch knew what kinds of hats women admired and the French names for their underwear has been snickered into limbo, as has the more recent day when Sheldon's plays were accepted as surgical portraits of the male on the ground that he didn't make a tough mug speak like a Harvard graduate and occasionally allowed him a measure of carbonated biology in the presence of an inviting lady. Our playwrights, even certain of those of unfortunately minor talent, are more and more, in the great Dr. Brisbane's phrase, looking nature and fact straight in the eye. The whilom sentimentality and equivoque are disappearing, and truth is gradually finding itself in stage surroundings hitherto strange to it.

Do I seem to be full of an unaccustomed and alarming optimism? Not so fast, brother! For though the American drama is in better state than ever it has been, there is still an immense amount of room for improvement and development. Europe, on the whole, for all its immediate doldrums, is still so far ahead of us that, O'Neill alone excepted, the combined American calliope is far from earshot of the foreign drum major. But the wind is stirring in the cities and on the prairies. In time, maybe, in time. . . .

—October, 1928.

The manuscript of Eugene O'Neill's new work, *Dynamo*, to be produced next Spring by the Theater Guild, has also been duly read. While I shall reserve an expression of critical opinion for the time being, I may hint that the play deals with the battle of divine belief opposed to atheism and with the heart-tearing search of modern mankind for a god that shall be satisfying. The technique of *Strange Interlude* is repeated, though in relative moderation. The drama has eight characters and is in three parts. The characters are a clergyman, his wife and son, the atheistic superintendent of a hydroelectric plant, his wife and daughter, and an operator and floor-man at the plant. The first part of the play shows the exteriors of two small houses in a small town in Connecticut, the scenes and lighting, as in *Desire Under the Elms*, revealing different rooms in the houses. The second part is laid in the same general setting after a lapse of fifteen months, but shows chiefly the sitting room in the house of the clergyman. The third part is laid in a hydroelectric power plant near the town, four months later. Scenes one and three reveal the exterior of the plant; two and five the interior of the generator room, switchboard room, and upper- and lower-switch galleries; and scene four the interior of the switch galleries. The play will be fitted into the customary theater length. More anon.

—December, 1928.

THE FIRST OF A TRILOGY

In connection with *Dynamo*, his latest play, which I touched upon briefly in these pages last month, Eugene O'Neill writes me his purpose as follows:

It is a symbolical and factual biography of what is happening in a large section of the American (and not only American) soul right now. It is really the first play of a trilogy that will dig at the roots of the sickness of today as I feel it—the death of the old God and the failure of science and materialism to give any satisfying new one for the surviving primitive religious instinct to find a meaning for life in, and to comfort its fears of death with. It seems to me anyone trying to do big work nowadays must have this big subject behind all the little subjects of his plays or novels, or he is simply scribbling around on the surface of things and has no more real status than a parlor entertainer. . . . The other two plays will be *Without Endings of Days* and *It Cannot Be Mad*. These two plays will be greater in writing scope than *Dynamo*—which has a direct primitive drive to it and whose people are psychologically simple as compared to *Strange Interlude*'s—and will give me a great chance to shoot my piece as a writer. But *Dynamo*, believe me, has taken all I have to give as a dynamist of the drama and it should make its power felt when once it is skilfully produced. It is going to bring all the pious sectarians down on my neck in hell-roaring droves, I prophesy—and should be as much argued about, I think, in its different way as *Interlude*. It will require some expert directing to get its full values across. . . . In addition to the plans for near-future plays, I've also done a lot of thinking on my idea for the Big Grand Opus. I want to give about three years to it—either in one long stretch or, more probably, that amount of working time over a larger period with intervals of doing a play in between times. This G.O. is to be neither play nor novel, although there will be many plays in it and it will have greater scope than any novel I know of. Its form will be altogether its own—a lineal descendant of *Strange Interlude*, in a way,—but beside it *Interlude* will seem like a mere shallow episode.

As for *Dynamo*, I amplify what I set down a month ago with a brief and very crude narration of its plot scheme, reserving critical comment until the play reaches the stage.

The Reverend Hutchins Light, a fanatical Christian, and Ramsay Fife, superintendent of a hydroelectric plant and a dogged atheist, are neighbors in a small Connecticut town. They are bitter enemies. Fife, who is gifted with an ironical humor, plans to utilize the clergyman's son's love for his own daughter to sardonic ends. Knowing that Light hates him and would do anything in his power to get rid of him as a neighbor, Fife, after swearing the clergyman's son to secrecy, confides to him the fabricated story that he, Fife, is a fugitive from the law and is wanted in a Western state for murder. The boy, brought up in the faith but gradually finding himself torn by doubts, beset by the prayers of Light on the one side and by the derisions of Fife on the other, finds Fife's secret betrayed out of him by his vindictive father—as Fife duly anticipated. The betrayal maddens him and, as his bigoted and frenzied father shouts his potential triumph over Fife, the boy, seeing in the betrayal the meanness, hypocrisy, and utter rottenness that lie under his father's principles, shouts in turn his hatred and contempt for his own family and what they profess to stand for.

In the boy's heart and mind, however, there is nothing to take the place of the faith that he has been robbed of, of the principles that he has found were built upon quicksand. His father, the pseudo-saint, and Fife, the rabid unbeliever, keep up their futile taunting and futile acrimony. But the boy can find no path to truth either through the one or the other, or even between them. His mind wanders to the great hydroelectric plant, the scene of Fife's labors. The notion begins presently to dawn upon his confused, adolescent brain that there, in electricity, may be at least a semblance of something to respect, to stand in awe of, to worship as a positive. The idea becomes a fetish.

"It all comes down to electricity in the end," he babbles. "What the fool preachers call God is in Electricity somewhere—and I'm going to give up my life to find it. But I won't find it in books, I know that now. They help, but they don't go back far enough. They're outside. You've got to get inside it somehow, go back in it and *be* it. Did you ever watch dynamos? What I mean is *in* them? They stand for it the same way the old stone statues stood for gods—but the dynamos are living and the statues were only dead stone. *Dead* stone? Where do I get that dead stuff? Stones are atoms, and atoms are alive. I never thought of that before. Those old gods were electricity in the end, too!"

A different phase of the father's fanaticism presently takes hold of the son. The dynamos at Fife's plant take on in his mind the aspect of gods, the plant itself the aspect of a place of worship. There, his tortured, groping thoughts seek solace, peace, truth. And, in the end, half-crazed, he goes to his death in the whirling embrace of one of the generators. "Poor Reuben," mutters Fife's wife, "she wouldn't tell you the secret after all, would she? Or maybe she did and you couldn't stand it."

—January, 1929.

ERVINE ENCORE

In a review of Eugene O'Neill's *Strange Interlude*, Mr. Ervine vouchsafes us the following critical observation:

The famous "asides" left me, for the most part, unimpressed. In any event Mr. O'Neill cannot claim any credit for their invention. They are part of the oldest form of theatrical technique, and they were rightly abandoned as the craft of the actor improved. Their revival by Mr. O'Neill is either an attempt to prevent actors from acting or a sign of laziness in the author.

With all due respect to friend Ervine, I have the honor to believe that on this occasion he has pulled what may politely be described as a boner. In the first place, while he is perfectly right in saying that O'Neill cannot claim any credit for inventing asides, as they are part of the oldest form of theatrical technique, he exposes himself, by the very nature of his statement, to the charge of criticizing *Strange Interlude* simply on the ground of its novelty or lack of novelty, surely—as he would be the first to admit—the most trifling and defective of critical viewpoints. Secondly, when he says that asides "were rightly abandoned as the craft of the actor improved," he not only argues that the forthright dramaturgic genius of Ibsen proceeded less from within Ibsen's dramatico-literary conscience than from Ibsen's external consideration of mummers, but, also, by implication, that the craft of the actor improved as asides were abandoned. The fact that the greatest actors since Ibsen's time have in the majority of cases achieved their eminence and reached the highest peak of their craftsmanship in classical plays full of asides appears to have escaped Mr. Ervine. In the third place, our friend's assertion that the revival of the asides "is either an attempt to prevent actors from acting or a sign of laziness in the author" must, so far as the first of its allegations goes, be big news to the ghosts of Coquelin, Salvini, Bernhardt, and Mantell no less than to all the living Moissis, Bergners, and Anglins and, further, in the case of its second, must appear to many an exceptionally dirty crack at such lazy dogs of the past as Shakespeare and Sheridan and at such low loafers of the latter-day as Edmond Rostand.

The objection to the old aside is simply another critical symptom of the lamentable over-sophistication that has come upon the theater of our day and age. We have arrived at a point where familiarity with the theater and consequent satiety have brought about a critical *Katzenjammer* of which the most conspicuous characteristics are a tendency to hail what is merely new, however essentially dubious, and to disparage whatever is old, however sound. Personally, I list myself a champion of the sophisticated theater, but only when that sophistication has marks of integrity, experience, understanding, culture, and wit. The so-called sophisticated theater of the present time is, on the contrary, largely a bogus thing, with the air of a movie actor imitating an English gentleman and with the smarty manner of a Bernard Shaw talkie.

The belief that the theater must be sophisticated or play to empty seats has impelled a horde of undertrained, unpolished, dumbbell play concocters to leave off the writing of their erstwhile species of innocent balderdash and to posture a recherché sliding-panel, false-bottom drama as idiotic and common as it is integrally spurious. Europe is full of playwrights who imagine that sophistication is simply a matter of denying what everyone has believed for three thousand years and setting their denial in front of some bughouse scenery, while America is hardly poorer in stage scribblers who believe that the height of sophistication consists in making faces at adultery and transferring the scene from Shore Acres to Park Avenue. The so-called sophisticated stage of today, as a consequence, is sophisticated largely in the sense that a college boy out with a chorus girl and reinforced with some very bad liquor is sophisticated. It is worldly in speech and juvenile in mind. It has the aspect of a grandfather in diapers.

The really sophisticated playwrights active in the contemporaneous theater may be numbered on the fingers of both hands. The others who affect sophistication run into the hundreds.

These, unable to transcribe life in terms of authentic character, seek to pleasure their little reputations by an arbitrary nose-fingering at life and character as the latter are depicted and portrayed by their superiors.

—February, 1929.

A Non-conductor

Dynamo, Eugene O'Neill's latest, produced by the Theater Guild, fails to foment me. There is in it, doubly and even triply exaggerated, that note of swollen emotion and indignant vociferation that made *Welded* ineffective and occasionally even absurd and that robbed *Desire Under the Elms* of the slow, smoke-curling force which is drama's most vital attribute. O'Neill betrays himself in so feverish a personal mood that one achieves much the same feeling that comes over one when listening to that boiler-works symphony of Antheil. In place of smooth persuasiveness there is shillaber lapel-tugging and coat-tail pulling; in place of suggestive harmony there is simply an earsplitting racket.

I look at the script of the play and scrutinize it somewhat in the light of a musical composition. It is almost completely without shading. The brasses, with the characters' chests and bosoms heaving and with faces a violent purple, hold the field. The emotional din is overpowering. The final effect is of a calliope going down for the third time and tooting at the top of its remaining strength for help. At the risk of filling altogether too much space, but in the thorough conviction that in no wise more accurately may the nature and pitch of the play be indicated, I set down seriatim, from beginning to end, the list of stage directions:

Arguing tormentedly within himself.
With angry self-contempt.
Furiously clenching his fist.
His eyes lighting up with savage relish.
Suddenly horrified.
Protesting petulantly.
With indignant anger.
With evangelical fervor.
With life-long resentful frustration.
With bitter self-contempt.
With a grim resentful side-glance.
With a gloomy glance.
Nettled.

Sharply and challengingly.

With a stubborn counter-challenge.

Presses his thick lips tightly together, clenches his teeth and the cords along his jaw stand out—an effort that gives his face the expression of a balky animal's.

Her face is suddenly set in the intense expression of concentrated purpose that his strives after.

She thinks bitterly.

Determinedly.

With melancholy.

He interrupts her stubbornly, his voice booming assertively.

She frowns.

Hearing his father's raised voice Reuben jumps to his feet resentfully.

A look of passionate anger sweeps into his face.

Defiantly and sneeringly.

He looks around uneasily, afraid of where his thoughts are leading him.

The lightning flash has caused him a nervous, apprehensive start.

With annoyance, turns his back on her.

With a sad longing, he sighs.

Her voice turned bitter.

Echoing her bitterness.

In a hard voice.

Irritably.

Thinking bitterly.

Fife's voice is thin, sardonic and malicious.

Chuckles with malicious satisfaction.

Growls contemptuously.

Sniffs the air critically.

With glum humor.

He calls her impatiently.

She gives a start.

Muttering with concentrated rage.

Turning on his wife angrily.

Impatiently; stung—angrily.

Defensively impatient.

Grimly.

With a scornful smile.

Stung—bitterly.

She goes deadly cold.

In a hard metallic voice.

Bitterly.

With a bitter sneer.

Winces as if he had been struck.

Starts a bitter retort.
Determined to push her advantage.
The Victrola starts a blaring jazz record.
Fixes his eyes on his wife combatively.
His expression growing stubborn and set again.
His voice taking on the direful tone in which he warns sinners of the hell-to-come.
Sharply.
Thinking gloomily.
Despairingly.
With a groan.
This thought drives him frantic—he paces up and down vainly trying to calm himself.
He waits nervously.
With sudden fear.
With fierce jealousy.
A strong flash of lightning.
She gives a gasp.
Fidgets uneasily.
The storm gathers over the hills.
With scornful superior comments.
Disgustedly.
Confidently boastful.
Thinks exasperatedly.
With a grunt.
Rapturously.
Laughs scornfully.
Gives a start at another flash of lightning.
With a snort of rage and disgust.
Boiling over with indignation.
With a start.
With fiery indignation.
With fierce sarcasm.
With indignant disgust.
Rebelliously.
With a malicious grin.
Resentfully.
With a forced laugh.
Confused, she turns on her mother angrily.
With sardonic scorn.
With a challenging air that has grimness in it.
Insistently.
With a grim smile.
Tauntingly.
Frowning uneasily.

Worriedly.
Venomously.
Frightfully.
Scornfully.
Terrified, pulling back and stammering.
With taunting scorn.
Stung.
Sneeringly.
There is a flash of lightning—he gives a frightened start and glances up furtively.
With fear.
A wave of passion coming over him.
He grabs her.
With a little cry of pain.
With passionate oblivious intensity.
Frightened in her turn—with an almost hysterical flippancy struggling away from him.
She adds tartly.
Her temper ruffled.
In miserably shame and contrition.
Completely crushed.
In a bullying tone.
His mind full of tortured remorse.
In a tone of mingled rage and grief.
Irritably.
In exasperation.
Thrusts paper at her.
A grin of malicious expectancy on his face.
Slinks hurriedly across.
Peers stealthily around in an extreme stage of agitation.
Starts frightened.
Staring moodily.
With bitter self-scorn—thinking gloomily.
His resentment smouldering up.
Dissolves into abject shame and fright.
Cowers weakly.
With bravado.
With exaggerated cordiality.
His face flustered.
Forces him into chair.
His confusion increased.
With a challenging smile.
With a meaning grin.
In a solemn severe tone.
Stares at him appalled and bewildered.

Jeeringly.
Raising his voice defiantly.
With horrified stupefaction.
Strains her ears.
Smiling mockingly.
With defiance.
With a malicious leer.
His face flushed with mingled indignation and fear.
Opens his mouth to make an indignant retort when a vivid flash of lightning comes.
Gives terrified start.
Half rises—his body tense with the struggle with his will.
With mingled anger and fearful awe.
Mockingly.
Shrinking back in a turmoil of guilt and fright.
Thinking remorsefully.
Worriedly.
Indignantly.
Protestingly.
Glances at her impatiently and gives her a meaning challenging look.
Solemnly.
Peremptorily.
Sternly.
With an appalled look of shocked stupefaction.
With offended indignation.
Leaning forward indignantly.
His voice booming.
With sudden confusion.
Hangs his head in acute embarrassment.
Stunned.
With growing rage.
Takes a determined step out.
Weak with fright and on the verge of collapse.
Weeping hysterically and trying violently to stifle it.
She sinks down on the ground and lies flat on her face, clutching her throat to choke her sobs.
One hand over her mouth.
Staring calculatingly at him.
Solemnly.
Visibly uneasy and apprehensive.
Worriedly.
With a tragic sigh.
Very solemnly.
He stares somberly at Reuben.

Indignantly.
Gripped by all sorts of nameless dreads.
His nerves set more on edge by a rumble of thunder.
With feigned guilty furtiveness.
With savagery.
Stares at Fife with bewildered horror.
In a strange bewilderment of mind.
His horror turning to a confused rage.
Harshly and condemningly.
Staring at him, thinking in astonishment.
Denouncingly.
With a furious threatening look.
Uneasily.
With a threatening glare.
Piteously.
A flash of lightning.
Clutches the arms of his chair in superstitious terror—all the passion drained out of him, leaving him weak.
Glancing at Fife with horror and fear.
Staring at him apprehensively.
Eyeing him keenly.
Somberly.
Torturedly.
Mournfully.
Filled with horror.
Conscience-stricken.
Frantically.
Furtively.
Insistently.
With hatred.
Angrily—his voice booming denouncingly.
Taunting scornfully.
Angrily and threateningly.
Giving him a scornful look.
Turns her back on him contemptuously—thinking bitterly.
Tears of mortification—she brushes them back angrily.
Wounded—his anger rising.
Turns with a triumphant chuckle.
Turns angrily.
She flings herself on the chaise-longue and begins to cry.
Stares at her in astonishment.
Angrily.
Remorsefully.
Jumps up angrily.
Thinking with a grin.

A vivid flash of lightning.
Jumps nervously to his feet.
Intently and uneasily.
Jerking herself up.
Slinks back.
Uneasily.
His mind is a turmoil of conflicting emotions.
With a shudder of horror.
With a sudden desperate cynical bravado.
A great flash of lightning.
He stands paralyzed with terror.
Thinking incoherently.
Obsessed more and more by a feeling of guilt.
His teeth chattering.
A growling roar of thunder.
He cowers trembling.
Cries with desperate longing.
With malicious satisfaction.
In alarmed surprise.
With increasing uneasiness.
With trembling fingers.
Weakly and frightenedly.
Sinking down on the bed.
Slumps down on his knees and prays frantically.
Comes in excitedly from hallway.
He springs to his feet.
She hurries in breathlessly.
Kissing her frantically.
With agitated preoccupation.
Breaks away from him excitedly.
Her words pouring out.
Completely stupefied.
Stares at her.
Calling desperately.
Commandingly.
Vindictively.
She gives him a shove.
He bounds upstairs.
He rushes in.
Distracted.
With a cruel hard expression.
He breaks down and sobs heartbrokenly.
Alarmed.
Indignantly.
With a start of surprise.

Sharply.
Clinging to her.
Thinking eagerly.
A vivid flash of lightning.
He shrinks and blurts out.
Startled.
With sudden strong revulsion—angrily.
She pushes him away—thinking resentfully and determinedly.
Harshly and condemningly.
A roll of thunder comes crashing and rumbling.
He sinks down on his knees—hiding his face in her lap.
Frightened.
Uneasily.
Insistently.
In a passion of eagerness.
Indignantly.
Listening greedily.
With fierce revengeful joy.
Dumfounded.
Defensively.
Angrily gives him a vicious shake.
With a furious glance at his wife.
Trying to break from his mother's grasp.
Angrily.
In a sudden panic of guilty shame.
Pleading.
Still gripping him and staring into his face vindictively.
Stung—with a violent effort he shakes her hands off his shoulders.
Shrinking back from her.
Still on his knees—passionately protesting.
Pleadingly.
In a voice hard with fury.
Grimly.
Takes a threatening step forward.
Stupefied—his mouth open—stares with amazed horror.
Her face is gloating and vindictive.
In a tortured agony of spirit.
Cries out in an agony of reproach.
Sobs heartbrokenly.
Grimly unmoved.
With hysterical sobbing anger.
Furiously.
Cowers and scrambles into corner.
His horrified eyes fixed on the belt his father has raised in his hand purposefully.

His thoughts whirling madly.
With defiant determination.
Whirls belt over his head and brings it down heavily across
Reuben's bent back.
Reuben's body quivers.
A glaring flash of lightning.
Starts back with a frightened exclamation.
With a convulsive cringing movement.
Wincing painfully.
With an exasperated sense of frustration.
Defiantly jumps up with hatred in his eyes.
Vindictively.
Reminded of vengeance.
Roughly.
A crash of thunder.
Staring with the same fixed look of hate.
Jeeringly.
In sneering triumph.
Frightened.
In a bullying tone.
Sneeringly.
Determinedly.
Harshly.
Vindictively.
Pitiably.
Bitterly.
Breaks down miserably.
Resentfully.
Accusingly.
Furiously.
Furious in turn.
Thinking wildly.
The door slams.
Jeering cruelly.
Glaring with intense hate.
Flings herself on bed and sobs.
Jumps to window.
Desperately.
Excitedly.
With an ugly sneering expression.
In a malicious mocking tone.
With a hard ugly laugh.
Stares at him with a rage that chokes him.
With a pretence of guilty terror.
In a booming ecstasy.

Cursing in a frenzy of rage.
Drives at door with his whole body, crashes it open and stumbles out.
Horrified and frightened.
Staggers to her feet calling frightenedly.
With mockery.
Suddenly flares up into a temper.
With furious disgust.
With sneering contempt.
In fury.
Advances threateningly.
Overwhelmed.
Threateningly.
Furious.
Wildly.
Weeping hysterically.
Aghast.
Grief-stricken.
Thinking bitterly.
Yelling in a frenzy of anger.
Pushing her away roughly.
Threateningly.
Throwing herself in front of him.
Stupefied.
Bursting into a rage.
Fiercely pushing his mother to one side.
A startling vivid flash of lightning.
In wild defiance.
With a sneer.
A tremendous crash of thunder.
With a wild laugh.
Shrinks back in abject terror.
Shouts.
Trembling and pale with fright.
With scorn.
With a wild mocking laugh.
Grabs father by the lapel.
With insulting insolence.
Squeals with terror.
Tries to break from his hold.
Mother screams.
Light runs off panic-stricken dragging his moaning wife by the arm.
Defiantly.

Shades of *Pirate Pete* and *The Queen of the Highbinders*—and that is only the first act! To save space and avoid repetition, I decide not to go on. You have my word for it that the second and third acts are every bit as rich in *fuming impatiences, snorts of contempt, fuming longings, flyings into a rage, defiant sneers, taunting laughs, dire booms of foreboding,* and *terrible looks.* Are these, I beg to ask, symptoms of dramaturgical excellence? Are they not rather symptoms of internal misgiving and weakness, suggestive of ill-assimilated Strindbergianism, or the clamor manufactured by a German street-band to conceal its musical deficiencies? I have before me the scripts, on the one hand, of various old ten-twenty-thirty tin-pot melodramas and, on the other, the scripts, among other things, of such representative emotional dramas as Ibsen's *Ghosts*, d'Annunzio's *The Dead City*, Gallarati-Scotti's *Thy Will Be Done*, Haupmann's *Rose Bernd*, Wedekind's *Erdgeist* and Strindberg's *The Dance of Death*. The stage directions of the former read almost exactly like those of O'Neill's play; the emotions of the latter are hardly visited upon the characters by any such lung and lightning injunctions but are brought to proceed from the secret depths of their souls. A quiet answer may not always turn away wrath, but it generaly turns out vastly sounder and more moving drama than a yell.

We come now to the philosophical content of *Dynamo*, the theme and plot scheme of which I outlined a month or two ago in these pages. That theme, I may recall to you, deals with mankind's search for a new god that shall take the place of the unsatisfying present gods, with the implied belief that in electricity lies the true deity. Granting, with considerable reluctance, the validity or even adultness of O'Neill's thesis and conclusion, let us glance at the nature and originality of his metaphysical exercises. To save time and space, I boil down direct quotations from his text:

1. It's Bible-punchers like Light that do more harm than all the jail-birds past, present and to come! They stand like balky old mules and block up the path of progress.
2. How does God call you, tell me? I'm thinking He wouldn't use the telegraph or telephone or radio, for they're contraptions that belong to His arch-enemy Lucifer, the God of Electricity, the Bringer of Illumination to the black, ignorant, God-struck minds of men!

3. Your Jehovah might aim a thunderbolt at me but Lucifer would deflect it on to you—and he's the better electrical expert of the two, being more modern in his methods than *your* God!

4. Your sin and your Hell and your God mean no more to me than old women's nonsense when they're scared of the dark!

5. I should think God would have to punish adultery and murder —if there *is* any God.

6. He looks scared—it was that lightning—it didn't phase me—he's yellow! "The fear of God in my sinful heart"—it's the fear of Electricity in *his* heart, that's what!

7. God was simply using Reuben as His instrument to bring retribution on your head!

8. It all comes down to Electricity in the end. What the fool preachers call God is in Electricity somewhere!

9. Did you ever watch dynamos? What I mean is *in* them! They stand for it the same way the old stone statues stood for gods, but the dynamos are living and the statues were only dead stone. *Dead* stone? Stones are atoms and atoms are alive! Those old gods were Electricity in the end, too!

10. Did you ever think that all life comes down to electricity and that the man who first really knows it will know the secret of life and have power over everything?

11. Machinery's a queer thing. It's only fools think it's dead—if they'd lived with it like I have they'd know different.

12. How long, Dynamo? I feel as if any minute You'd at last found me worthy—that You'd open your heart to me, the heart of Electricity, and take me in. And then I'll come back with your secret and your power. I'll be born again out of You, Dynamo. I'll be the first true Son of the real, living God!

13. Why does everyone call on God when no one so far has ever dared to face what God really is? The Bible boobs like my old man and the atheist boobs like yours—they're both sick with the fear of knowing the real God, of facing Dynamo! . . . Dynamo's song is the hymn of eternal generation, the song of Eternal Life!

14. I assure you, my dear sir, that all the atheists in the world could stand for days with watches in their hands daring Almighty God to strike them dead and His merciful failure to do so would no more prove that He didn't exist than—

15. But I should think your God, if He is just, would jump at such a fine chance to punish the impious and at the same time prove to everyone that He's on the job! He might do that much for us poor creatures that He'd made in His image—without our consent—that is, if you can swallow the Adam and Eve fairy tale and believe He made us at all!

16. How else could life have begun except by a divine act of creation? . . . And you can say that after all the facts of Evolution that Science has proven?

17. You prefer the perverted nonsense that you are the descendant of a filthy monkey rather than believe that a wonder-working God created you in His image.

18. The sea is only hydrogen and oxygen and some minerals—and all those things are only atoms when you go back in them far enough —and when you dig deep into atoms they're only protons and electrons—all things are Electricity in the end!—the air, the earth, the cells that make up our bodies. And look at the stars! And space and time! They're only conductors for Electricity! There must be a center around which all this moves. That center must be the Immortal Soul of all life, Electricity—the new Saviour who will bring happiness and peace to man!

Now, ladies and gents, I ask you!

I thus permit O'Neill's play to criticize itself, with small intrusion of my own opinion. Surely the O'Neill who dug deep into the human heart in *The Great God Brown*, who in the same play—in that speech about the young man's mother—showed himself to be the first of American dramatic poets, who in *The Moon of the Caribbees* showed himself a rare dramatic painter as in *Beyond the Horizon* and *Strange Interlude* he showed himself a brilliant interpreter of the hopes and disasters and pitiable bravery of mankind, and who in other of his works has achieved an unmistakable importance—surely that O'Neill is not the O'Neill of this amateurish, strident, and juvenile concoction. When O'Neill feels, he often produces something that is very beautiful, very moving, and very fine. But when he gives himself over to science and philosophy, as in *Dynamo*, he would seem to be lost.

—March, 1929.

THE AMERICAN DRAMATIST

Let this chapter be devoted to a consideration of American dramatists and to an effort to ascertain what place, if any, they presently occupy in the theatrical sun.

That O'Neill is the outstanding figure in the catalogue under discussion is now denied only by such critics as employ the denial, against their honest and better judgment, to lend to their writings that share of fillip which always attaches to a marching out of step. Their insincerity is easily penetrable, for while they eloquently argue that O'Neill is not the outstanding force, they do not tell us who is. With the production this last season of *Dynamo*, a very poor piece of work, the hostility toward its author and the skepticism over his hitherto loudly proclaimed talents took on full sail, and we were entertained by an overnight shifting of the critical course. Because he had written a bad play, O'Neill, his antecedent work forgotten, was denounced as an overestimated and even ridiculous dramatist, and it was argued that, since this one play was so bad, doubtless his previous good plays were not really so good as they had previously been thought to be. In this we engaged no novelty, for the tactic is a commonplace one in American criticism, whether literary or dramatic, and familiar to everyone who follows the critical art as it is maneuvered in God's country.

If O'Neill is not the leader among American playwrights, *Dynamo* or no *Dynamo*, it is pretty difficult to make out who the leader is. While it is perfectly true that in one or two of his other plays as well as in *Dynamo* he has exposed at times a juvenile indignation, a specious profundity, and a method of exaggeration that has verged perilously on travesty, he has nevertheless written a number of plays of a very definite quality, a number of plays that outdistance any others thus far written by Americans and, whether in his better work or poorer, shown an attitude and an integrity—to say nothing of a body of technical resource—far beyond those of any of his American rivals. The truth about O'Neill is that he is the only American playwright who has what may be called "size." There is something relatively distinguished about even his failures; they sink not trivially but with a certain air of majesty, like a great ship, its flags flying, full of holes. He has no cheapness, even in his worst plays. *The First Man, Welded*, and *Dynamo*, for example, are mediocre affairs as drama goes, but in them just the same there is that peculiar thing that marks off even the dismal efforts of a first-rate man from those of a second-rate.

—August, 1929.

VIII

H. T. PARKER

"Green Grow the Lilacs"; "Hotel Universe"

The Guild, a Folk-Play, and Acting

To begin—the circumstances. . . . At the Tremont last evening, the usual notable audience awaited the first performance on any stage of *Green Grow the Lilacs*, first play of the five that the Theater Guild is dispatching to Boston; to be fourth or fifth in its New York sequence. Upstairs and down, numbers and interest implied hearty welcome and deserved support. A third time it was testing in Boston a play new to its repertory—as the event proved in a much more forward state than was the lot of either *Caprice* or *Meteor*. A day or two for correction and easement, and *Green Grow the Lilacs* should be in order for well-rounded performance. Thanks to this preparedness and to the quality of play, players, and production, the audience listened and watched intently, were quick in response and plentiful in applause. After the final curtain it lingered to clap the assembled company: would plainly have had the author, Mr. Lynn Riggs, join it. But that young poet-playwright, like the magnates of The Guild, scattered about the house, preferred a modest obscurity.

Next—the externals. . . . The action of *Green Grow the Lilacs* (which title is the name of a folk-ballad) passes in Oklahoma, while it was still the Indian Territory, on a day or two in the summer of 1900. As Mr. Sovey sets the stage, there is a permanent horizon of hazy Southwestern sky, soft blue and white. There is also a picket fence (as New Englanders, if not Oklahomans, would say) interposed between stage and spectators. Once the curtain has risen, it ascends to right and left in two sections to descend at the completion of the scene. Before this fence and an inner curtain, repeating the Southwestern blue and white, pass interludes of local balladry, A.D. 1900, sung by six cowboys and seven Oklahoman maidens. The Northern phrase

Reprinted from *The Boston Evening Transcript*.

for this exercise would be "porch-song"; but the chanting, as it often seemed, was both pungent and amusing; while primi donné of the opera house might have envied these children of earth such clear and colorful diction. This balladry, increased by other examples sung at a porch-party, was shrewdly chosen. It ranged from cowboy ditties to songs of homely sentiment or amorous narrative. It smacked of time and place; smelt of the soil and of those going to and fro upon it; was folk music become integral part of a folk play.

Between horizon and fence we spectators looked simultaneously upon the opened living room and the opened smokehouse of an Oklahoman farm; upon a girl's chamber in the same house, with the closed smokehouse across the way; upon the opened smokehouse again; upon the long porch, with cleared space in front, of Old Man Peck's house; upon a stacked hayfield in sultry, moonlit night; upon the living room once more. All these structures were movable wooden blocks, seemingly a little less than natural size, conforming to the architecture—the word is polite—of time and place. What with a parlor-organ in the living room, a scattering of family portraits, wild flowers in the bedroom washbowl, a range on the porch; ladders against the hay-ricks, the furnishings—to the untutored eye—were plausible and atmospheric. From scene to scene the aspect and air was of the homeliness proper to the play; while throughout, the lights kept the Southwestern softness before the wayfarer passes to the glare of New Mexico and Arizona. How much settings and atmosphere owed to Mr. Biberman, the producer, Mr. Sovey, the designer, and Mr. Riggs as native to Oklahoma, it was impossible to disentangle. Certainly they seemed the happy union of stage quality, literal truth, and imaginative suggestion, that is source of illusion in the theater.

Now to the players . . . Miss Helen Westley, appearing for the first time in Boston as actress for The Guild, took the part of a mothering aunt in this Oklahoman Israel. She wore its calicoes and ambled about its furnishings as to the habit born. She excelled in unelaborated, unobtruded, and also responsive listening, when the talk ran from other lips. Sitting still, when the action passed to others, she remained animation to the scene. Meeting the playwright halfway, she caught and communicated Aunt Ella's mother-wit and homely humor, neither averse on occasion to the candors of frank living. She was as apt with the rough of Auntie's tongue as she was with the honest and affectionate sympathy underneath. She timed, spaced, and colored her speeches with the craft of old experience. In sum Miss Westley, free and full.

On the distaff side Miss June Walker companioned her as the girl, Laurey, who backs and fills before the cowboy lover, because her heart beats so hard that she cannot keep a steady gait; who plays with the preliminaries to marriage in gay young confidences and anticipations; who is Curly McClain's elated and whole-souled bride; who endures the rude mockeries and coarser jests of a Shivaree; who quivers out of swift dread into hysterics of humiliation; whose prideful resentment cracks finally under prideful devotion. Within recent memory Miss Walker has entertained us in Boston with the sophistications of Miss Loos's gold digger and Mr. Belasco's bar-sinistered daughter. She returns now to homely simplicities and honesties, to the unvarnished stress and the mute self-torture of an abased but still wilful girl. Her actress's skill and feeling persuade the character into warm illusion, yet hide the means.

On the masculine side, few professional abilities were concerned—Mr. Strasberg's for a quick, passing sketch to type of a voluble Jewish peddler, bringing (as the natives believed) the air as well as the wares of the great world into this distant Oklahoma; or Mr. Richard Hale's for a villainously jealous, lustful, morose, and murderous farmhand drawn by Mr. Riggs in the unrelieved blacks of melodrama, tempered by the actor into a dehumanized denizen of this Oklahoman soil. Perhaps Mr. Tex Cooper, from the circus tent, should also be counted professional; but he had little to do save to exhibit a tall, spare, gray and goateed presence as Old Man Peck, to wear a genially paternal air, both of which he did easily and well.

The natural actor, as the phrase goes, was Mr. James Patterson, cattleman to play a cattleman. At moments his Curly McClain was plainly remembering and accomplishing what Mr. Biberman had schooled him to feign and suggest. Far oftener, he deployed a native shyness or swagger, a native humor, candor, reticence, or passion that found natural means of expression in tune with the character. Evidently Mr. Biberman had only to touch them up to theater-illusion. The young producer—a rising talent in The Guild—could not quite work this miracle with his ensemble of cowboys and Oklahoman maidens. Touches of self-consciousness, the pause to remember, still lingered. But once cut loose, as in the party at Peck's or the tumult of the hayfield, they were vivid and pliant, earthy and folksy, alive and urgent. Nor, to the casual eye, was Mr. Biberman at fault in the coloring, the building, the whole saliency, of the action.

Lastly to the play itself. . . . For new adventure (which it is the privilege of The Guild to encourage) it is folk piece of this fertile American earth, remote from cities and seaboard, midway across our lusty continent, in time both near and far in our world of quick changes. In these days we are grown-up enough to write, mount, and enjoy such pieces, to consider them discriminatingly. Our theater will not be full-rounded until it gives them just place. Our playwrights, having the instinct for them, will not do their full duty until they set to the writing, naturally, spontaneously—not with the preachy, apostolic, aggrieved assumption that have already turned one into a three-ply bore. Mr. Riggs escapes this pitfall. He knows these Oklahomans, not analytically, but sympathetically and affectionately. They are memories of boyhood, adolescence, and later returns, living memories but also slightly glamoured. He can still breathe the atmosphere around them; yet feel it in heightening retrospect. He leads them into the theater, on no mission bent, but that he may extract from them such human goodness or badness, truth or beauty, such pungent native quality as may dwell in them for us, who, with all our veneer of urban sophistication, are brothers and sisters under our American skin.

Mr. Riggs accomplishes this purpose as chronicler, as poet, as playwright. As chronicler he has chosen aptly a time when the antipathy of the settled farmer folk and the wandering cattlemen was smoldering into final flame. As chronicler again, he has remembered "characters" in the local American sense of the word—Aunt Ella, above all the rest; Curly McClain who is individual as well as cowboy type; in minor place, the girl who plays about with Laurey, Old Man Peck as well. As chronicler once more, he has set in the folk scenes of the peddler's visit, of the songs, dances, and games at the porch-party. Likely enough he also chose the decorative balladry. As chronicler, fourth and finally, he has made the local rite of the "Shivaree" on a wedding night instrument of the theater. Its uncouth din and dirt, its

rude derisions, its nuptial malevolences he has transmuted not
only into stage-spectacle of a soil, time, and custom, but into his
dramatizing means. Coarse-tongued inevitably goes this folk
sport.

Time and again, moreover, Mr. Riggs is poet by inclination
and by habit. Listen to the homely talk that characters Laurey
and Curly through the opening scenes. It is touched with a
native poetry to which we Americans, if we are not over-
civilized, instinctively respond. Hear Laurey and Curly solitary
in the moonlight before Peck's house, the echoes of the party
faint in the background. In homely, humble words, Mr. Riggs
is writing their idyll. Recall the last scene when Curly comes
back from the jail in longing loyalty; when, but only for the
while, pain and pride stay the girl from as loyal loving. Then
find in it, under Mr. Rigg's poet-touch, the simple beauty of
devotion, homely flavored of the soil that begot it.

Minded to enter the theater, Mr. Riggs must also be playwright. As such he lacks the native instinct, the congenial practice, guiding him as chronicler and poet. Now he is on unfamiliar
ground, so eager for means that he cannot be choice, so little
experienced that he does not exhaust them. Unconsciously,
rather than deliberately, he leaves to players, producer, and
scene-designer much that shall shade and round and intensify.
Fortunately for him, the resourceful Guild stands by. Seemingly
he meditates upon the simplicity, homeliness, folk quality, with
which he would invest his play; then chooses melodrama for
theater-means. For it he shapes and colors his lowering villain;
sets him to overhearing sneakingly Curly's talk with Aunt Ella
about the girl. Proceeds then to the ominous talk of the two men
in the smokehouse, with the politeness of the plains half-veiling
mutual repugnance, with the antipathy of farmer and cattleman
thrumming underneath, with foil in the happy expectancy of
the girl almost within hearing. Pistol shots and a knife for momentary climax.

Next, this black-hearted Jeeter Fry haunting the girl lewdly
in the very hour of her marrying. Then the mockery and skull-
duggery of the Shivaree, to climax again when Fry slips and
falls on the knife with which he would kill. Last the shading
into the piteous epilogue, with the truer Riggs putting behind
him his crasser theater-means. Yet who shall say for certain that
he has not chosen advisedly? To the homeliness of a folk play,

the theater-counterpart may be the rudeness (as we like to call it in superior righteousness) of melodrama. Poetry, as Mr. Riggs has shown us, may gild homeliness. Rudeness is more resistful.

—December 9, 1930, p. 12.

OFF THE DEEP END PLUNGES PHILIP BARRY

In *Hotel Universe*—the play that the Theater Guild is presenting in New York and that it may, or may not, bring to Boston next season—in *Hotel Universe* Philip Barry has taken to himself a method. The oldest inhabitants of his stage world report traces of it (as the analytical chemists say) in the half-remembered *White Wings*. They deepened, though they remained few, in the more recent *Paris Bound*. In *Holiday*, they ceased to be traces and became a procedure. Whoever saw the comedy will remember that, every now and then, two or three of the more sprightly wits among the personages imagined themselves some one else in another situation and a different setting to that which actually inclosed them. Having achieved this mild feat of humorous fantasy, they embarked upon a conversation, brief or longer, proper to the imagined characters and occasion; ran through it with such humor and mockery as Mr. Barry put into their mouths; returned summarily to their place and quality in the play; only to repeat and vary the excursion, whenever the fit seized the playwright. Some might say that they halted the course of the piece to diversify it with a charade. Others called the process the acting of miniature comediettes within the comedy. Aided by the skill of Miss Hope Williams and of Mr. Donald Ogden Stewart, these Barryesque exercises in fantasy, humor, and playful illusion proved fresh and amusing. They also suited the personages engaged.

In *Hotel Universe* this procedure becomes a method. Mr. Barry persists in it; enlarges and deepens it; uses it rarely for mere diversion; upon grave issues plies it seriously. No longer are the personages concerned acting high-humored, mocking charades. Rather, they are reenacting, in all gravity, not to say intensity, remembered episodes out of their own past. The playwright begins indeed as though he were resuming the procedure of *Holiday*. With amusement we spectators listen to a humorsome, capricious, quasi-fantastical conversation between three in an office; pass to further interchanges, for the most part derisive, between a financier and a trust company. At the next turn

121

Mr. Barry leads us a step forward. He bids three young men imagine themselves boys "under the old apple tree." They play at Father Damian—a priest who worked among South Sea lepers, one of Stevenson's heroes—fall to quarrel and fisticuffs over bandied words like "Jew," "heretic," "Catholic"; soon are deep in strife recollected out of their several lives.

Thereafter, Mr. Barry uses the method for no other purpose. We see an actress recalling a bitter scene with a brutal father; a youth at confession to a priest whom in his school days he had venerated. By an extension of the method we hear yet another personage recounting graphically to the woman he loves the suicide that had ended an earlier amour. In all these instances, as will presently appear, Mr. Barry uses this method for the release of the chief personage concerned from a besetting memory. Plainly he believes that it is valid with the deeper issues of life.

Scene and Characters

First, however, to set Mr. Barry's scene, array his personages, outline the basic situation and the variants upon it. The action of *Hotel Universe* fills an hour and forty-five minutes and proceeds without intermission—an "innovation" that set tongues wagging in provincial New York but which is common experience in any German city with a revolving stage in its municipal theater. Possibly, that American tongues should stay still, outside sleep, for one hundred and five successive minutes is an extraordinary requisition. This action passes upon a terrace overlooking the summer sea in the environs of Toulon, under the shadow of a house that was once, with the French liking for grandiloquent labels, a "Hotel de l' Univers." There hangs about it an uncanny attribute—of recalling to those within scenes in their lives that have befallen elsewhere; nay, of evoking the very surroundings, say a hawthorn bush in the rich bloom of an English spring or a cheap furrier's shop in a bystreet of New York. By these signs Mr. Barry is preparing for a play of modernistic fantasy and for the practice of the method aforesaid. Mr. Simonson, for The Guild, has designed a setting that suggests spacious isolation, dilapidated beauty, the encircling stillness of lustrous Mediterranean night. He is also fantastic and in the key of the piece with the intermittent play upon the scene of a search light, presumably at the neighboring naval station.

Upon this terrace Mr. Barry assembles nine personages. One is merely incidental, yet aid to the implication of uncanny fantasy—a butler who, at the end of each half hour, stalking gravely through the company, calls it as reminder that nearly all have a train to catch back into the world. Another of these personages is an old and failing man, once an eminent physicist, now obsessed with a mysticism that keeps him ever hovering between the real and the unreal. He is as one who dwells, thinks and speaks at a triple borderland of past, present, future.

The other seven are young persons—the spectator guesses—at the late twenties: the daughter who cares for the aging scientist; an actress of the New York stage, scrawny-voiced, nervously restless, coarse-grained; a wife content with the care of her children, though her husband puzzles her; an overripe damsel of sensual allure and neurotic temperament. To these add three men: one who wanders the world in search of adventure, whose present penchant is perilous mountain-climbing; a second of Jewish blood already risen to great position in finance, yet resenting the obligations thereby laid upon him, like the actress of a different breeding from the rest; last the fine-strung husband of the wife aforesaid, once a publisher, now preferring life to books, yet finding it hardly more rewarding.

FAMILIAR FIELD

It is to be observed that Mr. Berry is again peopling his play with the sort of personages that are his theatrical stock-in-trade. They need take no thought of the financial morrow, since their balances in bank are renewed like the widow's cruse of Scripture. It is their privilege to rise up and depart, to sit down and linger, the world around, as impulse without obligation—save in the case of the financier—may prompt. Their occupations are chiefly mental and tongueful; for it is Mr. Barry's custom to equip them with minds that work quickly, if not too deeply; with lips that open readily to darts of humor, jets of capricious fancy, thrusts of wit, intimate, and, therefore, piercing gibes. All are surfaced with a manner no smoother than is postwar custom in this western world. (It is thinnest and roughest in the actress, the financier, and the woman of amorous allure.) All are also veneered with what passes in their world for sophistication. Detached observers of maturer years may now and again find it amusingly ingenuous and shallow. To Mr. Barry, how-

ever, and to the personages of his creation, it is honest, earnest—
cherished.

It is pleasure to find the playwright concerned again with
such characters, aptly remolding and retouching them for the
theater, regarding them with both insight and sympathy, treat-
ing them, perhaps, as so many emanations of himself. Almost
alone, among American playwrights he can lead them to the
stage; array them in becoming environment; accord with their
manners; set their minds and tongues in motion; release both
their surface-chatter and their inner moods. It is, perhaps, no
grave blasphemy to suggest that they are as much entitled to
place in the American theater as aspiring Negroes of the South,
middle-western bourgeoisie, the dwellers in Harlem flats, or
Jersey suburbs. To some of us, with distorted minds, they seem
more interesting. We are also prepared to believe that they experience genuine emotions, though they neither whine, yap,
nor shout.

Preluding

Mr. Barry's next concern is to weave closer at atmosphere. It
appears that another guest has that afternoon taken his own life,
diving into the sea, leaving behind him the well-turned but
slightly enigmatic message that "he is off to Africa." The reaction among his companions is a natural perturbation; preoccupation in thoughts and speech with life and death, present and
future; irritation of temper and tongue; short-lived eagerness
for this, that or the other distraction. There are nervous drum-
mings upon an ill-tuned piano; shuttings on and off of a
gramophone; nervous recourse to cigarettes and drinks; uneasy
breaks and hasty resumptions of talk; a pervading irascibility
that now and then nips or snarls; a certain wildness stirring in
the air. Mr. Barry, as everyone knows, is fertile and adept with
this sort of thing—the right touch of manner, the light stroke,
the unexpected turn. If at moments he contrives and conducts
too obviously, the other merits are an amend more than honorable.

Now in this first three-quarters of an hour of *Hotel Universe*,
he ventures deeper. Recurrently the talk spins about suicide.
The impulse to it has haunted this one and that one among these
others, even as it obsessed the vanished youth. They also have lost
illusions and found nothing to replace them. They are at odds,

in their own fashion, with living. As Mr. Barry puts some of this talk into the mouths of his personages, it is in character, graphic, pungent. Again, he clouds it with Freudian vapors. It does not always escape a desire to be "literary." It misses occasionally the semblance of precision that the commerce of the theater exacts. Some reproach it as "young talk," forgetting to note that it must necessarily be such, from young personages neither deep nor clear-minded. The method, as already noted, has had at least two turns.

THE PLAY

By this time Mr. Barry is well embarked upon his play of mental states and inhibitions, upon his inset and individual dramas of illusion lost and illusion regained. For illusion, possibly, substitute faith in life. The mountain-climber, for example, loves the physicist's daughter; is loved by her. The obstacle to union is recollection of an amour that culminated in a girl's suicide. Therefore is he base; would be rid of the memory, even at the cost of his life. (There are slips and precipices.) Yet once he has told the tale to the physicist's daughter, the memory and the pang are dispelled. The comedienne is ambitious to act Cordelia in Shakespeare's *Lear*. She is withheld by the memory of a paternal doom that condemned her to the dance and the lighter stage. The old man, who has the faculty of divination, perceives her plight. They re-enact the scene of the angry father visiting his wrath upon the girl-dancer. The memory is lifted; the comedienne goes forth to her ambition.

In turn, the financier is drawn to the sensual woman. Yet wherein does she feed his ambitions? He has fed nothing else since he had his first job at the furrier's. The lady walks in her sleep; a betraying tongue discloses a willing mind. (Mr. Barry is not always fortunate; can be tasteless in his inventions.) Restraining recollections slip away from the financier. The pair are mated. Last, the instance of the young man who would have been priest, who put by occupation for brooding solitude; who still finds life without plan or purpose. He goes, as to the confessional, to the old physicist; by him is comforted and enlighted as by the exercise of a mental priesthood; rises with faith renewed. So are inhibiting memories banished; sadness scattered; the will to live rekindled. . . . One by one the guests go their ways. Only the mountain-climber and the physicist's daughter linger. . . . "Lord, now lettest thou thy servant depart in peace." And the curtain falls upon the old man dead in his high-backed chair.

RESIDUE

Now Mr. Barry succeeds, again he fails, in this high adventure of play making. He dares to put by realistic drama: to swing back and forth between the actualities of the terrace, the phantoms of memory, the quasi-mystical prescience of the old scientist. These differing planes (as the learned call them) are sometimes imaginatively placed; while the transitions from one to another are poignant. Yet again, and all seems contrived, cloudy, awkward, as though the playwright had made shifts with halting means and obscured purpose. The method of individual dramas acted within a larger whole obtruded here and there as a preferred, insistent machinery. Even so, Mr. Barry lays hand upon the malaise of a time and a breed that lack illusion and want faith. The bystander may or may not take this state of mind too seriously in these young personages. Yet it is all to the good that a young American playwright should come to grips with it for his generation, if now and then impotently. The healing mysticism of the old man with his breezes blowing out of past across present, into future, with his faith in ends that are but beginnings, may not be too valid. There are moments when the radiant vestrue of words in which Mr. Barry can wrap it, is at least emotional persuasion. At others that vesture hangs in faded tatters remembered out of Freud or Einstein; moments again when the spectator cannot find the saving sun through the verbal fog. There are even one or two gross errors of taste, especially in the handling of the sensual woman, strange indeed in a playwright of Mr. Barry's sensibility and breeding. There are fortunate symbolisms as in the timing butler and the flicking lights; unfortunate as in the unctuously crowing cock of dawn.

So it goes, even in an acting that rises now to fine-grained and subtly tuned accomplishment as with Mr. Carnovsky (the old man), Miss Alexander (his daughter), Mr. Tone (the youth beset by the priesthood); to clear the true nervous vigors as with Mr. Anders (the mountaineer) or Mr. Larimore (the financier); only to fall away into such implausible semblance as Miss Gordon lends to the comedienne. What *Hotel Universe* signifies for Mr. Barry's future deponent knows not, being unblessed—alone in his calling—with the faculty of divination. Having no place in the inner counsels of the Theather Guild, he does not know, either, why it produced *Hotel Universe*—unless possibly for clear interest, merit, rarity. Both matters are best left for speak-easy debate—at the third round. . . . But Mr. Barry shall have the last word out of the mouth of the old physicist:

I have found out a simple thing; that in existence there are three estates. There is this life of chairs and tables, of getting up and sitting down. There is the life one lives in one's imagining, in which one wishes, dreams, remembers. There is the life past death, which in itself contains the others. The three estates are one. We dwell now in this one, now in that—but in whichever we may be, breezes from the others still blow upon us. . . . There are no words for it. It is a sense, a knowing. It may come upon you in a field one day, or as you turn a corner, or one fine morning as you stoop to lace your shoe.

—May 27, 1930, p. 12.

IX

JOHN HOWARD LAWSON

The Law of Conflict

The history of dramatic theory gives us certain general principles, upon which we can base at least a preliminary definition of the art of playwriting.

We have seen that three very broad principles are involved: action, unity, conflict. One cannot say that there is complete agreement either on the meaning or the necessity of any of these elements. It has been noted that Andreyev, Maeterlinck, and many others have questioned the idea of *action*. *Unity* has been variously interpreted. Brunetière's law of *conflict* has also been strongly questioned and hotly debated.

It seems to me that conflict is the most fundamental of these principles, and that we can properly use this as a starting point. Since drama deals with social relationships, we may also say that dramatic conflict is of a social nature. Then our preliminary definition can be as follows: The essential character of drama is conflict: persons against other persons, or individuals against groups, or groups against other groups, or individuals or groups against social or natural forces. Play construction, then, is concerned with presenting, developing, and resolving conflict. But it is self-evident that, while every play may be a conflict, every conflict is not a play. In order to be intelligible to an audience assembled in a theater, the conflict must be presented in a certain manner, which can be summed up in the following four laws of construction: (1) it must be presented in action; (2) it must possess unity; (3) it must be logical; (4) it must be based on knowledge, both of individual psychology, and of the social forces which condition the psychology of individuals.

These points must be considered in detail. But first of all, it is necessary to examine the law of conflict and make sure that it is really a sound and inclusive definition.

Reprinted from *New Theatre*, June, 1935, pp. 10, 27, by permission of the author.

Brunetière's law, as quoted in the previous chapter, emphasizes the element of *conscious will*, "the spectacle of the will striving toward a goal." As Brander Matthews points out, "he subordinates the idea of struggle to the idea of volition." William Archer objects to Brunetiere's theory: "The difficulty about this definition is that, while it describes the matter of a good many dramas, it does not lay down any true differentia, any characteristic common to all true drama, and possessed by no other form of fiction." As illustrations of plays in which there is no assertion of the human will in conflict, Archer mentions, among others, *Oedipus* and *Ghosts*. He also says, "No one can say that the balcony scene in *Romeo and Juliet* is undramatic," yet he feels that there is not "a clash of wills" in this scene.

It seems to me that these examples offer very strong proof of Brunetière's theory. To be sure the "clash of wills" in the balcony scene in *Romeo and Juliet* is not between the two persons on the stage. But Brunetière never maintains that any such direct opposition is required. On the contrary he very specially emphasizes that the theater shows "the development of the human will, attacking the obstacles opposed to it by destiny, fortune, or circumstances." And again: "This is what may be called *will*, to set up a goal, and to direct everything toward it, to strive to bring everything into line with it." Certainly Romeo and Juliet are setting up a goal and striving "to bring everything into line with it."

The doom of Oedipus lies in the fact that his will to escape his doom is thwarted. If there were no will, no conscious effort to escape, there would be no tragedy. In *Ghosts*, the struggle carried on by Oswald and his mother is by no means a passive one. Mrs. Alving is a woman of strong character, who has very actively endeavored to shape her environment and control her son's career. Oswald does not accept his fate, but fights against it with bitter violence. The end of the play shows Mrs. Alving faced with a terrible decision, a decision which strains her will to the breaking point—she must decide whether or not to kill her own son who has gone insane. If this is not a struggle involving conscious will, I don't know how such a struggle could be imagined.

What would *Ghosts* be like if it were (as Archer maintains it to be) a play without a conscious struggle of wills? It is very difficult to conceive of the play in this way: the only events which would be partly unchanged would be Oswald's insanity and the burning of the orphanage. But there would be no action whatsoever leading to these situations. And even Oswald's cry, "give me the sun," would of necessity be omitted, since it expresses conscious will. Furthermore, if no exercise of conscious will were concerned, the orphanage would never have been built.

To be sure, I am here using the term, "conscious will" in a very broad sense. But this is the sense in which it is generally understood. If one is going to limit the use of the term, one must be careful to define the way in which it is limited. This, I think, Archer has not done.

While admitting that conflict is generally (but not universally) present in the drama, Archer maintains that the word, *crisis*, is more characteristic of the special quality of theatrical presentation: "The drama may be called the art of crises, as fiction is the art of gradual developments."

The truth of this is so obvious that it really admits of no discussion. While it in no way contradicts the law of conflict, it adds something very essential to it. One can readily conceive of a conflict which does not reach a crisis; such a conflict would by its nature be undramatic. However, simply to maintain (as Archer does) that "the essence of drama is crisis" is insufficient. An earthquake is a crisis, but its dramatic significance lies in the reactions and acts of human beings. Thus conscious will comes into play. If *Ghosts* consisted only of Oswald's insanity and the burning of the orphanage it would include two crises, but no conscious will, and no *preparation*. The idea of conflict includes the struggle of wills, the interplay and opposition which make crises inevitable.

Henry Arthur Jones, in analyzing the points of view of Brunetière and Archer, tries to combine them by defining a play as "a succession of suspenses and crises, or as a succession of conflicts impending and conflicts raging, carried through ascending and accelerated climaxes from the beginning to the end of a connected scheme."

This is a remarkably inclusive, and richly suggestive definition. Although it is not very specific about the *conscious will*, one may assume that it includes it, because "a succession of conflicts" among human beings involves the exercise of will. A conflict without will is an unimaginable abstraction, because there would be no motive for the conflict to continue—or, for that matter, to begin.

However, I think this definition, in spite of its value, is unsatisfactory because it deals with dramatic *construction* rather than with dramatic *principle*. As a definition of the construction of drama, it is not perfect, because it does not clearly present the ideas of unity, logic, and social content. On the other hand, in defining the principle upon which dramatic art is based, it seems to me that greater clarity and simplicity are desirable.

The law of conflict is both simple and fundamental. But it is evident that this law must be so phrased as to include the idea of a crisis. A crisis is, one may say, the breaking point of a conflict, the point at which the strength of the opposing forces is so strained that there must be a cracking of the strain. If this is the case, then there is a very important new point which must be considered: we are concerned not only with the *consciousness* of will, but with the *strength* of will. The exercise of will must be sufficiently vigorous to sustain and develop the conflict to a point of issue. A conflict which fails to reach a crisis is a conflict of weak wills. In Greek and Elizabethan tragedy, the point of maximum strain is reached with the death of the hero: his will cracks in the struggle with destiny or environment.

Brunetière is clearly aware of this point: "One drama," he says, "is superior to another drama according as the quantity of will exerted is greater or less, as the share of chance is less and that of necessity greater." One may well question Brunetière's statement that "the quantity of will exerted" determines the superiority of one drama to another. In the first place, one cannot measure the quantity of will; in the second place, the struggle is relative and not absolute: the quality of the forces and the way in which they are opposed cannot be reduced to such an easy formula as "the quantity of will exerted."

Nevertheless, it cannot be doubted that strength of will is an important factor—and that it must be sufficient to create a balance of forces and to attain a point of crisis.

We may then go back and rephrase our earlier statement of the law of conflict:

The essential character of drama is social conflict—per-

sons against other persons, or individuals against groups, or groups against other groups, or individuals or groups against social or natural forces—in which the exercise of conscious will is sufficiently strong to bring the conflict to a point of crisis.

X

MALCOLM GOLDSTEIN

Clifford Odets and the Found Generation

Our machine had been in a smash-up too. But we wanted to remain on the scene of the accident and see if we could fix it. We thought we could save it. Instead of a *lost* generation, I guess you might call us a *found* generation. We found out what was wrong. We were pretty damn sure we'd have something new out of all this mess that would be better than anything you had before.

Budd Schulberg, *The Disenchanted*

The death of Clifford Odets in August, 1963, at the age of fifty-seven, was followed by obituaries in the *New York Times* and *Variety* resembling in their complaining tone the notices of a play which has not quite come up to expectations. The playwright, it was recalled, had been recognized in the thirties as a "writer of promise," the American reviewers' standard description of any new dramatist whose work is tolerable; the question now was whether in his twenty-eight years of fame Odets had ever passed beyond the promising state. Two months later NBC television inaugurated the weekly series of plays on which Odets had spent his last months; the producers' plan was that he should write a few of the pieces himself and choose the rest from new scripts submitted by other writers. Although his well-wishers were hopeful that the series would belie the strictures of the obituaries, the program was too dismal to last beyond an initial thirteen weeks. All the plays were dull, the two by Odets no less than the others. The most recently completed and produced work by the playwright before the posthumous debacle was a 1961 film, *Wild in the Country* starring Elvis Presley.

The thinning of Odets's once considerable talent over the last dozen years of his life was and is a loss to the American theater. The talent was never of such magnitude that it could be con-

This essay has been written at the editor's invitation, for inclusion in the present volume.

fused with genius, but it was substantial enough to create at least four plays of broad popular appeal and to leave traces of itself on passages of dialogue in even the meagerest of the remainder. Moreover, in number alone the works are impressive: eleven plays produced on Broadway do not constitute a negligible record. Yet it is true that all but three were staged between 1935 and 1941 and that the plays of 1949, 1950, and 1954, though better received than a few that preceded them, are ill-composed. Some of the causes of the decline are likely to remain permanently hidden from readers, if indeed they did not remain hidden from Odets himself. However shrewd our guesses, we cannot confidently account for such symptoms of disorder as the sloth and narrow attention-span that cursed his later years—cannot, that is, know why after 1954 he began play after play with enthusiasm, only to let each drop before completion. But there is much in the troubled, fitful career that is not concealed, and it makes up part of the history of not one playwright alone, but of an entire generation in the theater.

The principal problem for Odets was the difficulty of finding appropriate focal points for his abundant sympathies. Plots came easily, themes did not. As late as 1949 he continued to write the best American plays of the thirties, and nothing else. Much the most skilled of the radical playwrights of the Depression stage, he wrote his first plays of economic injustice with such flair that the political right and left alike acknowledged their theatrical viability. Nevertheless, he was capable of no greater judgment than may be credited to the less intelligent dramatists of his generation; in attempting to develop class-consciousness among the Depression's victims for an attack upon their presumed oppressors, he did not recognize that he was merely substituting one brand of materialism for another. More damaging to the growth of his talent was the inability to free himself completely, as the years passed along, from the materialist theme with which he began his career. His perception of the world around him dimmed with the beginning of the national economic recovery late in the prewar decade, and the mind that should have taken cognizance of the new situation contented itself with after-images of the poverty of the Depression's worst years. It is true that Odets took up other issues in certain works, particularly in his late plays; but whether subsidiary or paramount, class-consciousness is never absent, regardless of the year and the remoteness of his characters' concerns from money worries. Having taken a stand with the destitute proletariat, he could not recognize the fact of a rising employment index. After the first six plays, handsomely brought together in an omnibus volume in 1939, Odets's work dwindled in relevance to the age, until finally, after 1954, he could give the stage nothing at all.

At the beginning, however, it was another matter. Odets's ability and interest revealed themselves in precisely the right place and time. Few would-be playwrights can have been more fortunate in their circumstances than was Odets as a young man. Employed as an actor in the perennially embattled, hard-pressed Group Theater, he received, to be sure, not a scrap more than a living wage, but he was at least secure—secure both economically and emotionally. The Group's historic position as the most seminal organization in American theatrical history was achieved by the determination of its original directors, Lee Strasberg, Harold Clurman, and Cheryl Crawford, to exert maximum effort for the security of the company which they had assembled at the beginning of the decade. In the midst of general economic dislocation, the Group members were assured food and shelter by their directors and were encouraged by their sense of community to give the best of themselves in performance. Their willingness to live as a collective on a slim margin was indicative of their social attitudes. A few—far from enough to control policy—joined the Communist Party; none stood further to the right than the position occupied by the New Deal administration, which the President himself described as being a little left of center. In this society it did not matter that Odets was not a notable actor, since he only accepted inconspicuous parts; on stage and off, each performer used his resources for the benefit of all and took according to his needs. Despite occasional comments to the contrary, all were committed to the idea of social theater, and it was a rare play that could attract them unless it embodied a cry of protest against poverty, militarism, fascism, or bigotry. With such certainty that it is stunning to contemplate, they knew precisely where they stood, what they wished to achieve for themselves and for the populace in general, and how, as craftsmen, to express their feelings to advantage. When in 1933 Odets began to work on the play ultimately titled *Awake and Sing!*, he wrote with complete awareness of his colleagues' virtuosity and social commitment. Always troubled by a shortage of appropriate plays, they were pleased to discover an effective dramatist in their own ranks.

But for all its theatrical skill, the Group lacked literary discrimination. Of the two dozen pieces mounted between 1931 and 1941, more than half were ineptly written. Often, however, as with Sidney Kingsley's *Men in White*, the company could add out of its own technique the strength missing from the material submitted by an author. Their passion was altogether too strong to allow for good judgment. It is, moreover, conjectural whether greater flexibility on the part of the directors and actors could have affected Odets's work, since he was as eager as they to record with intense heat the new social awareness of his age. His haste resulted frequently in a marked crudeness of construction and the employment of ill-conceived symbols and awkward stage-groupings. In such successes as *Awake and Sing!* and *Golden Boy*, as well as in lesser plays, stretches of bathos fall between moments of lively dialogue.

The zeal and self-righteousness constituting the manner that the Group displayed to the world are present not only in these plays but in *Waiting for Lefty*, *Till the Day I Die*, and *Paradise Lost*. All are class-conscious, revolutionary plays, and with the exception of *Golden Boy*, a tragedy, all embody elements of *agitprop* (short for "agitation-propaganda"), the optimistic, aggressive dramatic form promulgated after the crash of 1929 by workers' theaters close to the Communist Party. Providing for maximum dynamism and minimum logic, the form posits two forces which clash bitterly on stage in brief but harrowing action. In the first examples of *agitprop*, the forces are groups of industrial overlords—the "bosses"—on the one hand and underpaid workers on the other. Unlike their employers, the workers lack organization at the outset, but with the help of a strong and usually young leader they unite to win their demands. In due course as the form became popular the contentions exposed on stage took place between Communists and fascists, Communist unions and the A.F.L., Negroes and bigoted whites, and the *Daily Worker* and the Hearst press; for broad distribution, many were published in *Workers' Theatre*, a leftist monthly of the early thirties. Odets along with the rest of the Group was aware of this new form and sensitive to its impact; for its second production the company had offered an elaborate work modeled directly on the *agitprop* format: Claire and Paul Sifton's *1931–*.

In 1934 two members, Art Smith and Elia Kazan, collaborated on an *agitprop* piece titled *Dimitroff* which presented to American audiences the events of the trials following the Reichstag fire, and Group personnel performed in it to benefit the New Theater League, a federation of workers' and other social-minded troupes. The entire company, and especially those members dissatisfied with the directors' refusal to move further to the left, took a sharp interest in the radical theaters of the city. Some worked in various capacities with the Theater Union and the Theater Collective, new professional troupes organized in the hope of attracting intellectuals as well as workers to programs of social drama. Odets himself gave acting classes to members of the Theater Union. It is understandable that when a few of the Group became dramatists, they should turn to the agitational mode. Having joined the Communist Party late in 1934, Odets composed a play expressing the firmness of his commitment: *Waiting for Lefty*, an *agitprop* drama which took the form to a level of excellence it had never before reached. After an opening night on which the audience in delirium stormed the stage to congratulate the actors, it played across the nation. According to the playwright's count, recorded in *New Theatre* (the successor to *Workers' Theatre*) for January, 1936, it played in 104 cities in eight months of 1935; through the thirties it continued to be performed.

The play is unique among the works of Odets in its over-all adherence to the basic *agitprop* design. Although the strike of the New York taxi drivers, his point of departure, had been settled early in the year, the memory was fresh enough to provide strong pro-labor material. In the approved manner, the play presents a power struggle between opposing classes; since the taxi union officers act as the mouthpieces of management and not as the standard bearers of the men who elected them, they are the oppressors of the honest rank-and-file drivers. The traditional young leader of the poorly organized union dissidents is one Agate, who at the close draws the drivers together for an overwhelming strike vote, despite pressure from the officers to keep them at their work. Agate, however, is the leader only because of the absence of the better-known Lefty—such is the significant nickname of the chairman of the strike committee. As Kazan and others had done before him, Odets strove to give more substance to his play than the short *agitprops* printed in *Workers'*

Theatre had possessed. While waiting for the elected chairman to arrive at their strike-vote meeting, the drivers act out terse scenes commenting on the conditions which brought them to their underpaid occupation and which now make them wish to call a strike. These five episodes, the core of the play, reveal the strength of Odets at his best; from the start he was capable of compounding moving dialogue of homely images. Yet they also reveal him at his worst, for the situations of at least two of the drivers appear, as he reveals them, to be the visions of a man suffering acutely from hysteria. It is difficult to understand why in even the exacerbated climate of 1934 a gifted intern, released from his hospital primarily because he is a Jew, could find no more lucrative or appropriate work than driving a cab. Nor is it quite possible to accept the story of the lab technician, another skilled professional man, that he was asked to write a weekly report on the honesty of his superior, the inventor of a new poisonous gas, and for the sake of secrecy to live inside the plant. A third episode, the tale of an unemployed actor, is no less naïve, though possibly more credible. Unable to make an impression on a hard-bitten producer, the actor reveals his despair to the producer's stenographer, who thereupon offers him a dollar. On hearing his refusal of the gift, she promptly reminds him that with it he can, after all, buy ten loaves of bread. Or, more to the point, he can buy nine loaves of bread and a copy of the *Communist Manifesto*. When preparing the volume of *Six Plays* in 1939, Odets had the delicacy to excise this scene. However, it was present at the first "New Theater Night" performances on Fourteenth Street in January, 1935, and was still present when the Group brought the play to Broadway at the end of March, along with *Till the Day I Die*, a shaky piece on Nazi Germany hastily prepared to fill the bill.

Given the speed under which it was written and the special audience of radicals it was originally intended to reach at leftist benefits—not necessarily the Group's own audience of Broadway customers—*Waiting for Lefty* should be spared criticism. The day is long past when it can be taken seriously. To ignore it, however, is to leave unexplained the distraught, evangelical tone of the plays which followed. *Awake and Sing!* and *Paradise Lost* allegedly present close investigations of the American middle class caught in the confusion of financial disaster from which the entire nation suffered. Like all the Odets plays for the Group,

they are in the form of the well-made play; that is, they are constructed on a cautious design to show cause and effect in a logical pattern which culminates in emotion-laden confrontation
scenes. To this mode of construction, first used by Ibsen for
serious social drama, Odets added an overlay of Chekhov, one of
his most admired writers. The Chekhovian influence is evident in
the oblique expression of strong feeling, as in Moe Axelrod's
first-act curtain line for *Awake and Sing!*, when, his heart breaking for a lost love, he spits out, "What the hell kind of house is
this it ain't got an orange!" Like the two European playwrights,
Odets reached, after *Lefty*, an audience for the most part middle
class. Yet the pull of the revolutionary theater was too strong to
be denied, with the result that Odets jeopardized his new plays
with hortatory *agitprop* conclusions. That such scenes were
neither structurally nor emotionally valid and that they offered
scant comfort to the Group audience was, in the passion of the
moment, of no importance. In *Awake and Sing!* young Ralph
Berger's last-act cry of determination to read Marx, spread the
revolutionary word in the warehouse where he works, and "fix
it so life won't be printed on dollar bills" at a time when his emotional life is in collapse bears a heavy air of unreality. It was felt
by many of the play's first critics, who charged the author with
a last-minute revision to render his work revolutionary in its
final effect. In a lengthy taped interview printed in two numbers
of *Theatre Arts* (May and June, 1963) Odets denied having done
so with this play, but admitted tacking revolutionary endings on
to others. Although he named none of them, it is most likely that
Paradise Lost was in his mind, for its revolutionary conclusion is
so out of keeping with the rest of the action as to take the play
into a kind of fantasy world. Leo Gordon, Odets's spokesman,
finds life marvelous to contemplate at the close, despite the bank-
ruptcy of his business, the loss of his home, the death of one son,
and the fatal disease of the other: "Ohh, darling, the world is in
its morning . . . and *no man fights alone!*" He has lost the paradise of the middle class, but has found a better life among the
homeless proletariat. The phrases that he and Ralph trumpet
forth in their respective plays are proclamations of self-discovery—that is, each man sees himself as a fighter for a better
society. But the scenes, coming after unrelieved calamity, suggest self-intoxication as much as self-discovery. In real life, such
indulgence usually results in a hangover of chagrin.

Like his characters, Odets himself soon became something of an *agitprop* visionary in his personal life. Generous with his time and royalties, he took up a position of leadership in the left-wing theater movement. In May, 1935, he provided a brief monologue, *I Can't Sleep*, on the stricken conscience of the American businessman for a performance to benefit the Maritime Workers Industrial Union; it was acted by Morris Carnovsky, one of the best-known Group performers. In the summer he served as nominal head of a Communist Party–backed organization calling itself the American Committee to Investigate Labor and Social Conditions in Cuba. As he later told the Un-American Activities Committee, the investigators fully expected to be arrested on arriving in Havana; they were pleased when, indeed, the incarceration occurred on schedule, since they knew it would receive full coverage in the American press. At some time soon after this incident, Odets gave up his membership in the Party, but on November 19, 1935, he ran the following announcement in the *New Masses*, the Party's cultural organ: "Clifford Odets will be glad to advise DURING REHEARSALS of First Run Production of Any 'Valuable' Play. No Charge." After the closing of *Paradise Lost* the next year, he accepted the offer of a Hollywood contract and, amid his friends' protests of "sellout," left New York. Yet he remained with the Group in spirit; part of his salary came back to support the Group actors, and with *Golden Boy* he attempted to provide the company the glossy material which would draw in the Broadway crowd.

These activities are the evidence of self-consciousness; with his initial success on Broadway Odets had come, it would seem, to sense that he had a certain role to play in life. The result to his new work was an obvious, labored literary quality. Both *Paradise Lost* and *Golden Boy* are burdened with a clumsy system of symbols which, though possibly less evident on the stage than in print, sorts uncomfortably with their class-conscious theme. It is surely no coincidence that Leo Gordon and Sam Katz, the two Depression-hounded businessmen of *Paradise Lost*, are manufacturers of ladies' handbags, items useless, or nearly so, when money is scarce. Another of the play's complaints against the idea of a capitalist society is embodied, awkwardly, in the dying younger son of the Gordon family, a one-time bank clerk now afflicted with sleeping sickness. Such strength as remains to him he uses in making paper profits on the stock market. To his mother falls the task of reporting the barely audible words he speaks before taking to his deathbed in the hospital: " 'United Aircraft'—it's an active stock, he says." In *Golden Boy* the symbols lack such simple-mindedness, but nevertheless create doubt as to the validity of the work as a whole. The life of the spirit is presented in young Joe Bonaparte's love of music and in the violin bought for him by his father. The dangerous, crippling battle for wealth which Odets finds, to his sorrow, inescapable under the capitalist system, is symbolized explicitly by prize-fighting. When Joe, believing that money alone will bring him self-respect and general acclaim, turns from music to the fight ring, he acts out a parable of despair which provides the audience with a series of moving incidents. Yet we may wonder about the play. To quarrel with the author's social view at this late date is simply to waste time; but it is possible, even so, to take issue with his presentational means. The professions of fiddling and boxing are separated by so great a gulf of emotional and intellectual distance as to make almost a freak of the man who can perform competently in both; Joe's situation is special pleading on a grand scale. Viewed dispassionately, he is not much less astonishing than the young women encountered occasionally in the newspapers who divide their time between courses in law school and the burlesque stage.

But at the same time that Odets's zeal to reform American society drew him into such errors in judgment, his perception of the problems of the individual deepened. The agitational fury of the first plays inhibits the development of the characters as individual persons with special goals and private problems; Odets tells so little of their anxieties, except for those caused by poverty, that the differences among them appear only in such superficial matters as age and accent. With *Golden Boy* however he began to let his mind speculate at greater range. It is not only the desire for money that goads Joe Bonaparte to the fight ring, but the desire to make up for the indignities he suffered in childhood and youth because of his odd name and strabismic eyes. In his adulthood the old taunts remain in his mind, and he fights to work off the hostility they induce. Again in *Rocket to the Moon*, produced in 1938, rooted dissatisfactions with no economic cause are at work alongside the financial worries. Ben and Belle Stark, a middle-aged dentist and his wife, are unhappy together, and although Ben's lackluster career is one cause of distress, another is that they have never been able to have children. Belle, moreover, cannot tolerate her father and prefers to remain in relative poverty if the alternative is to accept a loan from him. Among the most ingratiating characters in any of the plays is Steve Takis, a boy in *Night Music*, Odets's last Group Theater production, who is also driven by problems of the mind. It is true that he is poor and in danger of losing his job as a minor employee for one of the Hollywood studios, but equally powerful among his griefs is the early death of his revered mother; whenever the worries grow too fierce, he thinks of her. None of these plays is lacking in sociological interest, but in each of them Odets gives equal weight to psychological determinism. It is chiefly through the revelations of the mind which he was willing to vouchsafe his audience that the plays have staying power. This is not to say that Odets was ignorant of inner pain at the start of his writing career, but that before *Golden Boy* he chose not to round out his characters with the kinds of problems from which at one time or another each man suffers privately, the better to stress the problems from which, in his vision of American life, all men suffer in the mass.

Had Odets given more attention to character analysis, the result might well have been rapid growth in the direction later taken by such writers as Arthur Miller and Tennessee Williams, for whom the study of personality is of paramount importance. As it was, he continued to fill up his pages with references to hard times and the problem of maintaining honor and dignity in the economic battle. *Rocket to the Moon* (1938), *Night Music* (1940), and *Clash by Night* (1941) all refer to the scarcity of ready money to lengths extravagant for their day. On having a belated first glance at them, a reader today may forget that the national economy, though nothing like the boom of the fifties and sixties, had changed for the better by the end of the decade and that with the coming of war to Europe in 1939 the American "defense" industries were priming the pump still further. Although he had long since given up his Party membership, Odets continued to write in the querulous Communist style, forswearing reason and magnifying grievances at every turn. In *Night Music* this tactic is particularly oppressive. Written during the period of the Soviet-German non-aggression pact, it makes a plea for American non-intervention, since an American alliance with England and France would mean war against Russia. In his despair Steve Takis contemplates joining the army—one way to make a living—but is dissuaded from doing so by the advice that it is better to work as a civilian for the good of the nation.

In his postwar plays Odets continued, in various ways, to demonstrate unwittingly the perils of his commitment. *The Big Knife*, like *Golden Boy*, is melodramatic tragedy, and once more the theme is class warfare. With an almost intolerable shrillness the playwright demonstrates his conviction, that the artist, a worker like any other, is at the mercy of an exploiting class, the men who will use his talent for profit. Charlie Castle, a sensitive film actor, is so baited and affronted by the head of production at his studio that in the end he can escape only through suicide; the bosses, well-organized as always, win the battle even though they lose their star, for they are better off with Charlie dead than Charlie alive and looking for an opportunity to strike back. The play is Odets's gesture of revenge on Hollywood, the lotus land whose easy way of life dulled his flair as a writer. The characters are drawn in the starkest black and purest white, as in a shabby western or *agitprop* diatribe. All that is lacking to take the play back to the early thirties is a way out for Charlie from the trap his studio has cunningly set for him, and perhaps a proclamation of his personal independence. On looking at this play again, the present writer is reminded of the brief sketch of Jean Harlow which the *Daily Worker* printed in lieu of an obituary after the actress's death in June, 1937. The paper had not been able to bear her performances, and had been infuriated by her appearance in an anti-labor film titled *Riff Raff*, but on this occasion a reporter recalled having seen her in a Hollywood drugstore not long before her death and thinking that she looked faded and pinched—a healthy American girl sapped of her vitality by the ruling class, and not such a bad actress after all.

In the fifties Odets came to sense that something was wrong. He was brought forcefully to recognize that times had changed by the flagging of interest in his work. Under pressure in the McCarthy period to make a public confession of his political activities or lose his value to Hollywood, he chose at first to ignore the threat and write a foolproof, money-making play: *The Country Girl*. It is a bland piece concentrating on psychological disorders to the near-exclusion of sociological comment. With great effort, an alcoholic actor is persuaded to return to the stage, and, helped by his vigorous wife and a young, optimistic director, succeeds in the part. But he too has a class enemy: the producer, who wishes the director to fire him lest he turn back to the bottle and ruin the play. The money motive, once more, looms as a destructive force. The play tries for suspense as the audience wonders whether the actor will regain his self-confidence, but the happy outcome is clear enough from the start. Too long trained to work with social motives, Odets could not bring himself to make a thorough-going investigation of the hero's problem; the victory comes about with preposterous ease. To his credit, Odets revealed in *Theatre Arts* (May, 1963) that he was fully aware of the meretriciousness of the piece. In 1952, following the paths of old friends, Odets took the next step indicated by the fall in his fortunes and made the obligatory trip to Washington for a confession of his political past. What he had to say was scarcely new; the names he gave had all been given before by others—actors, directors, and playwrights—who had come to prominence in the thirties. But had he not given in, it is unlikely that Hollywood would have filmed *The Country Girl*. Screened in a slick production, with Odets's name prominent in the advertisements, it became one of the most profitable films of the mid-fifties.

With his last produced play, *The Flowering Peach*, Odets tried to explain to himself and to his public the reason for his appearance before the Un-American Activities Committee. At once moving and amusing, the play is a reworking of the story of Noah and the flood in the idiom of the lower–middle-class Jews of New York. The religious tone, unexpected of the once-rebellious writer, is sustained throughout with no trace of embarrassment, but is set off with mild comedy as Noah protests the burden God has inexplicably placed upon him. A looseness in the second act, however, obscures the shifts in Noah's character and prevents the play from reaching its potential level as the most convincing of all Odets's works. It is as though a scene or passage of dialogue were left out that might bring the play into focus by accounting for God's mercy toward this particular family. Brooks Atkinson, writing in the *New York Times* on September 3, 1963, explains that Odets was aware of the flaw and promised his producer to correct it during the Washington try-out performances, but instead spent the days attending Congressional hearings. Possibly he hoped, by listening to some of the scores of ex-Communists still arriving to make their reports, to understand the motive behind his own willingness to comply. At the close of the play he gives the reason as best he can. It sounds in Noah's decision to make his home, after the landing on Mount Ararat, with Shem, his obsessively materialistic second son. Life in Shem's household will be, in Noah's words, "more comfortable."

Thus too late, and for what many of his audience would take to be the wrong reason, Odets tried to alter the direction of his life and art. With his original subject taken away from him, he wrote without stimulus, and soon his reserves of emotion and energy were gone. For the creative artist the failure to grow always results in disaster. Although he may not regress in his craft, but merely stand still, he *seems* to regress as the current of intellectual life swells and sweeps beyond him; it is an optical illusion affecting the inner eye.

Odets's particular problem, or what we can understand of it, was not his alone; the pages of theatrical histories are filled with the names of playwrights who failed to concern themselves with changes in the values of the world around them, and more will be added as the decades flow on. At present the American theater suffers acutely from the influence of members of Odets's generation—more precisely, of his one-time associates in the Group—who have not grown sufficiently with the times. The two producing units in New York of which much was to be hoped in the sixties, the Lincoln Center Repertory Theater and the Actors Studio Theater, showed every symptom after their first full season, 1963–64, of what may be called the Group Problem. Both were headed by men trained in that remarkable organization who could not free themselves of the grip of the past.

Of the Lincoln Center company's new plays, both Arthur Miller's *After the Fall* and S. N. Behrman's *But for Whom Charlie* have the stale flavor of the thirties. Miller's play treats candidly the issue of Congressional clearance of persons with a history of Communist affiliation—an important subject, but no longer fresh, and robbed of its edge by opaque dialogue. Behrman's piece is merely a flashy drawing-room comedy such as would have delighted the well-to-do Theater Guild audiences who saw his *Biography* and *End of Summer*; it is an unbelievable choice for a supposedly dynamic company. Among the Actors Studio productions of the first year were June Havoc's *Marathon '33*, a play attempting to recapture the atmosphere of the Depression, and thus of little appeal to present-day audiences, and James Baldwin's *Blues for Mister Charlie*, a throwback to *agit-prop* with Negroes and whites lined up in crucial scenes on opposite sides of the stage, the whites united from the outset and the Negroes gradually coming to see that in union there is strength. For all their shortcomings, the plays by Miller and Baldwin show great skill; what is needed by the writers and producers alike is a sufficient lessening of the straitjacket of passion to allow them to recognize the passages of incoherent, overwrought writing. But what is needed even more is the passing of leadership to younger, less self-assured practitioners of the theater arts, along with the proviso that they too will be heeded only as long as their minds are free.

XI

VINCENT WALL

Maxwell Anderson: The Last Anarchist

Now that the echoes of the present European war are being
clearly heard in this country, it is obvious that another period of
national culture is at an end, just as 1914 marked the end of a
different era. Hence it is not too early, perhaps, to criticize the
work of the foremost dramatist of the decade who sometimes
expressed so exactly the temper of the times, yet who was often
at complete variance with it.

Maxwell Anderson dominated the American theater of the
thirties as Eugene O'Neill dominated that of the twenties.
O'Neill's pessimism, his odd combination of realism and mysticism made him the most representative dramatist of the postwar
period. To an almost equal extent Maxwell Anderson expressed
the period of financial readjustment and chaos that followed.

In another sense, however, Maxwell Anderson's independence
set him apart from his time. Not only as a literary craftsman—
since he alone was writing poetic and romantic tragedies—but in
other respects, his was an alien voice. In an age of increasing
collectivism this voice could be heard praising individualism,
independence, and the frontier spirit. In an age of increasing
govern mentalism he could still maintain that the best government was that which governed least. As the last champion of
what almost amounts to a laissez faire and rugged individualism,
he is an isolated figure, almost an anachronism. And since anarchy has few apologists even among the radicals, Anderson is
a lonely and puzzling figure—at least until the nature of his anarchy is examined. As a rebel he has been a part of many an insurrection, yet always in a quiet, academic manner without personal aggrandizement. He seldom attends the openings of his
own plays and seldom answers or discusses criticism of them,
although he is a fine critic himself and has contributed several

Reprinted from *The Sewanee Review*, XLIX (1941), 340–69, by permission of the publisher. Copyright 1941 by the University of the South.

penetrating essays on the drama. Yet during the last decade in which he has produced his mature drama he has maintained a remarkably consistent point of view other than the mere blanket condemnation of war, fascism, and industrial tyranny which satisfied so many writers; and as a craftsman he has written in several different mediums ranging from prose realism to poetic tragedy.

Thus on two scores he has aroused the interest and ire of his critics and peers. First, he has dared to write plays which were romantic and tragic and in verse when a good many of his critics felt that contemporary life could only be expressed realistically and in prose, and when some of them thought that tragedy could not be written at all. This, however, is less important than a second dispute which arose concerning the ideas which lay behind his plays and repeat themselves in them. This criticism has been mostly from the left-wing critics who have found Mr. Anderson of slight stature according to the Marxist critical yardstick. Their charge is that his brand of anarchism makes him a defeatist —that he has achieved his popularity in the theater by escaping into the romantic past.

The fact that the critical wolves have been in full cry whenever an Anderson play has been produced may have been responsible for his remarks on a playwright's qualifications on the occasion of receiving the Critic's Award for *High Tor*:

> But of all these qualifications, necessary as they may seem, only one is central . . . his priesthood, his belief in what he is doing, his belief in the theater and its destiny, are the essentials to significance. . . . If a civilization has any meaning at all, that meaning will be found concentrated in its arts, and the theater is our national art.

This ringing affirmation of his faith in his art in the face of adverse criticism is both noble and heartening, for he not only takes it seriously but applied himself seriously to the preparation for his service in the temple. This included apprenticeship in several professions before he became a dramatist. Before that he had been a journalist and editor but what is perhaps more important he had also been a poet and teacher.

Long before he turned to the composition of his first play at the age of thirty-four he had been experimenting with verse patterns. Together with Padraic Colum and Genevieve Taggard he had aided in founding a magazine of poetry, *The Measure*, and in 1925 he collected his own verse in a volume, *You Who Have Dreams*.

Of no less importance, however, was his appointment to the faculties of several Middle West and Western colleges. In the classroom and library he no doubt picked up the historical details which has given authority to his historical tragedies, and more particularly to his interpretation of the American scene. And it is particularly important to remember when watching the development of the art forms used, revised, and discarded that Anderson brought to the theater not only the journalist's and editor's awareness of contemporary events, and the poet's depth of feeling and sense of language but also the scholar's knowledge of the heritage of the theater from Aeschylus to Ibsen.

It was hardly by accident, however, that Anderson's career as a teacher ended when he was dismissed from Whittier College for his pacifism. He told his class one day after reading a poem, "A Prayer Before Battle," that, "if the enemy had offered the same argument for victory, the Lord of heaven might have been placed in an embarrassing predicament." Similarly he lost his job on the *San Francisco Bulletin*, it is said, for declaring that "it was hardly reasonable to suppose that Germany could pay the entire Allied War Debt." During the tumultuous teens such statements were radical and dangerous.

With such a history it is small wonder that his first successful play was a collaboration with Lawrence Stallings, *What Price Glory?* Here war is treated realistically, so much so that the authors admit grudgingly that, "There's something about this profession of arms, some kind of damned religion connected with it you can't shake." In the light of later and more searching plays and novels on the shattering effect the war had on the lives of those engaged in it, this is still "romantic," as is the ending when Quirt, ill and tired after boozing, calls to his captain as he prepares to go back to the front: "Hey, Flagg, wait for baby!" Yet it is at the same time more real than if either of them had delivered himself of an editorial on war as a capitalistic enterprise which sacrifices the lives of citizens for profit. It is a realistic appreciation of the romantic appeal which war has always had.

On the technical side, *What Price Glory?* is as fine a job of playmaking as the theater had seen since Eugene O'Neill's early sea plays. It was, in fact, so notable that the authors tried twice to collaborate on historical plays in prose but without success. Anderson, apparently, knew what he wanted to do but had not as yet discovered quite the pattern. Still, even in *First Flight*, their next play, there is something of the formula of several later plays, notably *Winterset* and *Mary of Scotland*, namely a form in which the first two acts are racy, filled with adventure and action, while the last is a lyrical scene of deep emotional appeal. Also in this play we meet that salty, voluble, alcoholic Major Singlefoot who reappears with his whiskey jug as Sol Fitzgerald in *Both Your Houses*, little changed indeed after a century of debauchery.

Other than this, little importance can be attached to these collaborations, nor indeed to *Saturday's Children*, his first independent play to succeed. It is his most appealing play in many respects, and may hold the stage long after the more pretentious costume pieces are forgotten. But, like *The Star Wagon*, it has little connection with those plays which reveal the growth and development of the dramatist who is to write *Elizabeth the Queen* and *Winterset*, and who is to dominate the theater of the thirties.

Of greater importance is his next play, *Gods of the Lightning*, which was a collaboration with Harold Hickerson. This play is a moving narrative of the trial, conviction, and execution of two I.W.W. agitators for a crime which they did not commit. Coming as it did, however, little over a year after the execution of Sacco and Vanzetti, it found scant favor with metropolitan audiences. Although praised by some it added little to the author's reputation as a dramatist, and when Burns Mantle published *American Playwrights of Today* in 1929 he failed to include Anderson in the honor group, although he found him "promising." It is true that these years had been years of incubation and preparation but only one independent play, *Saturday's Children*, had been a real success. However, Anderson had ended his apprenticeship to the drama and the next decade is full of brilliant achievement.

In fact Anderson's initial effort in the thirties indicated clearly that he was more than a "promising" playwright. He had previously written much poetry, he had collaborated on historical plays and he had pondered deeply the nature of tragedy. As a result, *Elizabeth the Queen*, when submitted to the Theater

Guild in 1930 was considered worthy of the talent of its brightest stars.

In 1929 Joseph Wood Krutch had published *The Modern Temper*, a study of that loss of faith in the gods and in man which had once in more happy, vigorous, and confident ages resulted in the writing of great tragedy. In a chapter entitled "The Tragic Fallacy" in this volume, Mr. Krutch analyzed this. "Tragedy arises, then," he asserted, "when, as in Periclean Greece or Elizabethan England, a people fully aware of the calamities of life is nevertheless serenely confident of the greatness of man, whose mighty passions and supreme fortitude are revealed when one of those calamities overtakes him." The "tragic fallacy," however, is that today, owing to some enfeeblement of the human spirit we are no longer confident of our own or anyone else's ability to rise "serenely confident" and face a calamity which may result in destruction but which so ennobles the observers of the action that they achieve a "tragic reconciliation to life." Having lost all belief in the gods as well as arbitrary rights and wrongs, modern authors can only write tragedies which are an accusation against the world rather than a justification of it.

In 1929 Maxwell Anderson had written just such a play. The heroine of his prose tragedy, *Gypsy*, is a neurotic creature, dishonest and emotionally unstable, a victim of heredity and environment. Mr. Anderson has never published this play, and apparently felt that this—his only independent prose tragedy—was a failure, artistically as well as commercially.

In 1929, therefore, almost in refutation to Mr. Krutch's theory of the tragic fallacy, Schoolmaster Anderson turned his back on studies of psychological misfits and malcontents and turned to a golden age. *Elizabeth the Queen* was to be a tragedy—if not a modern tragedy, at least a tragedy by a modern author; and in it he peopled his stage with those very men and women whose passing Mr. Krutch had so lamented: Elizabeth, Cecil, Essex, Raleigh, and even Richard Burbage who appears *in propria persona* acting Falstaff by royal command.

It is hard to tell whether or not the Theater Guild's subscription audience achieved that night of November 3 quite the tragic exaltation that the Elizabethans felt when Lear bent over a dead Cordelia or Othello found too late that his wife was innocent of adultery. But for his part Mr. Anderson acquitted himself handsomely. The protagonists were heroic: a queen, capricious, fierce tempered, proud, and lonely, and a young and an ambitious courtier. Here was sufficient grandeur of theme for most audiences; here a man and woman were working out their own inevitable destruction; yet it was one which must leave the audience with the satisfaction that it was not only inevitable but that the characters were somehow ennobled by it. There is recognition of this in their last speeches to one another:

> ESSEX. It's better for me as it is
> Than that I should live and batten my fame and fortune
> On the woman I love. I've thought of it all. It's better
> To die young and unblemished than to live long and rule,
> And rule not well. . . .
> ELIZABETH. Oh, then I'm old, I'm old!
> I could be young with you, but now I'm old.
> I know how now it will be without you. The sun
> Will be empty and circle round an empty earth . . .
> And I'll be queen of emptiness and death . . .

Lord Essex is destroyed by his tragic flaw, ambition, just as surely as was Macbeth; he has realized that he would have ruled Elizabeth's kingdom rashly and heedlessly, that she was cautious and wise in intrigue and diplomacy. And he comforts himself with the same stoic wisdom with which A. E. Housman comforts the athlete dying young:

> Smart lad, to slip betimes away
> From fields where glory does not stay.

What Mr. Anderson has done in this play is obvious, and it is interesting to contrast it with Mr. Krutch's observations on the present state of tragedy. He would agree with Krutch that one of the difficulties of writing modern tragedy is our loss of faith in the gods and the nobility of kings; he would disagree in that he does have faith in man, for Anderson once wrote in an early poem:

> Now that the gods are gone,
>   And the kings, the gods' shadows, are gone,
> Man is alone on the earth,
>   Thrust out with the suns, alone.

And although man himself has a bitter destiny, Anderson at least has a belief that he is capable of facing it with dignity.

It is true that in *Elizabeth the Queen* he dodged the issue to a certain extent. Granting, perhaps, that we are unable to believe in the grandeur and nobility of our contemporaries, we are more likely to believe in a hero and heroine of "heroic" times. And he further evades the issue by what many believe his romantic attitude towards these characters. Whatever the "real" Elizabeth and Essex might have been like is naturally hard to say; but Anderson has been at some pains to give us the best of them both. This is one of the elements which marks him as a romantic dramatist, and the critic's only concern is whether he adequately establishes the characters for what he wishes them to be. In this he is successful, for we find him turning to advantage the lessons in dramaturgy which he had learned in earlier plays. The power of love to change and to raise men and women to unexpected heights we shall see him using again and again; just as we see him again and again speculating on the nature of government and the effect of individuals exercising it; and, as in *Winterset*, there is the same tragic catharsis which comforts the audience witnessing the untimely end of the hero, since like Cyrano de Bergerac he carried forth his plume unblemished and unbent.

That these elements in the play which distinguish it as tragedy were introduced and developed quite consciously is proved by the fact that Anderson later produced an essay of his own on the subject. "The Essence of Tragedy" was written when Anderson was asked by the Modern Language Association of America to prepare a paper for the American drama section. The foundation for the theory of tragedy there expounded is one which applies to some, if not all, of his own plays. It is based on the Greek conception of the "identification scene," which is that point in the drama wherein the protagonist discovers something in his environment or in his own soul of which he was not hitherto aware. This should occasion the crisis, and should dictate the end of the play. Its effect on the hero is such that his direction in the play is altered.

An identification scene of this sort is present, Anderson believes, in all the plays we choose to remember. It is present, in some form or other, in most of Anderson's tragedies. In *Elizabeth the Queen*, for instance, it is the scene at the end of the second act wherein Elizabeth, after she has promised to share her kingdom with Essex and after he has dismissed his followers, orders his arrest. "I have ruled England a long time, my Essex," she says, "And I have found that he who would rule must be quite friendless, without mercy, without love."

It is true, then, that the tragic flaw which in this case is an essential in the character of each of the protagonists is that which dictates the end of the tragedy. Ambition, pride of place, prevents them from enjoying their love, since it causes them to doubt that love. Actually they do not realize this completely until the third act. The crisis, as in most Anderson plays, is too dramatic and full of action to admit much introspection. Only in the lull that follows, in the lyrical third act, do we find it given statement.

As a corollary to this theory of the identification scene, Anderson feels that the hero, after achieving this new realization of his tragic destiny, must learn to suffer. He cannot change, but he can bear his grief with dignity and spirit. He must try to correct this tragic flaw, and the correction may or may not result in his destruction. In *Elizabeth the Queen* both protagonists are destroyed since Essex realizes that if he lives it will only be to wrest the kingdom from the woman he loves. Both, however, have risen to heights: Elizabeth, the queen, has offered Essex her kingdom; and Essex has preferred the scaffold rather than take it from her. Here is what Anderson calls "an excellence dimly apprehended," here is evinced man's belief in his own destiny. Or, perhaps, in Anderson's case it is a belief in the poet's dream of man's destiny.

This, then, is the author's conception of what tragedy should be; in another essay he has defended the poesy which he chose as the medium for the expression of these conceptions. Here again the defense is *ex post facto*, the latter essay being the introduction to the play *Winterset*. But once again it is only a codification of what the author had long felt about dramatic verse.

Before the production of *Elizabeth the Queen* it would have been possible to have counted on one hand those plays in verse written the last hundred years which had been really successful. Several playwrights of the Abbey Theater had experimented with the poetic form; several other famous poets had tried it. But success such as that achieved by Rostand's *Cyrano de Bergerac* was rare; Ibsen is chiefly remembered for his masterpieces of prose realism rather than for his sagas of Viking heroes. Nevertheless, there has always been an undercurrent of feeling that the drama of naturalism wherein the prose of life is exhibited unadorned by passages of great emotional tension did not alone satisfy. As T. S. Eliot, who has himself written one fine poetic drama, has observed, the theater is the ideal medium for poetry:

. . . for the simplest auditors there is the plot, for the more thoughtful the character and conflict of character, for the more literary the words and phrasing, for the more musically sensitive the rhythm, and for the auditors of greater sensitiveness and understanding a meaning which reveals itself gradually.

Anderson, who was a poet before he was a dramatist, wrote his first play in poetry because, as he once told Barrett Clark, "all the great plays I can remember were in verse." In his essay, "A Prelude to Poetry in the Theater," he further defends the medium. Prose is the language of information, poetry the language of emotion. The best prose on the stage, he feels, is inferior to the best poetry. Hence, the plays of journalistic comment which fill our theater are inferior to those plays which reach occasionally into the upper air of poetic tragedy. For Anderson, as for Bernard Shaw, the stage is a cathedral of the spirit. Just now it is filled with plays whose purpose is to comment upon our social, economic, and political life. But in Anderson there has always been a belief that an age of faith in things unseen will follow an age of reason and that eventually the cathedral will again house the mysteries out of which our drama grew. This strain of mysticism which runs through Anderson's work, only occasionally coming to the surface but always a part of its foundation, is probably responsible for his experiments in verse.

Now there is no doubt that poetry does heighten the emotion of a scene, that the imagery and cadence of verse fires the imagination of players and audience. And there is no doubt that Anderson's dramatic verse has at times done just this. However, in order to determine how relatively successful he has been, it is necessary to inquire into the requirements and nature of dramatic verse, since there has been little understanding of really competent criticism of it during the past few years, largely because there has been so little written. Most of the criticism that Anderson's verse is stiff and prosy is from poets themselves who have not written a line of dramatic verse; or from critics who claim that poetry on the stage is a medium and idiom that does not express or interpret our society and times.

In *Elizabeth the Queen* and *Mary of Scotland* Anderson was taking legends familiar to theatergoers and decorating them with verse, much as the Elizabethans took scenes of faraway and long ago for their tragedies. For this he was labeled an historical and romantic playwright—two terms which he dislikes but which he will find difficulty in denying. With these backgrounds he was relatively successful. Certainly these plays, and *Night over Taos* as well, contain some fine passages. There is fairly judicious mingling of prose and poetry, for instance, in *Elizabeth the Queen*: the bustle and confusion of the council scene of the third act is entirely in prose. The dialogue turns to poetry only when Elizabeth and Essex face one another alone. In *Mary of Scotland* and *Night over Taos* his style seems to be more disciplined, at times almost becoming sparse and barren. However, John Mason Brown felt that Anderson achieved in the former play, "not only the best historical drama that has ever been written by an American, but a script which brings the full-flooding beauty of the English language to a theater in which its beauties are but seldom heard."

Certainly there is beauty here, not only in a lyric moment when Mary bends over the dead Rizzio murmuring, "He wanted to go to Italy," but also in the unforgettable scene when the two queens face one another in Carlisle Castle. However, these plays of faraway and long ago aroused nothing like the storm of criticism which greeted a play produced a few years later.

In *Winterset* which was produced by Guthrie McClintic in 1935 Anderson had written a play which was attended by as much criticism as was Victor Hugo's *Ernani*. The reason, of course, was that here was not only a tragedy in verse but an American tragedy. Here were gangsters, hoodlums, and a judge from the bench all speaking in iambics. As the author points out in his preface to the play, not even Shakespeare had ever attempted that. His great tragedies, while interpreting Elizabethan life, nevertheless all deal with foreign princes and gentlemen at foreign courts or with England's own historical past. Never were Elizabethan audiences asked to believe that their own contemporaries spoke in blank verse; and the scenes in Shakespeare which most vividly picture Elizabethan manners are nearly always in prose.

In *Winterset,* however, Anderson had chosen a theme hitherto treated only in terms of naturalism. Moreover, it was a theme which he himself had so treated a few years before when he and Harold Hickerson had protested the injustice of the Sacco-Vanzetti trial. In the intervening years Anderson had brooded over the fate of those men about whom he had once written so eloquently. He now approached the subject with the ripened judgment of the philosopher rather than with the zeal of the reformer. His speculation into the nature of social justice is now tempered and tinged with the stoicism which has colored so many of his later plays.

Winterset is in the nature of a sequel to *Gods of the Lightning*, inasmuch as the hero of the former drama is the son of an anarchist condemned to death for his political convictions much as were the protagonists of the latter play. The simple words of Vanzetti at the time of his sentence, "If it had not been for this thing, I might have lived out my life talking on street corners to scorning men. . . . Now we are not a failure," rang in Anderson's ears many years after they were spoken. In *Winterset* the son of this man appears searching for evidence to prove his father's innocence of the crime for which he is convicted, and the first two acts of the play are concerned with his struggle to wrest this truth from one of the surviving witnesses.

Gods of the Lightning is a bitter, searching melodrama but it is primarily a play of journalistic comment on the injustice of the conviction of Sacco and Vanzetti. Since *Winterset* is a play written by a poet who is interested primarily in the larger meanings of social justice and revenge, he accomplishes his purpose just as Shakespeare once did; in other words, he takes the melodramatic details of a simple revenge play and makes the hero of it a poet and a philosopher. There is little doubt that this was quite intentional, since Anderson had earlier realized the value of relying on English classic tragedy as a model in trying to bring back poetry to the theater. Now he felt that an audience which could accept Hamlet could accept Mio Romagna. The latter hero even has some of the former's tendency to speculation and conjecture although he is on the whole a much more incisive and vigorous personality. In fact, the tragic flaw of indecision does not appear until this Hamlet meets his Ophelia and they dance together under the huge spans of a Manhattan bridge to the strains of a hurdy gurdy. This changes the course of the play since his Ophelia is the sister of the man whose evidence could clear the name of his father. At the end of the tightly written second act he is betrayed by his Ophelia, and—as in so many Anderson plays—there ensues a lyrical third act in which these star-crossed lovers become more like Romeo and Juliet. This, indeed, is a tragedy of fate rather than of a doom sealed by the overgrowth of any complexion. In fact, the third act in some respects introduces a new theme. For Mio, thwarted in his search for justice, turns rather to a consideration of forgiveness and mercy, and these he finds before both lovers are felled by a gangster's bullets.

This, then, is the play which so engaged the attention of the critics that comment concerning it filled not only the columns of the morning papers, but those of the entire season. The importance of the theme, the beauty of the production, the novelty of a modern play in verse—all claimed their serious attention. Few could fail to commend it on some score. However, as to the quality of the verse and as to the appropriateness of allowing gangsters and hoodlums to speak in blank verse, opinion was by no means unanimous.

Obviously, any character in any play has a right to speak in verse. In the most naturalistic drama in the world there is some editing of the speech, for men and women are rarely so articulate and so given to revealing their emotions as characters must be in a play. However, there must be an illusion of reality, and whether gangsters should speak blank verse is another matter. Joseph Wood Krutch pointed out in *The Nation* that it was as fitting for them to do so as it was for a Venetian general to deliver his order in iambic pentameter or a fourteen-year-old Italian girl to extemporize immortal verse. This, of course, is true, yet Shakespeare never attempted to make the robbers at Gadshill speak in verse, although it must be admitted that the bitter, clipped idiom of the doomed gangster is highly effective.

In fact, Anderson in the highly successful character of Trock proved that blank verse could have a vigor and freedom and need not impede the action of the play. Moreover, during scenes of action the speech frequently turns to prose. In the radical's denunciation of the law there is an amusing parody of Union Square jargon:

SECOND GIRL.   Please, officer, we want to dance. . . .

POLICEMAN.   Sorry. Can't help you.

RADICAL.   And there you see it, the perfect example of capitalistic oppression! In a land where music should be free as air and the arts should be encouraged, a uniformed minion of the rich, a guardian myrmidon of the Park Avenue pleasure hunters, steps in and puts a limit on the innocent enjoyments of the poor!

Similarly, when Judge Gaunt's mind is wandering and, Ophelia-like, he begins to chant scraps of vulgar ballads, his speech is prose. This, of course, is again in the best Elizabethan tradition.

At times, however, there are speeches which might well be in prose which are in verse which then becomes bombast and rhetoric. This has given rise to the criticism that the play was too full of cosmic platitudes, that the author was too preoccupied with figures of wind and rain and the stars. It should be remembered perhaps that these figures have always been the figures of poetry; and that Shakespeare himself was preoccupied with the figure of the poor painted player who so frequently struts and frets upon his stage. And at times the verse rises to real intensity and feeling, as when Mio discovers Miriamne's loyalty to her brother has betrayed him:

MIO.   The bright, ironical gods!
    What fun they must have in heaven! When a man prays
    hard for any gift, they give it, and then one more to boot
    that makes it useless
                (*To* MIRIAMNE)
    You might have picked
    some other stranger to dance with . . . Or chosen
    some other evening to sit outside in the rain.
    But no, it had to be this; all my life long
    I've wanted only one thing, to say to the world
    and prove: the man you killed was clean and true
    and full of love as the twelve-year-old that stood
    and taught in the temple. I can say that now
    and give my proofs—and now you stick a girl's face
    between me and the rites I've sworn the dead
    shall have of me! You ask too much!

There is power and authority here and the voice of the poet rings clear and true. As to those other moments of bombast, it is perhaps well to remember that few Elizabethan plays are unmarred. As Mary Colum (herself a poet) has pointed out, the very nature of dramatic verse demands it. Which perhaps reduces the problem to the fact that few poets and critics are aware of what constitutes real dramatic verse. And Mr. Anderson, who is a competent critic and knows as much about it as any other, will only say at the conclusion of his essay on the subject that whether or not he has solved the problem in *Winterset* is of little moment, "it must be solved if we are to have a great theater in America."

Besides the wonder aroused by an American playwright's attempt to write a tragedy in verse, Anderson's plays of the thirties were a challenge in another sense. These were the years during which a new school of criticism was flourishing. The songs of the thirties were all songs of social significance, and if Anderson stood alone in writing poetic tragedy he was at one with his contemporaries in wanting to comment on contemporary problems. What he had to say about those problems, however, was at considerable variance with what his critics both to right and left were saying. And once again the discussion centered about *Winterset*. This was to be a drama wherein editor, poet, and scholar were to collaborate with the playwright. Heretofore, the poet and playwright had produced such a play as *Mary of Scotland* or editor and playwright had produced tracts for the times.

In *Winterset* Anderson's comment on the nature of class justice in America caused as much criticism as did his medium of expression. This time, oddly enough, the attacks were mostly from the left—from those same leftists who had cheered the earlier *Gods of the Lightning*. This play had been completely ignored by conservative critics, although ironically enough when it was produced at the Anderson Festival at the Pasadena Playhouse during the summer of 1939 it was vigorously applauded by the *haut bourgeoisie* who all but threw their orchids at the feet of the players. In fact, this production as well as *Winterset* is an illustration of the ironies of introducing propaganda in art. The only real criticism of either play came from the Marxists who have always resented Anderson's conclusion that although a great social injustice was done when the state of

Massachusetts condemned Sacco and Vanzetti, no power on heaven or earth could right it.

Miss Eleanor Flexner in *American Playwrights 1918–1938*, a series of essays appropriately subtitled *The Theater Retreats from Reality*, finds the seed for Anderson's defeatism in *Gods of the Lightning*. However, it is full blown in *Winterset*, for Mio, after wringing the confession of guilt from the murderers, does not go forth triumphant to attack the gilded walls of capitalism. The same steadfastness of purpose which had brought him three thousand miles to seek out these murderers should have made him proclaim their infamy, not only in order to vindicate his father but to forge new weapons for the class struggle. Instead of this, however, Mio is thwarted by the vision of a girl's face, and there follows a lyrical third act in which he wills to forget his purpose.

> Mio. Miriamne, if you love me
>   teach me a treason to what I am, and have been
>   till I learn to live like a man. I think I'm waking
>   from a long trauma of hate and fear and death. . . .
>   . . . But teach me to live
>   and forget to hate!

The final irony, of course, is that death awaits both lovers after Mio has discovered this secret of forgiveness. Perhaps here the author is guilty of failure to construct a completely inevitable conclusion. But that is no doubt the author's purpose and is no graver a defect than the delayed letter which brings Romeo to grief. Anderson believed that these young vagabonds had small chance of happiness; the world was not their friend or the world's law. And to die young and unblemished, as so many of Anderson's young idealists die—Mio, Essex, and Rudolph of Hapsburgh—this is a gallant and beautiful thing. This is what brings about that feeling of "tragic exaltation" which is so rarely felt in the theater today. Esdras, the father of Miriamne, reads the epitaph of the two lovers which is almost a complete statement of Anderson's stoicism:

> . . . this is the glory of earthborn men and women
> not to cringe, never to yield, but standing
> take defeat implacable and defiant. . . .
>   . . . On this star,
> In this hard star-adventure, knowing not

what the fires mean to right and left, nor whether
a meaning was intended or presumed,
man can stand up, and look out blind, and say:
in all these turning lights I find no clue
only a masterless night, and in my blood
no certain answer, yet is my mind my own,
yet is my heart a cry towards something dim
in distance, which is higher than I am
and makes me emperor of the endless dark
even in seeking.

It is evident that Mr. Anderson's conclusion concerning man's fate in this hard star adventure is not too cheery. When accused by Max Eastman of being a defeatist, however, Mr. Anderson felt called upon to reply in *Stage*. Here he claims that his hope for the human race is not that it will achieve perfection or apparently even improvement in magnanimity and mentality in the near future but only over a long period of time. Meanwhile civilizations may come and go and with them different disciplines and moralities. Of these it is futile to conjecture; only the poet may dream of them: "For what the poets are always asking for, visioning and projecting, is man as he must and will be, man a step above and beyond his present, man as he may be glimpsed on some horizon of dream, a little nearer what he himself wishes to become." To hold to this, Anderson believes, requires more courage than to cherish illusions that man with all his present limitations could save himself by revolutions—political or scientific.

Meanwhile, however, there is only that belief that there is in man—at least in most of Mr. Anderson's heroes—the courage of despair, a gallant conviction that they at least will meet their inevitable defeat with head bloody but unbowed. This is never better illustrated than in Mr. Anderson's latest play, *Key Largo*, which is in many respects a successor to *Winterset*, since it is a poetic tragedy dealing with contemporary events. It might almost be said to be an answer in dramatic form to the charge that his heroes have surrendered their lives and their missions too easily. In the prologue to this play a band of eight recruits, mostly Americans, are defending a machine gun nest in Loyalist Spain. Their leader, King McCloud has discovered that they have been betrayed by the Loyalists who are giving up the cause of Spanish democracy and are about to ask Franco for terms.

Meanwhile the foreign recruits are being sacrificed in order to cover the retreat of the other Loyalist troops. For McCloud, Spanish democracy has been a symbol of something far greater. It was an ideal made tangible, something to believe in, a standard to defend. It was to give meaning to an otherwise meaningless life. Yet now, the cause of Spanish democracy is being abandoned and this ideal has been betrayed: Franco, McCloud believes, will win in Spain. The English, the French will see to that:

> ... But if he didn't, Stalin would win in Spain
> and it's one blood purge or the other,
> > but never justice
> only the rat-men ratting at each other
> in a kind of rat despair.

These are almost the words of Queen Elizabeth when she discovers that Cecil has outwitted the Earl of Essex. The snake-mind, she concludes, is best; the free of soul, the valiant go down; "The rats inherit the earth." In this play, however, Anderson gives fuller voice to his conviction that there is in men some dim, indestructible belief that whatever the conduct of the rat-men may be, a lost cause is better than no cause at all. Victor d'Alcala, another of the Loyalist recruits, prefers to remain and face death defending the retreat of the other troops than to desert as McCloud counsels:

> ... if I die
> then I'll know that men will never give in;
> then I'll know there's something in the race
> of men, because even I had it, that hates injustice
> more than it wants to live. ...
> > And that means the Hitlers
> and the Mussolinis always lose in the end—
> force loses in the long run, and the spirit wins,
> whatever spirit is.

The rest of the play follows the *Winterset* pattern. Just as in *Winterset* the larger problem of the nature of social justice was complicated by a lurid gangster melodrama, in *Key Largo* another gangster and his mob offer the hero a chance to test these two attitudes towards living. Whether deserting and failing the Loyalist cause was "cowardly" or "sensible"; whether he should have lost his life in order to save it—this is the issue. As in the former play the hero spends the third act talking the matter over with a heroine and her wise old father. Once again the patriarch delivers the judgment, and the hero is convinced that it is necessary to believe that man is advancing millenium by millenium, from civilization to civilization, that the noblest action is to die in order to prove this to himself. Fortunately the rat-men offer him a second opportunity to vindicate himself. He dies in order to save two derelict Seminole Indians whom a corrupt Florida sheriff wishes to arrest for a murder they did not commit.

Anderson has used the formula of the gangster melodrama often enough to be fairly familiar with it. In the romantic fantasy *High Tor*, it is used as comedy; and in *Winterset* and *Key Largo* to provide sufficient action and suspense to relieve the philosophic conjecture which accompanies that action. However, how effective and honorable a device melodrama may be is of no prime importance. The fact is important, however, that Anderson in *Key Largo* absolved himself of the charge of defeatism, yet at the same time proved himself to be an uncompromising idealist.

Thus he has at least tried to rationalize his position, although few leftist critics would admit that he has answered them successfully. The brand of stoicism which he defends in *Key Largo* is as little palatable to them as was the utter despair reflected when the oriental heroine of *Wingless Victory* turns on her Puritan persecutors and flays them for their hypocrisy and cruelty. In Anderson's social philosophy there is scarcely more hope for immediate amelioration of the social problems besetting our age, than there is in Bernard Shaw's belief that some day there will be a race of Methuselahs wise enough to solve those problems. For comfort for those suffering from poverty in a land of plenty he can offer only a belief in the poet's dream.

This is not enough for the Marxists. They will neither forgive him for this stoicism or for his lack of faith that any collective action will solve our difficulties. Only twice in the Anderson theater do we find any great affirmation of faith of this kind. The first instance of this is when Alan McClean the crusading hero of *Both Your Houses* accuses of corruption the politicians in Washington who have just passed a ruinously extravagant appropriations bill which generously lines their pockets: "You think you're good and secure in this charlatan's sanctuary you've built for yourself," he tells them. "You think the sacred and senseless legend poured into the people of this country from

childhood will protect you. It won't . . ." Eventually their con-
stituents will turn them out of office. Just who will replace them,
however, since Anderson believes that the rat-men inherit the
earth, is not certain.

The second instance is in the tremendously moving speech of
George Washington in *Valley Forge* when he surveys the cold
and hungry men he is commanding in this last desperate stand
against tyranny and oppression. They are, he says, "an uncouth
clan, unread, harsh-spoken" but they are followers of a dream of
liberty and freedom. There will come a time when men will be
able to bear no burdens save of their own choosing, to worship
as they please, to walk upright—independent and masterless.
This is destined to be, even if they themselves fail. Yet it will
not be without travail. At the end of the play, as they are bury-
ing their dead, Washington grimly reflects that

> this liberty will look easy by and by
> when nobody dies to get it.

However, these two great affirmations, this faith in America,
is hardly a belief in any kind of radical action. In none of Anderson's plays is there a rallying cry for the proletariat to unite
and throw off their chains. This is for two reasons. First, Anderson is too much of an individualist; and second, he is too convinced that government is and always has been exploitation. He
believes in the class struggle and he even feels that the capitalistic
system is worse than the Marxists claim that it is: it is so bad that
it can't be changed. Secondly, he believes that radical action will
never be effective since the radicals are always too busy fighting
among themselves ever to present a comprehensive strategy that
could outwit entrenched greed.

On this score he has disappointed the leftists sadly. For instance, in *Gods of the Lightning* Anderson failed according to
their standards because of the character of Suvorin, who believes
all struggle against entrenched capitalism is futile. This disillu-
sioned anarchist delivers a vicious attack on radicals of all stripe
and color because of their failure to unite, for the continual bick-
erings within the party:

. . . How many years have I sat listening to fools' talk? Five years—
ten years. And what have I learned from you? . . . that you know
nothing—that you learn nothing! Uplifters you are, dreamers, reformers, thinking to make over the earth. I know you all and you are

fools—the earth is old. You will not make it over. Man is old. You will not make him over. You are anarchists, maybe, some of you social pap. The world is old and it is owned by men who are hard. Do you think that you can win against them, by a strike? Let us change the government, you say. Bah! They own this government, they will buy any government you have. I tell you there is no government—only brigands in power who fight always for more power!

This is indication of how little Suvorin believes in that perfectionism which is the essential core of socialism. And one of the characters in *Key Largo* offers much the same sentiment to his comrades. One of them has remarked that they actually have little knowledge of what they're fighting for.

We thought we did before we started. We said, no matter what they do with this freedom, they have a right to keep it. But suppose the first thing they do with their freedom is to put on chains? We believe in the rights of minorities, don't we? Well, there are fifty-seven minorities in Loyalist Spain . . . Anarchists, Communists, Leftists, Rightists, Leftist-Rightists, Rightist-Leftists, Socialists, Leftist-Socialists, Rightist-Socialists, Anti-Clericals, Clerical-Communists, Loyalist soldiers, police, crazy people. . . . But if they won and it came to a vote, and one party was in power, would it make hash of the other fifty-six varieties!

The ultimate reason, however, for the Marxist's criticism of Anderson's stoicism and his lack of faith in collective action, is that fundamentally he wished to write tragedies, they wished him to write propaganda. *That* his integrity could not permit. Since he could not accept the Marxian dialectics he could hardly make plays of the themes of the class struggle as outlined by Marx and interpreted by Lenin. Or rather when he did as in *Winterset* take the theme of class justice he gave it his own interpretation, and shows that the judge who condemns the anarchists to death is himself a victim of class justice.

Judge Gaunt in this play is not made the villain of the play. Anderson has reserved for that position the gangster Trock. The Judge he portrays as the victim of the system he represents just as is the man whom he sentenced to die. In the play, the Judge is an outcast wandering the streets, the victim of amnesia, trying to find justification for what he has done. He defends his position when Mio confronts him with the evidence which proves his father was innocent:

> ... there are things a judge must not believe
> even though they should head and fester underneath
> and press in on his brain. Justice once rendered
> in a clear burst of anger, righteously, upon a
> common laborer, confessed an anarchist, the verdict
> found and the precise machinery of the law invoked
> to find him guilty—think what furor would rock the
> state if the court then flatly said all this was
> lies. . . .
>   A vendor of fish
> is not protected as a man might be who kept a
> market. I own I've sometimes wished that was not
> so, but it is. The man you defend was unfortunate—
> and his misfortune bore almost as heavily on me—
> I'm broken—broken across. You're much too young
> to know how bitter it is when a worn connection
> chars and you can't remember—can't remember.

Miss Flexner, of course, has no sympathy for this note of pathos. She reprimands Anderson for not vigorously prosecuting a judge who could admit as clearly as he does the nature of class justice. Other critics—Grenville Vernon in *The Commonweal* for example—found Gaunt the only truly tragic figure in the play. Certainly the intensity of the torment of the conscience-stricken old man made him an unforgettable, if not a tragic figure, and Anderson's pity and understanding of both the judge and the condemned anarchist as victims of class justice recommends him as a tolerant, and perhaps very shrewd, critic of the radical movements of the third decade.

This impartiality, this passionate sense of justice which is revealed in so many of his plays is one of Anderson's noblest qualities. Consequently, perhaps, it has inspired some of his best poetry. He is magnificent in wrath, and when he rises in anger to denounce tyranny and sham he is extremely effective. If he has criticized radical ideology, he has certainly not spared conservative opinion.

In this he is not alone among dramatists, for since Shaw established the form of the drama of discussion, almost every item in the curriculum of the social sciences has been discussed. But Anderson is alone in that he has made the discussion an integral part of his drama. His favorite hero has been the rebel reformer; and he has set against him to represent the conservative position no man of straw but a worthy opponent who as often as not is the victor. Hence, there is almost always a real dramatic issue. Besides the two plays based on the Sacco-Vanzetti legend, he has discussed in *Knickerbocker Holiday* the meaning of democracy; in *High Tor* the possibilities of anarchism; in *Both Your Houses* he has attacked corruption in Congress; in *Night over Taos* he has dramatized the passing of the Spanish feudal order in the far west; and in *The Masque of Kings* has discussed the nature of kingship.

In fact, he has been so preoccupied with these problems that he has been the object of one of Wolcott Gibbs' pungent satires in *The New Yorker* entitled, "Eva's Deathbed Revisited." The author's note tells us that it is the account of a nightmare experienced by a man attending *Key Largo*, and then attempting to read himself to sleep by rereading *Uncle Tom's Cabin*. This parody illustrates the contention of many of his critics that his verse is empty and pretentious, that he is something of the pedant, certainly too much of the political scientist.

At times, it is true, it does intrude on the action. For instance, in *Night over Taos* the forward movement of the play is halted by Montoya, the feudal lord of Taos, who insists on giving advice to his son who is urging him to eat after the battle:

> MONTOYA.   Not when I'm about to fight, Felipe. Have
> the sons of Montoya never felt it . . . a fever in
> the lover so devouring that food is impure? No,
> no . . . you're young. There's an ancient belief
> that wisdom comes with age, and the twenties are
> the time of passion. It's for that reason they
> choose old men as judges . . . men who will have
> outworn the lusts of the flesh and blood and be willing
> to rule impartially over the sins of youth. But
> all this is a fallacy. For wisdom and justice we
> must depend on the young; for madness in devotion
> to a cause, for all madness, you must go among
> their elders . . . It's a thought for your stage
> should you ever govern, Felipe. Make no old men
> judges . . . Make the old men soldiers. Old men are
> swift, violent, crafty, lecherous, unscrupulous in
> winning, relentless in defeat, putting their cause
> before affections . . . Young men are much too
> tender, much too true. . . .

This advice Anderson thought so well considered that he repeated it in *Winterset*. But certainly in this previous play (which has other structural defects as well) it slows up the action to a standstill.

In other plays it is much more natural and frequently gives solidity to his drama, for he seldom indulges in such extraneous conjecture as the above, but makes the issue a concrete thing. As to his opinions themselves they are fairly clear-cut and they repeat themselves with sufficient regularity to be fairly obvious. He is first of all the anarchist, the arch-individualist who is actually of the opinion that the best government is the government which governs least. Hence, the best government probably is a democracy, since in its fumbling, stumbling inefficient way it brings about a maximum of civil liberty and personal freedom; hence, he condemns a dictatorship which although it may be more efficient nevertheless always ends by destroying personal freedom. For Anderson feels strongly that power (and wealth which is power) always in the end corrupts the individual and leads to tyranny. In *Valley Forge* when Washington is meeting with his officers to determine whether they shall continue their insurrection, one of their number complains bitterly about the inefficiency of Congress and its lack of support of the army so pitifully unprepared for the rigors of winter:

Do you know what I think of governments, by and large, I mean in general? They're run by pimps, who get kicked out of hot-houses for picking the customers' pockets. This one we've got—we made it, set it up, picked the best men we could find and put them in—and their brains began to rot before the year was out. It rots a man's brains to be in power, and he turns pimp and picks pockets; the scavengers! At least, when you have a king you can chop his head off.

Anderson would no doubt agree with Harold Laski who once maintained that after years of study of political science the only truth to which he could subscribe was that "power always corrupts, and absolute power corrupts absolutely."

This is aptly illustrated again in *The Masque of Kings*. This is Anderson's solution of the mystery which shrouded the double death of Rudolph, heir to the Hapsburg throne, and his mistress, Countess Mary Vetsera, at the Mayerling shooting lodge one January night in 1889. According to Anderson, this is the trag-

edy of a really liberal prince who wanted to lift the iron heel of
the Hapsburgs from the necks of his subjects. In this he is naturally opposed by that wily and cynical tyrant, Franz Joseph, his
father. Rudolph allies himself with the disgruntled Count Hoyos
who commands the Vienna garrison troops, and together with
other liberals surprises Franz Joseph in his study.

Rudolph tells his father that the absolutism of the Hapsburgs
is over. He himself will take the motto of the medieval kings—
"nothing for myself."

> . . . Let me drink plain water and eat
> plain food, and turn what mind I have to an·instrument
> of justice, clean of greed, despising politics.

But here Franz Joseph enters the opening wedge of his counter-
attack. He points out that Rudolph's first steps must be tyrannous and bloody; that is the nature of revolutions. Franz Joseph
offers to supply him with a list of seven hundred names of men
who must be liquidated. And he adds that there needs must be
military rule as well as complete censorship of the press. He
subtly points out that all governments are class governments,
that Rudolph must rise to power as he did himself. And Rudolph
admits that "A government's business is to guard the trough for
those whose feet are in it." As soon as he touched Franz Joseph's
power he felt the blight.

> . . . then virtue
> went out of me to him; I was not the same,
> and any man who sits here in his place
> will be as he was, as I am.

He turns to the desk wherein his father has advised him there is
a diary of one of the traitors, and finds it to belong to his own
mistress, Mary Vetsera. Thus, like Mio Romagna in *Winterset*,
he is turned aside from his purpose, not only because of the dis-
illusion of finding that he would have to take tyrannous measures
to establish himself but because of an unfortunate upset in the
course of true love.

Whether or not this is bad dramaturgy is hardly to the point
here, since what Anderson is essentially trying to do is dramatize
the destroying power of power. It is a pitch that defiles all who
touch it. It brings about the destruction of the Earl of Essex, of

Mary of Scotland, and Rudolph of Hapsburg. In this instance Anderson has gone so far as to show how even a liberal monarch cannot rule without being corrupted. Hence, apparently, it is better to have no government at all, or at least as little as possible, since then and then only can man's personal freedom and dignity be assured.

For this reason Anderson hates the totalitarian states even more than the corrupt monarchies which they replaced. State socialism with the dictatorship which goes with it leads to the servile state wherein men surrender their personal liberty and dignity for a mean dependence, for a social security which ill repays them. Anderson feared and hated this servile state with as violent a fear and hatred as did G. K. Chesterton and Hilaire Belloc in the early years of the century when state socialism was being so vigorously defended by Shaw and Wells.

The fact that in an age when nearly all liberal thought involves a certain amount of collectivism Anderson can still believe so intensely in individualism has made his exact position somewhat equivocal. The fact that he could rise to such a vigorous defense of Sacco and Vanzetti places him at once in the "liberal" camp; in fact, his defense of anarchy itself indicates a very radical stripe in his make-up. Yet here the radicals themselves will hardly own him since he has repudiated all kinds of governmentalism. During the past few years, when misery has been so widespread and when many youths—like Mio in *Winterset*—have been unable to find a place in society, many have come to the conclusion that it is the responsibility of the government to intervene in some way. Similarly the need of protection of the citizen as consumer against monopoly involves a tremendous amount of governmentalism. Yet, that way bureaucracy lies, and Anderson fears it.

In fact, he fears it so much that he wouldn't even trust the government to take care of the great army of the unemployed and the unemployables. This is probably the gravest flaw in Andersonian political economy. No one has greater sympathy for such outcasts: witness the hobo in *Winterset* who sleeps under the pipes in the Esdras tenement. Yet he has never in any of his plays or prefaces suggested how they are to be provided for, save by private charity; and he is realist enough to know that that is hardly a satisfactory solution.

For Anderson, in spite of his great compassion for human suffering doesn't look for much amelioration of that suffering. All he offers is a kind of personal salvation through individual initiative. Take for instance, the Indians in *Key Largo*. They are being hunted from key to key by a corrupt sheriff who ignores the activities of the gamblers on the waterfront. However, they have a fine defiance of a white man's laws and a white man's justice and prefer a miserable existence in the everglades to governmental charity on a reservation.

This fear of governmentalism which he feels is dangerously near to state socialism has led Anderson to the conclusion that democracy is best. Here civil liberties are protected at least, and —inefficient though it may be—the rats have less chance to inherit the earth. He has dramatised this to best advantage in a musical comedy, *Knickerbocker Holiday*. In this play Anderson has allowed his genial satire to play over the field of politics in general. To little old New York which is being ruled in a very haphazard way by the city fathers comes Pieter Stuyvesant who claims that government is always "a group of men organized to sell protection to the inhabitants of a limited area at monopolistic prices." However, Stuyvesant realizes also that as dictator, the populace must keep certain illusions about him; hence, he engages Tienhoven, father of the heroine, to negotiate the sale of weapons to the Indians. He also glorifies him in song as "the one indispensable man"—indispensable to any government.

> . . . In every government
> Whatever its intent
> There's one obscure official with a manner innocent
> His job invisible
> Is purchasing good will
> With wads of public money taken from the public till;
> He's the one indispensable man.

In setting up this very pleasant little dictatorship with much urbanity and charm, Stuyvesant finds it necessary, however, to hang the hero, Brom Broeck, who is a musical comedy version of Van Dorn of *High Tor*. Brom claims that since coming from Holland, and since living in the wilderness for a winter on wild turkey and Indian corn he has developed a strange malady: this is a peculiar inability to take orders. In other words, he has discovered independence and self respect. That, Brom and Washington Irving who occasionally appears on the scene, decide is what distinguishes an American:

> Yes, it's just that he hates and he damns all the features
> Of any mortal man set above his fellow creatures,
> ... He does his own living, he does his own dying
> Does his loving, does his hating, does his multiplying
> Without the supervision of a governmental plan—
> And that's an American!

For this Brom is about to have his neck stretched but saves himself by an appeal to the city fathers whose government Stuyvesant replaced. Their government, Brom tells them, was clumsy and corrupt as all governments are, but it has the immense advantage of being "incompetent in villainy and clumsy in corruption." Stuyvesant, on the other hand, is efficiently vicious and corrupt. And the former is infinitely to be preferred. "Let's keep the government small and funny," he says, "and maybe it will give us less discipline and more entertainment."

This idea appeals to the city fathers, especially to one Roosevelt who is supposed to be some dim, distant kin to Franklin Delano Roosevelt inasmuch as "ven he gets an idea it sticks." They refuse to hang Brom and Washington Irving, who once again appearing as a *deus ex machina*, conveniently placates Stuyvesant with the promise that he who is about to become the city's saint shouldn't blemish his reputation with such a bloody deed.

There is excellent fun in this operetta, for which Kurt Weil produced a score almost as lively as Mr. Anderson's book. The lyrics have a Gilbertian wit and irony that is delightful. *Knickerbocker Holiday* at least proved Anderson's versatility. He can handle light verse and farcical comedy to advantage. It may not be *The Beggar's Opera* of our day but at least it has topical wit and informing intelligence that is first rate satire. It illustrates the fact that perhaps Anderson's claim to a permanent place in the ranks of our first flight dramatists is that he has searched unfailingly for new forms. He has tried his hand at melodrama, realism, poetic tragedy, poetic fantasy, comedy, farce, and comedy drama. He has had the courage to revive dramatic forms which have not been used successfully since the closing of theaters in 1642. How much the scholar has betrayed the playwright; how much the political scientist has betrayed the artist—this is for another generation to decide.

As a document—and all Anderson plays have something of the document in them—*Knickerbocker Holiday* proves that as an anarchist he is pretty conservative; just as *Key Largo* proved that as an idealist he was a bit on the pessimistic side. These paradoxes are the key to Anderson, and their resolution is a secret to an understanding of his plays.

There is much wisdom in what Anderson has been saying in the past decade of dramatic composition. However, there are several fallacies implicit. First, it is very well to admit Anderson's claim that an American is one who can't take orders—for we are a nation of law-breakers. This is all right as long as the government is kept "small and funny." Yet, the government of the United States today, however funny it may be to some, isn't small. And as in the past few months we have seen most of the "small and funny" European governments steam-rollered by the infernal efficiency of fascism, Anderson's observation seems dangerously flippant. Certainly it is not an intelligent suggestion, since our complex national and international structure demands another and larger view of our governmental problems. Another dangerous irrelevancy is that Anderson's belief in individualism is such that he seems to approve of nineteenth-century laissez-faire economics. In *Both Your Houses* Sol Fitzgerald, a lusty and salty old man of Falstavian proportions, gives a brief lesson in history. He defends the congressional raid which has just been made on the national treasury by telling Alan McClean, the young idealist who is trying to reform Congress, that brigands built up this country.

They stole billions and gutted whole states and empires, but they dug our oil-wells, built our railroads, built up everything we've got, and invented prosperity as they went along. Let 'em go back to work! We can't have an honest government, so let 'em steal plenty and get us started again.

Now McClean does confront him with the threat that "there are a hundred million people who are disgusted enough to turn from you to something else." But what that is he doesn't say. And it can't be denied, Anderson has always had a reluctant but very real admiration for such lusty old tyrants as Pablo Montoya, Pieter Stuyvesant, and Franz Joseph of Austria. While they were brutal and perhaps corrupt they were at least men.

And if he would hardly agree to turning the country over to the robber barons again, he does look with nostalgia to the lost horizons of the nineteenth century. In *High Tor* his hero who owns a mountain on the west shore of the Hudson River finally decides to sell it to shyster real estate agents. The dying Indian in the play who is the symbol of a way of life opposed to the commercialism which is pressing hard upon them advises Van to seek wilder land and higher mountains. "You'll find them," says the Indian with supreme confidence. He bids Van dig his grave for him and to bury him as his ancestors were buried; and he leaves our hero looking forward to the time when the railroad bridges along the Hudson will be as picturesque as Roman aqueducts. No one can blame Anderson for disapproving of the less dignified aspects of contemporary life; but he is a little willful in insisting that our frontiers have not disappeared: we are living in a very different economic era and must face that fact.

There is a good deal of shrewd common sense in much of what he says, however. We can be grateful for his warnings against dictators and demagogues. Such are his convictions that we can expect him to be a vigorous champion of civil liberties in those trying times which may lie ahead of us. As the last anarchist, we may be sure that Anderson himself would retire to High Tor—he himself owns the property—and would defend it with his life against any encroachment on his personal freedom. However, Anderson's theater of the thirties was written before the European danger was so insistent. Just as much of the Marxist criticism written before the formation of the Berlin-Moscow Axis has become completely irrelevant, some of Anderson's observations seem to have been intended for a cycle of American life already far distant. Certainly the Anderson theater of the forties will no doubt have a different note. The current of mysticism in his plays will probably be deepened; perhaps there will be no more journalistic comment than in his most popular but least literate play, *Saturday's Children*.

One thing it is certain Anderson's work will always possess, however. This is his faith in his art and in the theater as one of the liveliest of the modern arts. In fact, it is more: it is a cathedral of the spirit and the playwright must be worthy of his service. It is Anderson's greatest service rendered that in this cathedral he has restored the wonder and the enchantment which the theater once had, but which it has lost in an age of realism and journeyman comedies. Anderson made it a place where Dutch skippers could reappear on the Palisades of the Hudson, where young lovers could meet and love and die under a Manhattan bridge, where men and women could sail away in a Wellsian star wagon.

And in this coming decade we may be grateful for that bitter wisdom which is to friend us in the dark and cloudy day. The bright ironical gods who look down on the lovers in the Manhattan dead-end alley are just as pitiless as those who looked down on poor Tess and Eustacia Vye on Egdon Heath. But at least Anderson will always have faith in faith and in the poet's dream.

XII

FRANCIS FERGUSSON

James's Idea of Dramatic Form

It has often been pointed out that James's attempt to write for the theater marks an important turning point in his career. He had behind him a certain success as a writer of fiction, but this success had begun to wane. He felt that his aims as an artist were becoming clearer, but that his public was losing interest. After his experience with the theater he returned to the novel. But at the moment of writing his plays he could not see what form his work was to take, and he seems to have considered the possibility at least that it would be drama. He had followed the theater all his life, and was aware that his fiction approached the form and texture of drama. He envied Dumas and Labiche their secure possession of a stage, an audience, a "theater."

But the theater he had to write for was the British theater of the eighties. The well-made play of the Scribe tradition, lightened and sweetened to suit the taste of the theatergoers of Victorian London, held the stage. Drama was understood as a plot or machine for holding the attention of an audience for two hours, and then releasing it in a good humor. The great Sarcey wrote, "The audience is the necessary and inevitable condition to which dramatic art must accommodate its means . . . . From this simple fact we derive all the laws of the theater without a single exception." When James set out to write his comedies he put the problem to himself in exactly these terms: to accept that audience and learn to obey the laws derived from its habits and its taste. "The mixture," he wrote, "was to be stirred to the tune of perpetual motion and served, under pain of being rejected with disgust, with the time-honored bread-sauce of the happy ending."

This narrow and cynical conception of drama is of course "true" as far as it goes. It is a necessary condition of drama that it

Reprinted from *Kenyon Review*, V (1943), 495–507, by permission of the author and the publisher. Copyright 1943 by *Kenyon Review*.

hold an audience. Yet on this basis we have no clue to the distinction between various dramatic genres, or even between drama and other devices for entertaining an audience in a theater. The notion goes back, I think, to the seventeenth century, when all the arts addressed themselves to a comparatively small and homogeneous society, the embodiment of all values and the arbiter of taste. The neoclassic theorists in their reading of Aristotle failed to notice the distinction between *mythos* and *praxis*, plot and action; they did not digest the Aristotelian notion of drama as the imitation of an action by means of plot. This left them without an explicit theory of the substance of drama, and hence with a purely mechanical and empirical idea of its form. They assumed that serious drama was substantially the conflict between love and honor, or passion and reason, or desire and duty. Subsequent generations of theatergoers were to lose their interest in this theme, but not their demand for entertainment. We have seen the tyranny of the consumer become as absolute in drama as in advertising, and the playwright study his trade in the same spirit as the layout man and copywriter.

James found no difficulty in learning the tricks of this trade, and he turned out four plays which are mechanically as neatly put together as one could wish. All four are perpetually agitated comedies, parlor games, the stakes "love" and money. At the beginning of each we are shown the characters paired off in a certain arrangement which is not quite satisfactory; by the end they have effected a shift into a new and happier pattern. The suspense, the speed of the story, and the succession of clear and stagey situations never flag for a moment. James had solved the problem which he as craftsman had set himself. But it was easy for him, as it is for us, to see why the experiment was not a success. It was not satisfactory to him because the nature of the form ruled out in advance any subject he would have been interested in trying to dramatize. He could only take a minor idea, he says, which, with the habit of small natures, proved thankless. It is too evident that he disliked his characters and that the happy ending offended his taste. This must all have been as puzzling and unsatisfactory to his audience as it was to him.

When he wrote the preface to the published plays he speculated a little ruefully about what the plays might have been. He thought that the tone of farce might have carried them off if the audience had not so inexorably demanded the "bland air of the little domestic fairy tale." In spite of his attempts at good nature, his plays do approximate now and then a cold, hard Jonsonian type of farce, based on flat external caricature, and boldly absurd situations—a form in which the mechanical ticking of the plot is part of the basic vision. I think it possible that if one produced a James play now in the costume of the eighties one might bring out this farce. Perhaps an audience would even accept it as a satirical picture of a society now safely remote.

He abandoned the stage, but without thinking that the drama or even the theater lacked the resources he required. It was rather that particular form of drama and that particular theater which baffled and thwarted him. As he turned away from the theater he wrote, "Give me an hour, just an hour; Dumas and Augier never lacked it, and it makes all the difference; and with it I shan't fear to tackle the infinite." It was about this time too that he wrote the article on Coquelin which contains the following fine description of that actor's art:

M. Coquelin's progress through this long and elaborate part, all of fine shades and pointed particulars, all resting on the keenest observation as well as appealing to it, resembles the method of the psychological novelist who (when he is in as complete possession of his form as M. Coquelin of *his*) builds up a character, in his supposedly uncanny process, by touch added to touch, line to line, illustration to illustration, and with a vision of his personage breathing steadily before him.

When James embarked upon his last group of novels and his critical prefaces he was free to tackle the subject which really interested him. It was in the effort to "dramatize" this subject that he made his great discoveries in dramatic form and technique. It is true that by rejecting the theater as he found it he also rejected some of the limitations which any theater imposes upon drama: the strict time limits, and the obligation to maintain a certain rhythmic tension in the face of that impatient crowd of Sarcey's. He clearly luxuriates in this freedom, multiplying his discriminations, taking his time, putting out of patience a large group of readers who accuse him of verbosity and hairsplitting. His novels are not literally dramas. I am not even sure that the phrase "described dramas" is very accurate for them. Yet both the texture of the writing and the large outlines of the form are truly dramatic. And I wish to suggest that his ideas of form and of techniques of presentation throw at least as much light upon drama as upon fiction.

The critical prefaces have been carefully studied by Joseph Warren Beach, Percy Lubbock, R. P. Blackmur, and others with whose work I am less familiar. Thanks to their work many of James's technical notions have become generally available. In the following notes I have taken some of the ideas, and indicated how they might be applied to drama, and what basic conceptions of dramatic form they constitute.

"Picture and Scene"

Percy Lubbock makes much of the distinction between "picture" and "scene" which James mentions several times in his prefaces. He writes:

It is the method of picture-making that enables a novelist to cover his great spaces of life and quantities of experience so much greater than any that can be brought within the acts of a play. . . . The limitation of drama is as obvious as its peculiar power. It is clear that if we wish to see an abundance and multitude of life we shall find it more readily and summarily by looking for an hour into a memory, a consciousness, than by merely watching the present events of an hour, however crowded. . . . But it needs a mind to create that vista.

A novelist may and often does break down and tell all, while a writer for the stage never can. In this sense the novelist commands a resource not available to the dramatist. But this resource, so conceived, James disdained. He felt how easily it degenerated into mere formless loquacity. He preferred to dramatize the picture too, by viewing it through a consciousness different from his own, that of a character in the drama. The method is that of the dramatist, and if you look at a drama which contains "great spaces of life and quantities of experience" you can see the dramatist employing it. Behind the chief characters in *Antony and Cleopatra, Troilus and Cressida, King Lear*, these great spaces extend, because the characters are aware of them. In the two hours of playing time of *Ghosts* Ibsen makes us feel many years of Mrs. Alving's life and experience by making the characters in their various ways feel them. Mr. Lubbock's analysis suffers throughout from his failure to understand the nature and scope of the stage medium. The actors are not there only to illustrate for us the facts of the story, but through their make-believe to create an imagined world for the eye of the mind to dwell upon. Good dramatic writing, like good acting, owes much of its quality to the establishment of these imagined perspectives behind and beyond the little figures on the boards.

THE FINE INTELLIGENCE AS "REFLECTOR" AND AS COMPOSITIONAL CENTER

James almost invariably used a fine intelligence to give us the clue to the other characters and to the issues and values of his dramas. It had to be a fine intelligence if it was to perceive what James wanted his audience to perceive through it, yet it could not be James himself, for then James would have been telling us *about* his subject instead of presenting it to us directly. The problem and the solution both belong to drama, and good drama is full of Jamesian "reflectors." Enobarbus in *Antony and Cleopatra* is one. In the first three acts he interprets Antony and Cleopatra for us. We come to depend on him for the clue even when we have the chief characters in the flesh before us. This function is very clear in Scene 13 of Act III, when Cleopatra receives Caesar's emissary and Antony has him whipped. Enobarbus not only shows us what to think of Antony and Cleopatra at various moments, he also sums up the impression of the whole scene for us several times and at the end. It is not too much to say that the scene is composed and pulled together for us in Enobarbus' consciousness of it. Shakespeare thus uses Enobarbus both as "reflector" and as "compositional center" for this scene.

These notions of the reflector, and of the fine intelligence as the center of composition, are as useful in the analysis of Chekov's or Congreve's plays as in the analysis of Shakespeare's. The practitioners of "well-made" drama, who usually conceive their subjects in terms of a single narrative line or a monolinear argument, the demonstration of a thesis, do not need the notion of the reflector. Any dramatist who conceives his subject in the round, capable of being looked at from various angles, needs and uses these devices. But it was James who defined them clearly.

SITUATIONS AS LAMPS OR REFLECTORS

James describes the structure of *The Awkward Age* as follows:

I draw on a sheet of paper . . . the neat figure of a circle consisting of a number of small rounds disposed at equal distance about a central object. The central object was my situation, my subject in itself to which the thing would owe its title, and the small rounds represented so many distinct lamps, as I liked to call them, the function of each of which would be to light with all due intensity one of its aspects. . . . Each of my "lamps" would be the light of a single "social occasion" in the history and intercourse of the characters concerned and would bring out to the full the latent color of the scene in question and cause it to illustrate, to the last drop, its bearing on my theme.

In this passage the Jamesian conception of the "round" subject is very clear. He thinks of it as a metaphysical or moral entity rather than as a sequence of events. It is, I think, an Action in Aristotle's sense of the word. The distinction between plot and action thus reappears in James's analysis of form, and he is then able to think of the story, or plot or arrangement of incidents as a means to an end: the end of revealing the Action which is the subject of the play.

He points out that the "occasions" which make up *The Awkward Age* are in effect the acts of a play. They are very much like the acts of a Chekhov play. The reviewers of Chekhov have not yet seen that his plays are composed, not as stories, in which the chief point of interest is to find out "what happened," but as a series of social occasions each of which throws its light upon the central subject. *The Cherry Orchard*, for instance, has a minimum of story in this sense, but a maximum of subject. The first act is the occasion of the return of Mme. Ranevsky's party to the Cherry Orchard; the second, a dilatory gathering on a warm evening; the third a rather hysterical party; the fourth, the departure of Ranevsky and her family. Each of these occasions illumines a facet of the subject, or action, "to possess the Cherry Orchard." By the time we are through we have seen this action from various angles and on various levels; and the completing of this vision, rather than the overt event which ends the little thread of story, completes for us the play.

There is of course no contradiction between the use of an intelligence as reflector and the use of the situation as reflector. The intelligent character reflects the occasion, and the occasion throws its light upon the central subject.

JAMESIAN SUSPENSE

Though the story is never the main interest in James's late works, they are very carefully composed in the dimension of time, having a beginning, a development, and an end in temporal succession. As Joseph Warren Beach points out, this order is that of the reader's developing awareness of the subject. We are finding out, not what happened, but what the true values in the situation are. And this process of discovery is itself dramatized. Sometimes it is dramatized for us in the growing awareness of the fine intelligence at the center of the composition. Very often the development of the investigation is controlled by switching from one intelligence to another. And in addition we are led from one social occasion or scene to another, whose succession (as well as their relation to the central subject) is significant.

If you once grant at all the interest of the subject, the investigation becomes a very intense and exciting project. Mr. Beach aptly compares this suspense to that of a well-planned detective story, which is an investigation on another level. But for some reason Mr. Beach seems to doubt that it is "dramatic."

There are many familiar dramas in which this type of suspense (once James has made us aware of it) may be demonstrated. It is very instructive, for example, to notice how in *Hamlet* our sense of the evil in Denmark is made to develop as we feel it now from the point of view of the soldiers, now from the point of view of the King, now from the point of view of Polonius, and now from the point of view of Hamlet himself. Perhaps the clearest example is *Oedipus the King*. This drama is primarily an investigation; and though it has the swift movement and the "plot interest" of the mystery story, it is also an investigation of the moral and metaphysical realities of Oedipus' situation. These interest the chorus even more deeply than the question, Who killed Laius?

James Subject as a Static Composition

When we have taken, in succession, the points of view of the various "reflectors," when we have seen the central intelligence, on various "occasions," complete its investigation, the drama is over, and the subject is revealed as a static composition. In *The Golden Bowl*, for instance, Maggie Verver is gradually revealed as the central intelligence. She understands, at length, herself and all the other characters in relation to the issues and the values of the action they have been through—she gets at last the "truth" of their situation. In her awareness and then in the mind's eye of the reader the whole comes to rest, and is perceived as motionless, like the composed canvas of a painter.

Mr. Beach has described the composition of James's later

novels in terms like these. He concludes that James's subject is essentially plastic rather than narrative or dramatic. He thinks that the narrative movement is lost in these later novels; and though he feels that they are full of the sense of "dramatic struggle" he cannot quite explain to himself how, granted the static subject, drama can still be there. I should prefer to say that the late novels are narrative *and* dramatic *and* plastic. The heresy would be to insist on one aspect of their form to the exclusion of the others.

As for the painter, he also may compose with a temporal succession of perceptions in mind; he also has ways of guiding the eye of the spectator from element to element to the final "stasis of aesthetic pleasure."

The notion of drama as a static composition is not popular with modern writers on the subject. Yet in what other terms are we to describe the full stop, the final rest, with which a completely achieved drama ends? This moment or this aspect corresponds to the epiphany in Greek drama. In Euripides the epiphany is characteristically presented in plastic terms—an arrangement of properties and corpses, with a visible *deus ex machina*. In Sophocles, though there may be a significant grouping of the characters, in tableau form, at the end, the final synthesis is made in the mind of the chorus as it at last "sees the truth."

It is easy to see, after the event, why James never found a public stage for his drama. The first answer is of course that the established and recognized public stage was too limited and too hard to crack. If you then go on to study the drama in his best novels, you see that this drama, by its very nature, postulates an audience which doesn't exist, so to speak, in public; and that it is founded upon James's anomalous and unique traditionalism, which is also far removed from the public consciousness.

James's drama is that of a fine, perceptive spirit which endeavors to secure for itself the best that the world has to offer: "Life," at its sharpest point of intensity and awareness. This fine spirit is always dispossessed, even disembodied. There is usually some circumstance to explain its having been deprived of life—an American upbringing, poverty, a fatal but hidden disease. Some of James's critics have tried to explain this deprivation in Freudian terms, as the result of some disturbance in James's own emotional life. It is true that James keeps sexual passion at the periphery of his consciousness; but his drama is no more disembodied sexually than it is in a number of other ways. His attitude to sex may be a symptom rather than a cause, and one can believe that if he had had a place and a name, "sex" also would have been added unto him. However that may be, his fine spirits exist almost exclusively on the plane of moral awareness and activity.

To "register" at all, they require therefore a stage, a setting, a "theater" which is based upon and embodies their awareness. James's fine spirits are usually American, but he hypostatizes the setting as "Europe," as a drawing room, like Shaw's secure, feeling eternal (so that even the Shavian bandits drink tea at five)— but unlike Shaw's the epitome of culture and the heir of the ages. Its architectural setting, its costume and its custom, its taboos and its heirarchies, all of its forms, embody the values the Jamesian Americans are seeking, and above all the value of concrete embodiment itself. For James's people, who must exist on what he called the "high plane," are extremely worldly, pagan, moral, and irreligious. The values they seek are traditional, but a tradition which no longer informed a society would be of no use to them whatever.

This drama is "dramatic" enough, even stagey, and James always felt it to be so. It is not subjective or private, being in the tradition of European moralists since the Greeks. But it is difficult to make its elements visible to a modern audience.

I have remarked that Chekhov was no more interested than James in the monolinear story or thesis, but saw his subject in the round; and that he evolved a form with many close analogies to James's. He also assumed a society—or rather (the distinction is important) found one—and stuck close to it. He was in this the physician rather than the moralist; he took the people, the themes and the situations he found around him. The material of his art was what his audience was already prepared to recognize, whereas a large part of James's ingenuity is spent in making the elements of his composition visible at all. Chekhov's people are perhaps more lost than James's, but being lost in the flesh and the feelings, they are not lost to public view. If James had known Chekhov he would probably have felt that he had "lapsed to passivity from the high plane."

James did know Ibsen's plays, and was among the first in London to recognize his mastery as a dramatist. The plays of Ibsen's naturalistic period start, like James's own comedies, with Scribe, and it is possible to read them as social theses or as well-constructed stories. But his plays are composed on a deeper level also. He is neither sociologist nor entertainer, but, like James, a moralist. James recognized this also, but with mixed feelings. In Ibsen's plays, he wrote, "the lamp of the spirit burns as in tasteless parlors with the flame practically exposed." He may have been remembering the America he left, which must have been similar in many ways to Ibsen's Norway. James could no more accept Ibsen's Norway as real and ultimate than he could the America of the seventies. Ibsen's characters are not trying to realize a life of the spirit in any sort of traditional cultivated society; it is doubtful whether, in their gloomy quests, they envision the possibility of *any* "life," and certainly they are unaware of a traditional wisdom that could have anything to say to them. James complains that Ibsen's dramas always end at the point where the true interest and the true comedy of things should begin. And I think one can see that if Rosmer and Rebecca, for example, had married under the eyes of a group of interested and intelligent friends, instead of jumping into the millrace together, a truly "bristling" Jamesian subject would have resulted. But at the same moment Ibsen would have lost his audience. The plays which do end on such a note, *The Lady from the Sea, Little Eyolf*, are still the least esteemed of all Ibsen's dramas.

Did James ever think that British society actually provided the setting and the awareness he needed? Probably not; certainly not for long—his early letters seem to show that clearly. He willingly admitted that his people were too intelligent and too gifted to be probable. Their ideal social intercourse was derived from James's experience of society, but eventually became almost independent of it. He seems to have been moving toward an unrealistic theatrical convention, based on the rules and the tensions of politeness; the kind of convention which makes possible a Bérénice, a Hippolyte, an Alceste, a Millamant. Such a "stage" was a fundamental postulate of his inner life and of his art, and even in the semiretirement of his last period he continued to live up to its ghostly urbanity and agility. It is this which makes his prose so entirely unlike that of Proust or Virginia Woolf. Though he left society, he clung to its values; and while Proust recorded the dissolution of the moral being, James, with his shadow-boxing, kept in excellent trim.

The drama that James knew did not survive the last war. The

most interesting writers for the stage between 1918 and 1939—among whom I should include Yeats, Eliot, Cocteau, Obey, Lorca—start completely afresh. The influences of the Moscow Art Theater, the Ballet, and the Music Hall, combine to produce a new conception of the theatrical medium. Not only nineteenth-century naturalism, but most European drama back through the seventeenth-century, is explicitly rejected in favor of medieval farce, Greek tragedy, peasant rituals, and entertainments. The new dramatists are likely to be interested in religion, in myth, and in types of symbolism designed to reach a popular audience. Most of them would I think approve of Cocteau's description of *poésie de théâtre* as like the cordage of a ship—a composition of large coarse elements easily perceptible at a distance. Their estrangement from the audience of before the war—if indeed it still exists—is complete. They neither ask for the support of the carriage trade, nor try, like James, to build a notion of the ideal cultivated spectator into their theatrical forms. The traditions and the symbols they like antedate the founding of the drawing room.

It is not yet clear whether this strategy is any less desperate than James's. The vision they get of a drama speaking directly to the population in simple, ancient, fundamental terms, is perhaps a flattering illusion, like that of the mythical drowning man who sees his whole life before him at the moment of going under for the last time. Paris in the twenties is already far away, and we see now some of the dangers in the new line. One needs, I think, to place against Cocteau's theatrical virtuosity, and Eliot's abstract theological framework, and Lorca's luxuriant popular imagery, the Jamesian and classic conception of an Action, seen in the round, seen from many angles. James paid dearly for his position above the battle, but he found there some curiously universal technical concepts, useful in contexts he never dreamed of; and a conception of dramatic form which we still need if we are to see the drama of his time and ours in the right perspective.

XIII

ERIC BENTLEY

The American Drama, 1944–1954

The economics of it. It costs anything from $40,000 to $150,000 to put a play on Broadway. It cost $23,000 to put on *Life With Father* in 1939, and $85,000 to put on *Life With Mother* in 1948. *Mother* cost three and a half times as much. One could cite wider differences. A famous Saroyan play was put on before the war for about $5,000. A famous Tennessee Williams play was put on in 1953 for $115,000.* That is twenty-three times as much. It would take a more expert statistician than I to say what is the average increase since 1939. Place it anywhere you wish between three-and-a-half and twenty-three, and you have an increase such as any business might find it hard to meet.

These figures help to explain the state of dramatic art better than any conceivable remarks about dramaturgy. However, instead of discussing union regulations, the "real estate situation," competition from movies and TV, I shall simply note the principal condition they impose on theater—namely, that no play shall be performed unless a small group of wealthy men will bet on its having a long run. For it takes months of playing to capacity houses for investors to so much as get their money back.

What kind of play is the safest bet? No one quite knows, and that is perhaps the one happy aspect of the situation: think how dreadful it would be if we knew for certain that good plays always flop! Nevertheless, though no one lays claim to certitude, and an extraordinary number of hits are surprise hits, there *is* a

Reprinted from *The Dramatic Event* (New York: Horizon Press, 1954), pp. 244–62, by permission of the author and the publisher. Copyright 1954 by Horizon Press.

* Extreme cases. *My Heart's in the Highlands* was done only at special matinees. Few straight plays in 1953 cost as much as *Camino Real*. Musicals, on the other hand, cost much more: *Kismet* cost $400,000. There are further particulars, highly relevant to this chapter, in two important *Harper's* articles by John Houseman: "No Business Like Show Business," September 1949, and "The Critics in the Aisle Seats," October, 1951.

general prejudice on Broadway against certain types of drama and in favor of others. Other things being equal, a play that can in any sense be defined as highbrow is considered a bad bet. It is not equally true that a play considered lowbrow is always considered a good bet. At this point, other criteria enter in. For example, all those who have opinions about plays seem to agree that *The Fifth Season* is an execrable play. Yet it was a hit; and its success was predicted by people with opinions, not about plays, but about garment workers, pretty girls, and Menasha Skulnik. A producer's job is not to judge plays but to "know the angles"—in more academic language, to know what criteria are relevant to success. That is, this *would* be his job, if it were possible. Since it has seemed to be impossible, what we witness is prejudice against so-called highbrow works and sheer guesswork among lowbrow works. "If only it were easier to tell good shit from bad shit," a producer said to me. We need not pity such a producer too much—we have our own troubles—but many of us do have some feeling about the prejudice against the so-called highbrow: we resent it. We have a prejudice against that prejudice.

I have simplified the producer-speculator's problem if I've suggested that he bets directly on the public's response. Actually, he doesn't ask about Tom, Dick, and Harry but about Brooks Atkinson and Walter Kerr. "What will the critics think?" When the first performance is over the producer presides over a dismal supper party till the small hours of the morning when the eight reviews are relayed to him by phone. If he has produced a serious play, and the reviewers don't like it, he is done for. If some of them like it, he is done for. Only if all of them write of it in a vein of corny exultation is he sure of a hit.

Many people still blame this state of affairs on the critics, but, as the latter are always pointing out, that is unfair: it isn't their fault if people take so much notice of them. And it is not true that they are unusually dogmatic men. On the contrary one might more justly complain of some of them that they play the role of the crumply little man who apologizes for having an opinion at all. They make such admissions of ignorance that one might say their motto is: "I thank thee, God, for my humility."

Why does the New York public pay so much more attention to the newspaper critics than it used to? Is it the higher price of a ticket that makes the customer more cautious? Is caution the best description of credulous dependence on eight reporters? Or is such behavior a straw in some more horrible wind? A token of an abject reliance on pundits that brings us nearer to George Orwell's *1984*?

The Fifth Season is a play that succeeded without the critics, as musicals and other light entertainments not seldom do. The paradox of the critics' position is that they completely control the serious drama which they hardly even claim to understand, while no one very much cares what they say of light entertainment which they are quite at home with. Where they have competence, they have no power, and vice versa.

I should not like to leave the subject of economics without admitting there are exceptions to the rule that no play shall be performed unless a small group of wealthy men will bet on its having a long run. There *is* a non-commercial theater which has three great sources of income outside the box office: private philanthropy, the local community (or group philanthropy), and the state legislatures. That is: there *are* producers who will put on certain shows—with little or no hope of profit—because they like them; there are community theaters, such as those of Cleveland, Pasadena, and Dallas; and there are the theaters of the great state universities supported by the taxpayer. Such are the American approaches to a subsidized theater. (Even the Federal Theater . . . was not a state theater in the European sense.)

Non-commercial theaters deserve all the encouragement we can give them except that of flattery. The fact that we want to get more and more money for them is no reason for overlooking their present limitations. Let us admit that they are more often a provincial substitute for Broadway than an alternative to it. To call them collectively the Tributary Theater is misleading. They do not pour their own waters into the larger stream. They are rather the Parasitic Theater drawing what little life they have from New York.

An extreme—if, therefore, special—case is the Summer Theater, which manages to be considerably more hidebound than Broadway. In New York, an actor's name is seldom enough to draw an audience; on Cape Cod, nothing else matters. In New York, a "name" actor usually—not always—has also to be a good performer; in a summer theater, any nincompoop from Hollywood will do. The formula is a movie star, even one who hasn't acted in twenty years, any old company, any old director, and any old hit play.

So if you come along with a new play which is not too easy or too stupid, which is not identical in pattern with a dozen accepted hits, it may be hard to get it produced on Broadway but it may well be even harder to get it produced anywhere else. A corollary of this fact is that many plays that are worth seeing are done in New York and never sent out on the road afterwards. The most recent works of Arthur Miller and Tennessee Williams are examples.

There is also the matter of how the plays are done. But before I tell what I have seen I should like to describe my angle of vision.

The criticizing of it. There is daily reviewing, and there is weekly reviewing. Most of the daily reviewers are weekly reviewers too, inasmuch as they add a Sunday article to their daily notices. But in principle daily and weekly reviewing differ. The daily reviewer is a reporter setting down right after the performance the responses of an "ordinary" playgoer. It is a very hard job—as reporting on anything, a football match or a street accident, is hard: it calls for a more observant eye and a more fluent pen than most of us possess. The weekly reviewer has the privilege of more time both to write and do his homework. And his aim is different. On most magazines the task he is called on to perform is dual: he has to judge the show as an expert on shows (not an average playgoer) and he has to entertain his readers with his thinking on and around the subject. Since the fate of a play in New York has been settled before the weekly magazine reaches the stands, weekly criticism has no immediate effect. To the weekly critic this seems both good and bad: it is a relief to know that you aren't doing anyone out of a living when you pan a performance and on the other hand it is depressing to feel that what you say has no practical importance. I sometimes feel my reviews have been dropped into a bottomless well, that they are contributions to a discussion that never takes place.

Even if I feel sure I am writing for a reader it is hard for me to know his identity. The weekly reviewer has to satisfy New Yorkers who have seen the play or will see it; he is also read by many outside New York who will not see it. Ninety per cent of *New Republic* sales are outside Manhattan. But then the Broadway audience is to a large extent composed of out-of-towners. So I have no idea what proportion of my hypothetical readers sees the shows. I find the thought of two distinct types of readers rather disturbing. I intend each article for both "inside" theater people and for non-theater people on the outside; yet there is some evidence that the former find my pieces too full of known information while the latter find them over-allusive and obscure. I should perhaps give the job up as hopeless but for the example of Stark Young who performed it so well for over twenty years. His procedure was simple: he set down what was of interest to him and left readers to fend for themselves.

The New Republic has a tradition in dramatic criticism. My two* predecessors on the magazine—Stark Young and Harold Clurman—stand apart from most of their colleagues in being less concerned with journalism than with theater. Both have worked on the other side of the footlights. The personal relations with actors which such an interest entails set the critic problems of tact that are susceptible of no perfect solution. It is impossible for him to be both as frank as he should be and as discreet as he should be, as ruthless as he should be and as charitable as he should be. He is always either bowing and scraping or bending over backwards. He knows too much. On the other hand, very few people have ever learnt much about acting and production from seats out front after the rehearsal period is over. These are arts you learn as playwright, actor, director, designer, not as theater-goer, nor yet as critic.

Whatever a man's estimate of the total intelligence of drama critics, high or low, he cannot fail to notice that—except for a Young or a Clurman—they know far less about acting and directing than about literature. Which is another funny thing about this remarkable class of men. They know something of literature though they are anti-literary; they are pro-theatrical but know little of acting. And so, as was noted above, a mediocre performance of a mediocre play is often greeted as a magnificent performance of a bad play. A brash actor who ruins a play will not be found out. He may very well be praised. The ruin is blamed on the playwright.

This scolding of the reviewers leads to my next topic.

The staging of it. Nowhere more than in stage design is the matter of expense the decisive one. America spends a lot on

---

* Strictly speaking, three; and the third, Irwin Shaw, has also had a lot of theater experience; but he stayed with *The New Republic* only a few months.

stage design and doesn't get very much for its money. Costs are so high that many of the best ideas have to be dropped as too expensive. This is the main fact to consider in making any comparison with the German or Russian stage. Producers breathe a sigh of relief if they are assured that a play can be done with one set. So we get stereotypes. The chief old-fashioned one is the stage drawing room with its familiar rows of bookshelves full of unread books, the couch here, the armchair there, the staircase, the door, the piano and of course the phone. The chief new-fashioned one is the interior-and-exterior-combined (*Death of a Salesman*, *Rose Tattoo*, *Streetcar*), of which the porch-and-surroundings is a variant (*All My Sons*, *Picnic*). Some sets of these two types have been very fine pieces of composition, but the possibilities of variation are limited; and the alternatives to the standard modern patterns seem also to run to type. Thus there is the gorgeous-gaudy show, lowbrow in musical comedies, highbrow in opera; brains and ingenuity and a certain lush taste go into these things; but no style is achieved. Then there is Shakespeare with platforms and drapes. Though the scheme has its points, they are not as many as at one time was expected. The same could be said of that more recent scheme: central staging.

If we look at the designs of Christian Bérard of Paris, Teo Otto of Zurich, or Caspar Neher of Salzburg, we find more of a style—more of a realized modernity—than even the most brilliant men are giving us here. We don't give our men enough practice, and we don't give them wide enough powers; so they find themselves caught between musical comedy with its miles of gaudy, old-fashioned scenery and the one-set play with its inevitable porch or its inevitable bookcase. We have fine craftsmen but they work under restrictions both artistic and technical that prevent them giving any adequate account of themselves. Ask why, and we are back again with economics.*

In this brief survey I shall not attempt to speak of directing: acting is more important. And, at that, directing today is less the mounting of giant spectacles, the marshalling of crowds, the unfurling of scenery, than it is the training of actors. Because we have no national theater and no network of repertory theaters

---

* There are other resources we don't use beside the human ones. I am not equipped to expound the theory and practice of George C. Izenour of Yale. But it is pretty clear that his researches have rendered the switchboard—and therefore much of the stagecraft—of all our theaters quite obsolete. . . .

we offer our young actors far too little either of variety or con-
tinuity. Still, certain remedial measures have been taken. The
creation of the Group Theater was one much measure—back in
the thirties. It was followed by the creation of the Actors' Studio
in the forties. In these organizations, a new generation of American actors has been trained, and a new type of American actor
has evolved. The easiest way of telling the layman about the new
acting is to inform him that he has seen it in *Death of a Salesman*
or *A Streetcar Named Desire*. It is a deliberate American alternative to the elocutionary "style acting" that we import from
England. It seizes on the nervous excitement of American life—
healthy or unhealthy—and communicates it. It makes older-fash-
ioned acting seem stilted, slow, and emptily declamatory. I never
felt this so sharply as when seeing *Tea and Sympathy* as directed
by the head of the Studio, Elia Kazan, the night after a Margaret
Webster production (*The Strong Are Lonely*). It was like finding myself on an express train after sitting yawning in the waiting room. On the other hand, reviewing plays which are acted by
members of the Studio, I have had frequent occasion to note the
narrow scope of the newer acting. It almost seems limited to the
portrayal of violent and neurasthenic types.

Two other kinds of acting are expertly practiced in America.
The first is musical comedy acting, which includes singing and
perhaps dancing. The second is light comedy acting. The lay
public scarcely distinguishes the two; yet the distinction is in fact
a fairly broad one. Musical comedy technique starts—I think—
with song: not so much with the music as such, not with singing,
but with the art of performing a song, handing it to the public by
means of singing, half-singing, interpolated speaking, and pantomime. Then the postures and gestures—the whole art of putting
a song over—extend themselves even into the parts of musical
comedy which are not sung; so that, if you see a musical
comedy actor in a straight play, you say: It seems as if he's always just going to sing. His bouncy manner, the little springs he
takes from one foot to the other, the way he keeps lifting his
arms in salutation, or extending his fist in a punch—all these
things come from the pantomime of a singer. It is quite a jump
from this to light comedy—from, say, Alfred Drake in *Kismet*
to Elliott Nugent in *The Male Animal*. Light comedy has an
inner connection with broader forms (like the musical) but
conceals it; and that is the joke. There is a portentous pretense

of grave reality. The vitality of a performance in light comedy depends on the degree of tension between the seeming reality and the concealed madness. The comic climaxes are reached when gay and furious imps of folly come surging up into a hitherto decorous situation. Any drunk scene is likely to be a simple instance of the pattern; and, in a sense, all light comedy is drunken comedy.

Domestic drama, musical comedy, light comedy—these are what American actors are trained to perform. They aren't all of theater. If we want to do Shakespeare or Wilde or Shaw or Eliot we are in trouble. British actors are called upon, and—to the extent that Actors' Equity lets them in—a provisional solution is arrived at. In the long run American actors have got to be trained to do these other kinds of work themselves. Shakespeare in particular is an author each country has to study and interpret for itself. The American Shakespeare might even be better than the British; at any rate it would be different.

The writing of it. Many of the most serviceable scripts of the past ten years have been in the less serious categories—musical and light comedy. The book of a musical is seldom impressive of itself; you go to musical comedy for everything except the words; yet, behind the music and dancing, the book may be efficiently doing its job.

Light comedy tends to have witty words wittily spaced out and arranged. If one were asked: What is the best American play? one might not have the temerity to say *The Male Animal* or *Born Yesterday*, yet they are better plays than most of those that have a higher reputation; and certainly, if you want a good evening, a light comedy is nowadays more likely to supply it than the so-called serious drama. During the 1953–54 season, for instance, one of the dullest evenings was an earnest treatise on the United Nations called *The Prescott Proposals*. One of the brightest was a joke about a comic-strip artist called *King of Hearts*.

Even inferior plays in the lighter vein often have something rather striking about them. It was agreed that a play called *Men of Distinction* was one of the very bad plays of the 1952–53 season; yet there was something very good about it. In fact it had one virtue of such a provoking sort that not only the deficiency of the play but also its merit militated against success. This virtue was a cocky satirical humor totally unsoftened by sentimentality. There being no nice character in the play "to root for" you were unable to detach yourself from the non-nice characters. What made matters worse, they seemed nice. One of them was a Harvard man as personable and charming as Harvard's representatives on Broadway, Brooks Atkinson and John Mason Brown. But he was a pimp. (I said at the beginning that the fate of a play at the hands of the reviewers was unpredictable; *Men of Distinction* is an exception.)

Turning to plays of more serious intent, I do not know which are the best of the past ten years. *The Iceman Cometh* would be a candidate, *The Autumn Garden* another, *The Country Girl* a third, yet all three are in the nature of postscripts to a communication written in an earlier decade. I prefer to pick out for discussion plays which belong more exclusively to the period under review. Of course they have traditions behind them. Two traditions in particular: that of the social drama and that of the psychological "mood play."

It is agreed that the most interesting social dramas of the period are *Death of a Salesman* and *The Crucible*. Sidney Kingsley's version of *Darkness at Noon* is just as skilful a piece of craftsmanship, is in subject matter much closer to the center of social conflict, and makes a much clearer statement, but, for all the exciting bits that are its component parts, it is not quite a satisfying play. One reason for this is that the statement it makes is not only clear but obvious, not challengingly a little ahead of public opinion but boringly a litle behind it. Why pay five dollars to be told that communism is unpleasant and immoral?

Maybe some people wish to. In that case I shift my ground and say they shouldn't. We shouldn't go to the theater to have our already inflated self-righteousness further blown up by ritual denunciation of an acknowledged villain's villainy. The theater should be less serious than that—or more so. It should be a place either of innocent frivolity—or of moral responsibility. There is an unending war to fight in our theater against those who are frivolous without being innocent and moralistic without being moral.

But not many people did wish to see *Darkness at Noon*.

They saw Arthur Miller's plays. Why? How could Mr. Miller's plays be more interesting if, as I have said, they are no better in craftsmanship, are less clear in meaning, and further from the center of social struggle?

At the center of things nowadays is the matter of communism. Mr. Kingsley put his play together to say so, and the play falls a little flat because we hold the truth of the proposition to be self-evident. What does Mr. Miller say about communism? He doesn't mention it; yet the word—spoken or not—is likely to be at the center of a discussion of Mr. Miller. Now which fact is more important—that Mr. Miller doesn't mention communism— or that you don't discuss him without mentioning it ?

Suppose we ask in any group of liberal intellectuals: do *All My Sons* and *Death of a Salesman* present a Marxian analysis of American society? Or: does *The Crucible* say that American communists should not be investigated? Some will answer yes, others will answer no; a certain heat and anxiety will get into the discussion; and a very vocal group will resent the fact that the questions have been asked in the first place. Mr. Miller may hold such and such a position, but, we shall be told, it is not— definitely not—playing fair to say so. In short, we encounter certain ambiguities and we find that these ambiguities have a strong emotional resonance among our fellows.

What is the nature of this resonance? What would explain so large an investment of emotion in Mr. Miller's plays on the part of those who don't wish us to ask questions? Take *The Crucible*. It is a play in which Mr. Miller complains that the accuser is always considered holy, the accused guilty. We think of McCarthyism; and we think of it again when we find that Mr. Miller's story is about a witch hunt. What is unusual about Mr. Miller's treatment of McCarthyism? One thing above all others: that he sets up as the offense which the seventeenth-century McCarthys accused people of an offense which it is impossible to commit: the practice of magic. If to the McCarthyites (of both periods) an accused man is almost automatically guilty, to Mr. Miller he is almost automatically innocent. If one were to ask: what fantasy would give most perfect expression to a communist's feeling of innocence in the face of McCarthyism? one couldn't do better than reply: Mr. Miller's story. Mr. Miller has missed the essence of our political situation. He has thereby missed a more interesting dramatic situation. But he has hit upon a wish-fulfilling fantasy that, conceivably, has a stronger appeal than either; and with it he has soothed the bad conscience of a generation.

Just as the good liberal is not supposed to mention communism when discussing Mr. Miller in general, so he is not supposed to mention communism—or McCarthyism—when discussing *The Crucible* in particular. The production of the play was preceded by a quarrel between Mr. Miller and Elia Kazan. Mr. Kazan went on record as a former communist and named some of his former comrades; in the last scene of *The Crucible*, Mr. Miller presented a man whose dignity consists in refusing to talk under pressure of the investigators. But that one is not supposed to find any connection between that scene and the Kazan incident I discovered when I tried to get some remarks on the subject into a liberal journal. The play, I was told, was about the seventeenth century. I gathered that, though I could have criticized Mr. Kazan's attitude, I mustn't criticize Mr. Miller's.

It is no business of mine—in this context—that Mr. Miller may be wrong. I am contending that he is ambiguous and this in a way that would amount to trickery were it deliberate. I assume that, like the rest of us, he doesn't deliberately deceive others but involuntarily deceives himself. What gives this fact public importance is that so many of our fellow citizens want to share these particular self-deceptions with him. Let me illustrate. Indignation is Mr. Miller's stock in trade: his writing has Attack.* But what is he attacking? And is he really attacking it? "He's attacking the American way of life," says someone. "Why nothing of the sort," says someone else, "he shows great sympathy for it." The punch is threatened; and then pulled. We are made to feel the boldness of the threat; then we are spared the violence of the blow. Now isn't this particular ambiguity strikingly characteristic of that large wing of the liberal movement which has been overawed by communism? They admire the audacity of communism all the more because they don't share it. They admire fearless outspokenness above all things; yet if outspokenness is actually to be feared, they fear it;** and

* "Daring is of the essence. Its very nature is incompatible with an undue affection for moderation, respectability, even fairness, and responsibleness."—Arthur Miller in "Many Writers: Few Plays," *The New York Times*, August 10, 1952.

** "But we have an atmosphere of dread just the same, an unconsciously —or consciously—accepted party line, a sanctified complex of moods and attitudes, proper and improper. If nothing else comes of it one thing surely has—it has made it dangerous to dare, and worse still, impractical."—Arthur Miller, *ibid*.

choose fearless silence. *The Crucible* is a play for people who think that pleading the Fifth Amendment is not only a white badge of purity but also a red badge of courage.

Another habit of the quasi-liberal mind has been to say that of course so and so is not a communist and yet, when it turns out that so and so is or was a communist, to register no dismay, not even surprise. Of course he wasn't a communist; but, if he was, so what? This ambiguity has been given rather powerful expression by Lillian Hellman in *The Children's Hour* which was revived in the 1952–53 season with changes expressly calculated to suggest the play's relevance to McCarthyism. The play can be translated into political terms as follows. Someone is accused of communism, and says "How absurd, I never heard of communism, this is a witch hunt, my accuser is psychotic," and you believe him and your heart bleeds. Then this someone says: "Well, maybe I do carry a party card, either it's all this red-baiting that's driven me into the arms of communism or, well, being a communist isn't as bad as you assume. The social system *is* pretty terrible. You admit *that*, I suppose? I'm going to kill myself in a minute. My death will make you feel awful. Please be indignant about it."

The Crucible and *The Children's Hour* represent a type of liberalism that has been dangerous and is now obsolescent. *Darkness at Noon* is more defensible on political or even moral grounds; yet it fails to stir us for reasons I have tried to state. If these are our best social plays, one wonders what the future holds for the genre. Shall we ever have a social drama with the purity and force of *The Power of Darkness* or *The Lower Depths?**

Perhaps the creative forces in America are no longer running into political art. More prominent, certainly, in our theater than social drama is the "mood play." I am referring to the school of playwrights—which is headed by Tennessee Williams and includes Carson McCullers, William Inge, and Jane Bowles. An older playwright, John van Druten, has hailed this school as a

---

* A couple of shows from the 1953-54 season—*End as a Man* and *The Caine Mutiny Court Martial*—suggest that the New Conservatism may have a vogue in the theater under the slogan: Respect Authority. Both shows have force; but it is scarcely the force of their message; and both are as impure and equivocal as any liberal effort.

fine new drama gloriously superseding the old in much the same way as William Archer hailed the school of Ibsen half a century ago. One has one's doubts.

The moral weakness of the social drama is that it scorns or neglects the self. Liberal idealism of the sort I have described springs from fear—even hatred—of the self. The new psychological drama, school of Williams, is equal and opposite. It springs from fear of the Other, of society, of the world, and from pre-occupation with the self. Now art that doesn't spring from the whole man but from one side of him tends, I think, not to become art at all but to remain neurotic or quasi-neurotic fantasy. The archetype of political fantasy is, perhaps, an imagined oration to a congress of the Party of your dreams. The archetype of non-political fantasy is an imagined confession to a psychoanalyst. Are the attitudes we find embodied in dramatic fantasies of either kind any more adequate for good drama than they are for the good life?

However this may be, one can certainly take exception to the view of form and structure implied in the new works and openly championed by their admirers. Mr. van Druten puts this view in a nutshell when he says he'd like a play to be all atmosphere and no plot. He says he finds inspiration and guidance in *Member of the Wedding, The Glass Menagerie*, and *The Cherry Orchard*.

These are not plays I should wish to attack: one is a masterpiece, all are good evenings of theater. However, none of them seems to me as mysteriously structureless as Mr. van Druten implies. Perhaps Plot is the name he gives to a structure he finds bad or at least obtrusive? Or is it just that he enjoys economy of means and the audacity with which a playwright can push big, tempting events into the background? Chekhov could push a duel-to-the-death off into the wings while the center of the stage is occupied by someone reading a newspaper and whistling a tune. Mrs. McCullers kills off the little boy between scenes of *Member of the Wedding*. This is not to say that either Chekhov or Mrs. McCullers has no plot, though Mr. van Druten admits that *Member of the Wedding* is open to criticism on the grounds that its action is too slender; which is to say it has a plot but not a very big—or perhaps a very good?—plot. Only by the beauty of the lines, the addition of music, romantic lightning, and the personality of two fine actresses could the play command a whole evening. It is a little story, prolonged by theatrical leger-demain.

Picnic I do not know in the state the author left it but only in its final state as directed by Joshua Logan. Mr. Inge clearly contributed admirable character sketches, group portraits, local color, anecdotes. . . . Can one venture to say that it took the showmanship of a musical-comedy director to give *Picnic* the size of a complete show?

Jane Bowles's *In a Summer House* posed a similar problem but met with a different solution. This play had rather a *succès d'estime* in New York largely, it is said, because of a performance by Judith Anderson which the critics called magnificent. Magnificent or not, this performance had little relation to the character Mrs. Bowles conceived. Yet—and this is my point—I don't know that the play would have stood up by itself. It needed a buttress made of harder material; and *that* Miss Anderson certainly is.

I am not interested in establishing that any of the plays I mention is weak but only that it might have been stronger had the author not followed current fashion and assumed he could get along without the traditional kinds of support. I do not mean that a bad playwright could ever become a good one by dropping one attitude and taking up another—only that mistaken notions can hamper a good writer. (I assume that writers we take an interest in are to some extent good.) Nor am I saying that Mr. van Druten's book is having a bad influence. Rather, it sums up—and is influenced by—the view of drama which the more sophisticated people in the theater had already come to hold.

This view is largely false. Chekhov's plays (for example) have a cast-iron structure, only it is concealed, like the girders of a modern building. Tennessee Williams (for another example) is no model of plotlessness. The fashionable components of plot may have shifted since Archer's day but *A Streetcar Named Desire* has a strong, straightforward story, organized on principles that would be familiar to any earlier generation. What is the play in fact but the American version of *Miss Julia?* Even *The Glass Menagerie* has what I would call a plot. In short, I cannot see that the plays Mr. van Druten admires were constructed according to the theory he expounds; on the contrary, they seem to me to have merit insofar as they contravene this theory.

Criticizing the criticizing of it. Having stated where I think our playwrights are going wrong, I should like to end by saying where criticism, including of course my own, may go wrong. I shall go wrong if I imagine that the playwright needs me to tell him what to do. Drama criticism is not a disguised and prolonged course in playwriting. If a man can write plays, he doesn't need a critic to push his pen. If he can't, he doesn't need a critic to dig his grave.

A critic is only a judge. A judge doesn't help you to commit your crime or even to abstain from committing it. His verdict—too late to influence the actions under consideration—has value, if at all, not for the prisoner, but for society at large. I inferred earlier that the drama critic mustn't be modest and pretend he's the man in the street. (Between aisle seat and desk chair he knows only the inside of a taxi.) I am insisting now that he also lay no claim to direct influence on writers. If by chance he does exert such an influence, and it is salutary, so much the better; this is service over and above the call of duty. All he regularly and imperatively does is help to create the climate of opinion in which the playwrights live.

That is no small matter. The cultural air has often become oppressive. And it has done so, not when criticism was keen and demanding, but when it was non-existent. One writer who resented the power of critics got himself made propaganda minister and legislated criticism out of existence, substituting *Kunstbetrachtung*—that is, reportage and eulogy. This was Goebbels. In Russia, critical analysis is dismissed as formalistic. A writer is praised as a yes-man or silenced as a saboteur.

Though the direct influence of dramatic criticism is small, its indirect effect could be considerable. Bernard Shaw stated the converse of this proposition when he spoke of the "ruinous privilege of exemption from vigilant and implacable criticism." There is, of course, a converse of this converse: that the right to criticize enjoins the duties of vigilance and implacability.

XIV

ARTHUR GANZ

The Desperate Morality of the Plays of Tennessee Williams

"Moralist," desperate or not, may seem a perverse appellation for a playwright whose works concern rape, castration, cannibalism, and other bizarre activities, but in examining the work of Tennessee Williams it is exactly this point—that he is a moralist, not a psychologist—that should be borne in mind. Williams's powers of characterization are real, but they are not his central gifts: witness *Cat on a Hot Tin Roof* which contains Big Daddy, one of Williams's most striking characterizations, but which fails nonetheless because in this play Williams's moral vision becomes blurred, and it is in the clarity and force of that moral vision that his strength as a playwright lies.

Admittedly, Williams's morality is not the morality of most men, but it is a consistent ethic, giving him a point of view from which he can judge the actions of people. Yet to say that Williams rewards those who, by his standards, are virtuous and punishes those who are evil is to oversimplify, for in the world of Williams's plays, good often has a curious affinity with evil. Beneath the skin of the Christlike martyr destroyed by the cruel forces of death and sterility lies the disease, the sin that has made his creator destroy him. The character who is most fiercely condemned may at the same time be the one for whom pardon is most passionately demanded. From the self-lacerating desire simultaneously to praise and to punish stems the violence that disfigures so many of Williams's plays.

To understand this violence in Williams's work we must first look at his gentlest plays, those in which the virtuous are rewarded, for here is most directly revealed the morality by which

Reprinted from *The American Scholar*, XXXI (Spring, 1962), 278–94, by permission of the publisher. Copyright 1962 by United Chapters of Phi Beta Kappa.

the guilty are later so terribly condemned. Surprisingly, one of Williams's most significant plays is an indifferent and undramatic one-acter about the death of D. H. Lawrence, only slightly redeemed by the audacious and successful title, *I Rise in Flame, Cried the Phoenix*. The play is significant because it gives us the central fact we must have to understand Williams's work, the nature of his literary parentage. In art, a son must seek out a father who will give him what he needs. Williams needed a rationale for the sexual obsessions that dominate his work, and it was this that Lawrence seemed to give him. In the Preface to *I Rise in Flame* Williams wrote, "Lawrence felt the mystery and power of sex, as the primal life urge, and was the lifelong adversary of those who wanted to keep the subject locked away in the cellars of prudery," and in the play he makes Frieda exclaim, "You just don't know. The meaning of Lawrence escapes you. In all of his work he celebrates the body."

Whether or not Williams assesses Lawrence correctly is, for an understanding of Williams's own work, irrelevant. The important thing is that from a very early point in his career (*I Rise in Flame* dates from 1941) Williams saw Lawrence as the great writer who "celebrates the body" and apparently saw himself as that writer's disciple. Like many disciples, however, Williams introduced his own variations on the master's doctrine. Williams betrayed Lawrence primarily by extending the approval of Lawrentian doctrine to areas of sexual experience beyond the normal, but first he did so by basing a very bad play on one of Lawrence's short stories.

The play, called *You Touched Me* from Lawrence's story of that title, is an early work, copyrighted in 1942. Although it shows little of the doctrinal variation on which Williams's later work is based, the distortions that were introduced as the story was transformed into a play are highly revealing. In addition, *You Touched Me* is important for establishing the structural pattern of two of Williams's most attractive plays, *The Glass Menagerie* and *The Rose Tattoo*.

Lawrence's story concerns the marriage between Matilda, the daughter of a retired pottery manufacturer, and his adopted son, Hadrian. Although the marriage is brought about by the father's threatening to leave his daughters penniless, it is a good marriage that rescues Matilda from her empty life and eases the spirit of the old man who, at the end of the story, asks the newlyweds to kiss and murmurs as they do so, "That's right! That's right!"

Williams's play, which he wrote in collaboration with Donald Windham, is a stunning vulgarization of Lawrence's story. The younger sister, Emmie, is changed into a frigid maiden aunt who represents, in Williams's words, "aggressive sterility." Matilda herself, a thin, large-nosed woman of thirty-two, turns into a pale girl of twenty, the cliché of the frail, sheltered maiden. Hadrian, in the story a neat, scheming little soldier with a common-looking mustache, is transformed into "a clean-cut, muscular young man in the dress uniform of a lieutenant in the Royal Canadian Air Force," much given to speeches about faith, the glories of the future, and the conquering of new countries of the mind. And the elderly pottery manufacturer is turned into a spry, if alcoholic, old sea captain, portrayed on the stage by Edmund Gwenn, everyone's lovable old grandfather. Given this set of popular-magazine characters, the play has no trouble reaching its predictable conclusion as the captain helps the handsome airman defeat the aunt and win the shy Matilda.

What is important here is not that, working with unfamiliar material at this early stage in his career, Williams should write a poor play, but that, while retaining the essential Lawrentian theme, he should so alter Lawrence's material as to produce an unmistakable Tennessee Williams play. The light but subtle characterizations around which Lawrence built his story are in the play coarsened to the point where the characters are as obviously broken down into the bad guys and the good guys as those in any television western; Hadrian, Matilda and the captain are in favor of sexuality while the frigid Emmie and her suitor, an impotent clergyman, are opposed to it. Williams is not a psychologist, and he "understands" his characters very little; rather, he is a moralist, although a very special one, and he judges them.

Although Williams has distorted Lawrence's work by sentimentalizing it and by introducing into it caricatures of frigidity and impotence, he is genuinely sympathetic to its real theme, the awakening of life, and particularly sexual life, in one who had previously been dead to it. In both the play and the story, Hadrian (the conquering emperor from the warm South) defeats the forces of sterility and rouses Matilda to new life. It was this action, which Williams sees as profoundly good, that he developed in this early play and then made the center of two of his most pleasing works.

Both *The Glass Menagerie* and *The Rose Tattoo* are variations on the material first used in *You Touched Me*. In each play the central character, a woman who has retired from life, lives in a closed world that excludes sexuality, "the primal life urge." Into this world comes a man, like Hadrian the sexual force designed to release the woman from her bondage. But although he succeeds in one case, in the other he fails. The reasons for this difference are worth noting.

The figure of Laura in *The Glass Menagerie* has clearly been developed from that of Matilda of *You Touched Me*, who is described by Williams as having "the delicate, almost transparent quality of glass." Both are shy, fragile creatures, remote from the life around them. But where Hadrian awakens Matilda and brings her back to life, Laura's gentleman caller gives her only a momentary glimpse of normal life before she drifts back into the fantasy world of glass animals. In Williams's moral system the rejection of life is the greatest crime, and those guilty of it are visited by the kind of punishment that falls upon Blanche DuBois in *Streetcar* and Sebastian Venable in *Suddenly Last Summer*. Laura, however, is innocent; she does not reject but rather is rejected, not because of her limp, which does not exist in "Portrait of a Girl in Glass," Williams's own short story upon which he based his play, but because she is the sensitive, misunderstood exile, a recurrent character in Williams's work, one of the fugitive kind, who are too fragile to live in a malignant world.

The vigorous Serafina Delle Rose of *The Rose Tattoo*, however, openly rejects life after the death of her husband. She lives an existence as solitary and sterile as that of Laura among the glass animals. Only when the truck driver Alvaro Mangiacavallo, who has the face of a clown but the body of her husband, appears does she disclaim her rejection and return to the world of life and sexuality. Again it was to this favorite theme that Williams turned when he converted his one-acter *27 Wagons Full of Cotton* into the script for the film *Baby Doll*. The vengeful sadist Vicarro becomes in the film the Lawrentian lover Vacarro who awakens the virginal heroine to sexual life.

Period of Adjustment, perhaps Williams's worst play, seems to belong to this group of gentle plays, for at its conclusion the two couples achieve sexual harmony as the phallically named community of High Point sinks further into the cavern beneath it. But before the playwright allows this to happen, each of the two men who are its central figures is humiliated and forced to admit his weakness. They have been great fighters and war heroes, but one has abased himself to marry for money, and before he can be forgiven he must be bullied by his father-in-law and forced to accept his unattractive wife. The other has rejected his homosexual nature, or at least pretended to a virility he does not possess. He must publicly admit his weakness before he is bedded down, blissfully it is assumed, with his hysterical bride. The play falls apart because Williams cannot decide whether his central figures are to be forgiven or to be punished.

When Williams does not doubt that a character who has transgressed his moral code must be punished, his work is at its most powerful. Of all the crimes in this code the greatest is that from which Matilda and Serafina are preserved, the rejection of life. This theme of punishment for an act of rejection is at the center of a group of Williams's plays very different from that already examined, but it is expressed most explicitly in a short story, "Desire and the Black Masseur," from the volume *One Arm and Other Stories.* The central character, Walter Burns, a man who has yielded completely to the loveless, conventional life surrounding him, is haunted by a nameless, unfulfilled desire which is finally satisfied by a giant Negro masseur in a Turkish bath. Under the manipulations of the masseur, Burns discovers that his desire has been masochistic, and gradually the masseur, the instrument of his destiny, beats him almost to death. As the story veers toward fantasy, they go to the masseur's room where he kills Burns and proceeds to eat him in the atmosphere of a sacred ritual.

Although this story is bizarre and perhaps a little ridiculous, it says a great deal that is revealing of the cast of mind of its author. To him, Walter Burns is not an individual but a broad symbol of human guilt, for Williams believes that the sins of the world "are really only its partialities, its incompletions, and these are what sufferings must atone for." He sees these sufferings as ritual, a device for removing guilt. This is the function of "the principle of atonement, the surrender of the self to violent treatment by others with the idea of thereby clearing one's self of his guilt." For all its macabre elements, in the mind of its author, as the end of the story shows, "Desire and the Black Masseur" is an example of a wider vision comprehending the world and the place of suffering in it. "And meantime," Williams concludes, "slowly, with barely a thought of so doing, the earth's whole population twisted and writhed beneath the manipulation of night's black fingers, the white ones of day with skeletons splintered and flesh reduced to pulp, as out of this unlikely problem, the answer, perfection, was slowly evolved through torture."

We need not believe that anything like perfection could be evolved from the process described in "Desire and the Black Masseur" to see its significance in relation to Williams's major work. The story concerns an elaborate, ritual punishment of one who has rejected life, and, more specifically, rejected sexuality. A whole group of Williams's plays including some of his most remarkable—*A Streetcar Named Desire, Summer and Smoke, Cat on a Hot Tin Roof*, and *Suddenly Last Summer*—is centered on this idea of the terrible punishment that is visited on one because of an act of sexual rejection.

The stage action of *A Streetcar Named Desire*, still Williams's finest play, consists almost entirely of the punishment that its heroine, Blanche DuBois, endures as atonement for her act of rejection, her sin in terms of Williams's morality. Since Williams begins the action of his play at a late point in his story, the act itself is not played out on stage but only referred to. Not realizing that she is describing the crime that condemns her, Blanche tells Mitch of her discovery that her adored young husband was a homosexual and of the consequences of her disgust and revulsion:

BLANCHE. . . . He'd stuck the revolver into his mouth, and fired—so that the back of his head had been—blown away! (She sways and covers her face.) It was because—on the dance floor—unable to stop myself—I'd suddenly said—"I saw! I know! You disgust me . . ." And then the searchlight which had been turned on the world was turned off again and never for one moment since has there been any light that's stronger than this—kitchen—candle. . .

While Blanche delivers this speech and the ones surrounding it, the polka to which she and her husband had danced, the Varsouviana, sounds in the background. At the end of the play, when Blanche sees the doctor who is to lead her off to the asylum, her punishment is complete and the Varsouviana sounds again, linking her crime to its retribution. As Blanche flees from the doctor, "the Varsouviana is filtered into a weird distortion accompanied by the cries and noises of the jungle." These symbolize simultaneously Blanche's chaotic state and the instrument of her destruction, Stanley Kowalski, the complete sensual animal, the equivalent in function to the black masseur. Although Kowalski's primary function, to destroy Blanche, is clear, there are certain ambiguities evoked by his role. By becoming Blanche's destroyer, Kowalski also becomes the avenger of her homosexual husband. Although he is Williams's melodramatic exaggeration of the Lawrentian lover, the embodiment of admired male sexuality, it is appropriate from Williams's point of view that Kowalski should to some degree be identified with the lonely homosexual who had been driven to suicide, for Williams saw Lawrence not only as the propagandist of sexual vitality but as the symbol of the solitary, rejected exile. (See the poem called "Cried the Fox" from Williams's collection, *In the Winter of Cities.* In it Lawrence is symbolized as the fox pursued by the cruel hounds.) By implication, then, Williams has extended Lawrentian approval to the rejected homosexual (an act that probably set Lawrence spinning in his grave). Yet this approval is never wholehearted; for the exile homosexual, as he appears in Williams's work, is always tormented and often despairing. He cannot, after all, be a martyr until Williams has had him crucified.

Those who crucify, however, can never be guiltless. Kowalski, although an avenger, is as guilty of crucifying Blanche as she is of crucifying her husband. For Blanche, who has lost the plantation Belle Reve, the beautiful dream of a life of gracious gentility, is an exile like the homosexual; her tormentor, the apelike Kowalski, from one point of view the representative of Lawrentian vitality, is from another the brutal, male torturer of a lonely spirit. But however compassionately Blanche is viewed, she remains a woman who, in effect, has killed her husband by her cruelty, and her attempts to turn away from death to its opposite—"the opposite is desire," as Blanche herself says—are fruitless. Even as she tells Mitch about her promiscuity, a Mexican woman stands at one side of the stage selling flowers for the dead. *"Flores para los muertos,"* she calls, *"flores—flores."*

A variant on the act of rejection is performed in Scene Six of *Summer and Smoke.* The characters are similar to those already encountered: the frail, spinsterish Southern girl with her sensuality repressed by a puritanical background; the man who is seeking spiritual relief through a sexual union. Like many of

Williams's characters he needs love as relief from solitude. At one point, while giving Alma an ironic anatomy lecture, he shouts, "This part down here is the sex—which is hungry for love because it is sometimes lonesome." At the crucial moment she rejects his advances and rushes off. Although Alma, like Blanche, has sinned and must atone, she has not sinned out of cruelty nor has she caused the death of her lover. After he has passed through his spiritual crisis and found a wife and a place in the world, Alma realizes what she had done. Like Blanche she is condemned to be tormented by the urges she had turned away from, and like Blanche she turns to promiscuity, but because her sin has been somewhat mitigated by her realization of it there is a suggestion at the end of the play that the traveling salesman she has picked up may lead her to salvation rather than destruction.

Williams's most recent play, *The Night of the Iguana* (a reworking of his short story of the same title), has, like *Summer and Smoke*, affinities with both the severity of *Streetcar* and the gentleness of *The Glass Menagerie*. Its heroine, Hannah Jelkes, a New England spinster artist, is placed in a position that closely parallels that of Blanche DuBois. But unlike Blanche, when confronted by an appeal for help from one with abnormal sexual inclinations (a homosexual in the original story, but converted for stage purposes to an unfrocked minister with a taste for pubescent girls), instead of driving him to suicide, she offers him what help she can. That help, however, is limited. When he asks to be allowed to travel with her, she cannot accept him. Because like Laura and Alma she is too delicate and too repressed to take on a full emotional relationship, Shannon's rescue is finally left to the sexually vital hotel proprietor, while Hannah must continue in loveless solitude. By her sympathy for Shannon and for the pathetic fetishist she had previously aided, she has earned, however, a fate far gentler than the breakdown meted out to Blanche and to her own predecessor in the original story.

In *Cat on a Hot Tin Roof*, however, Williams produces something much nearer the pattern of *Streetcar*. In fact, from one point of view *Cat* is simply a reworking of the materials of the earlier play, but with a crucial change that made it almost impossible for Williams to bring his play to a reasonable conclusion. Again we are presented with a work in which the motivating figure does not appear, and again that figure is the rejected homosexual. But now because the rejector, the sinner who must atone, is not a woman but a man, certain problems arise. The audience, although it sympathizes with Blanche, can accept her as guilty. She is a woman, and had she been able to give her husband love instead of contempt, she might have led him back to a normal life. Brick, however, confronted with Skipper's telephoned confession of a homosexual attachment, is hardly in a position to do the same—short of admitting a similar inclination. Yet Williams, although he is ambiguous about several points in this play, is not ambiguous about Brick's guilt. Big Daddy himself, who despises mendacity, condemns his son. "You! dug the grave of your friend," he cries, "and kicked him in it!—before you'd face the truth with him!" But it is beyond Big Daddy's power to explain how Brick was to do so.

Yet in a play designed for the modern professional theater, Wiliams cannot openly punish Brick for failing to be an honest homosexual. When he showed *Cat* to the representative of that theater, Elia Kazan, and Kazan suggested certain changes, Williams accepted his advice. As a result, the comparatively optimistic third act performed on Broadway contains the shift in Brick's character that leads to the suggestion that his castration, symbolized obviously enough by his broken ankle, will not be permanent. In the published version of the play, in which the Broadway third act is printed as a kind of addendum to the original, Williams claimed that he had agreed to Kazan's suggestions to retain his interest. There is no reason to disbelieve this statement, but it is worth noting that by mitigating Brick's punishment, Williams was relieved of the necessity of asking his audience to agree that Brick deserved to be castrated for an act which most members of that audience would not consider to be a crime.

Although the tentativeness of Williams's condemnation of Brick makes it difficult to know whether Brick was so condemned for rejecting his homosexual friend or for rejecting his own homosexual nature, in *Cat*, at least, homosexuality itself carries no stigma. In contrast to the castrated Brick, who has rejected, stands Big Daddy, who has accepted. Although he is a man of almost ostentatious virility, as well as the most powerful and sympathetic figure in the play, he had served and respected the two idyllically conceived homosexuals, Straw and Ochello, and received his land from them as a kind of benediction. Yet in *Suddenly Last Summer*, the last play to date of what may be called the "punishment" group, Williams has produced a work in which the homosexual—so often for him the symbol of the lonely, rejected exile—becomes the rejector, the sinner who must be punished. But neither this shift in Williams's usual pattern nor the *bizarrerie* of the play's atmosphere should conceal the fact that *Suddenly Last Summer* follows closely the structure of the other plays in this group. Once more the pivotal figure, the exile homosexual, has met a violent death before the opening of the play. As the sterile Brick is contrasted with Big Daddy, the life-giving father of *Cat*, so the cruel Sebastian is played off against the loving and merciful Catharine who gives herself not, it seems, out of desire but as an act of rescue. "We walked through the wet grass to the great misty oaks," she says, "as if somebody was calling us for help there." If we remember that this act of rescue is exactly what Blanche, Alma, and Brick failed to perform, we realize that Williams means us to accept Catharine as entirely good. Although Sebastian is, as we expect him to be, the loveless rejector who is punished for his sins, there is a surprising similarity between his vision of a world dominated by remorseless cruelty—as expressed in the description of the Encantadas, the Galápagos Islands, where baby sea turtles are killed and devoured by carnivorous birds of prey—and the vision of a world undergoing perpetual punishment expressed in "Desire and the Black Masseur." However, in punishing Sebastian, Williams is not disclaiming this vision. Sebastian's sin lay not in perceiving the world as, for Williams, it is, but in his believing, with a pride bordering on *hubris*, that he could exalt himself above his kind, that he could feed upon people like one of the devouring birds of the Encantadas. As always in Williams, the punishment monstrously fits the crime. As Sebastian had cruelly watched the turtles being eaten, as he had fed the fruit flies to the devouring plant, so he is fed to the band of children whom he had perverted and is devoured by them.

Sebastian's crime then is the very one committed by Blanche, Alma, and Brick. He has turned away from his suffering fellow creatures and, instead of offering love, has offered hate. He has not understood, as Catharine has, that although all men may be on a stricken ship sinking into the sea, "that's no reason for everyone drowning for hating everyone drowning." And yet there is a difficulty for the spectator in accepting the nature of Sebas-

tian's punishment, however fierce he knows Williams's morality
to be. It is not merely that Sebastian's fate is so violently grotesque but that, unlike Blanche and Brick, he has not performed
a specific act that brings his punishment upon him; he is punished
for what he is rather than for what he does. He is not only a
rejector but also a homosexual, always in Williams's work an
object simultaneously of sympathy and of revulsion. The ambiguity already noted in *Streetcar* appears in all Williams's plays
that touch on homosexuality. There is an intimate connection
between the guilty rejector and the martyred homosexual; the
punishment visited on the former regularly echoes the fate of the
latter, so that the two characters are not always distinguishable.
In *Streetcar* the rejector and the homosexual victim were separate, but both met desperate ends. In the ambiguous Brick these
figures began to converge, and in *Suddenly Last Summer* they
have completely coalesced. The pain felt by the cruel rejector is
also felt by the sterile and guilty homosexual; neither can escape
corruption and despair.

Here lies the source of that vision of universal corruption that
pervades so much of Williams's work and that makes it at once
so violent and so pathetic. In a world dominated by cruelty,
Williams maintains, the innocent are not only destroyed; eventually they too are corrupted. Williams has produced three plays
centered on this theme and on the figure that embodies it, the
wandering innocent. *Camino Real*, *Orpheus Descending*, and
Sweet Bird of Youth all tell the story of a wanderer who is or has
been innocent, who comes into the world of universal corruption and who is thereupon destroyed by it.

Williams has said flatly that the sinister fantasy world of the
Camino Real "is nothing more nor less than my conception of the
time and world that I live in." It is a time in which greed and
brutality are the ruling forces and a world in which those
pathetic souls who attempt to show some affection for their fellow creatures are remorselessly crushed and then thrown into a
barrel and carted away by the street cleaners. Although this is
admittedly a nightmare world, it does not differ in any essential
way from the American South as it appears in *Orpheus Descending* and *Sweet Bird of Youth*. This too is a nightmare world
where greed, brutality and sterility rule and where those who
love are castrated or burned alive. In these last two plays, Wil-

liams has attempted to give this world some resemblance to a recognizable social reality, but this reality is always closer to the mysterious country of the Camino Real than to anything in the southern United States. As an epigraph to *Camino Real* Williams has selected the opening lines of Dante's *Inferno*; the setting of that play is the place to which Orpheus descended, hell.

As we would expect, the ruler of hell is Death; more specifically, he is the god of sterility. In *Camino Real*, Gutman, the proprietor of the Siete Mares hotel, is cruel and sinister enough, but he always remains a little remote from the action. Had Williams personified the evil of the place in a single powerful figure, he might have been less able to end the play with its suggestion (however unconvincing) of optimism. Like Gutman, Jabe Torrance, the proprietor of the mercantile store in *Orpheus Descending*, takes little direct part in the action, but he is a far more heavily drawn figure and a far more violent antagonist. The evil creature who destroys life wherever he can find it is, as Williams describes him in a stage direction, "death's self and malignancy." He is not only "death's self," but the personification of sterility and impotence. Nurse Porter, who seems to have supernatural perception, can tell at a glance that Lady is pregnant and that Jabe is not the father. As he had burned the wine garden of Lady's father where the fig tree blossomed and true lovers met, so he calls upon the fires of the hell of impotence to burn her and her lover. (It should be noted that while Williams's work has changed in tone from the gentleness of *You Touched Me*, where the impotent clergyman was a figure of fun, it has not shifted in point of view.) Even more heavily than Jabe, however, Boss Finley of *Sweet Bird of Youth* is drawn as the symbol of malignant impotence. Miss Lucy, his mistress, has scrawled in lipstick across the ladies' room mirror, "Boss Finley is too old to cut the mustard." By implication, at least, he had presided over the castration of an innocent Negro and, as the play ends, is about to preside over that of its hero, Chance Wayne. (The anti-Negro social elements, like the Nazis of *The Night of the Iguana* who are also irrelevant to the drama, are no more than a ploy, a device to win for the hero the sympathy of a liberal New York audience.) The best description of Boss Finley is not in the play but in a poem called "Old Men with Sticks" found in *In the Winter of Cities*. In the poem, senile old men with sticks (lifeless phalli) clump about on "the iron earth of winter."

Drawn from the pouch that hangs
Like a withered testicle at the belted waist,
pearles without luster are passed without passion amongst them;
the dim but enduring stones of hatred
are trafficked amongst them by stealth.

As a result, "youth from his lover/draws apart in shame," and frost covers the land.

When Boss Finley's impotence is contrasted with Chance's attitude toward the emasculation of the Negro, the natures of the opposing forces in the play become clear. "You know what that is, don't you?" Chance cries. "Sex-envy is what that is, and the revenge for sex-envy which is a widespread disease that I have run into personally too often for me to doubt its existence or any manifestation." Boss Finley, Chance says, "was just called down from the hills to preach hate. I was born here to make love." Each of the three wanderers, Kilroy, Val, and Chance, had been born to make love, but each has been wounded by a hostile world. Kilroy's heart condition prevents him from continuing as a prizefighter or from staying with his "real true woman." Of the three he is the only true innocent and, significantly, the only one who is alone. Val and Chance both speak of the corrupt lives they have lived and of the waning of their youths, but in reality they are bound not by time or by their past lives but by their relationships with an older woman.

Williams developed this relationship most elaborately in his novella, *The Roman Spring of Mrs. Stone*. In that book a once beautiful actress, who had married lovelessly "to escape copulation," finds herself an aging widow at the end of her career and is reduced to buying sexuality from the lowest and most sinister of gigolos. What is most striking here is not the recognizable punishment-for-rejection pattern but the fact that Mrs. Stone's real inclinations are toward lesbianism. Her most vivid sexual experience had been an abortive moment with a schoolgirl friend. In addition, during a brief affair with a young actor, she had enveloped him in an embrace "in a manner that was more like a man's with a girl, and to which he submitted in a way that also suggested a reversal of gender."

If the suggestion of homosexuality that underlies the relationship between the older woman and the younger man in *The Roman Spring of Mrs. Stone* is extended to *Orpheus* and *Sweet Bird* (in each case the ostensible woman is an older person having a forbidden affair with a beautiful young man), these works fit very easily into the pattern of ambiguity we have observed in the "punishment" group. From one point of view we have the wandering love-giver—Val, whose phallic guitar is an obvious symbol, and Chance, who has a speech about his vocation as a love-maker for the middle-aged, the ugly, the sad and the "eccentric"—who enters the nightmare world of Hades in *Orpheus* and of what the Princess in *Sweet Bird* calls "the ogre's country at the top of the beanstalk, the country of the flesh-hungry, blood-thirsty ogre." There he attempts to rescue a lover, and in the attempt he is brutally destroyed by the giant.

From another point of view, however, the wanderer is not innocent but corrupt. Beneath the apparent heterosexual relationship lies one that is homosexual, and from it spreads an aura of corruption that pervades the plays. Chance calculates his age by the level of rot in him, and Val, who has been "on a party" in the bars of New Orleans since he was fifteen, is trying vainly to flee from his past. In his poem called "Orpheus Descending," Williams writes, "Now Orpheus, crawl, O shamefaced fugitive, crawl back under the crumbling broken wall of yourself." As before, the seeming-innocent is himself guilty and must be hideously punished. Once his moral sense has been appeased, however, Williams can allow himself the luxury of a sentimental apotheosis. *Orpheus* and *Sweet Bird* take place at Easter, and in both plays there is a suggestion that the dead wanderer should be viewed as a martyred Christ figure whose spirit is resurrected in Carol Cutrere and the Princess. (However, where the suggestion of resurrection is not incredible in *Orpheus*, the idea that the pathetic gigolo of *Sweet Bird* could be a Christlike martyr is merely bizarre.) It is the wanderer's sin that brings him to destruction and only after he has been punished and destroyed can he be revered.

It is from this conflict between the need to condemn and the desire to pardon that the weakness of Williams' work stems, for it is ironically the strength of his moral temper that forces him to censure what he wishes to exalt. Williams is passionately committed to the great Romantic dictum inherent in his neo-Lawrentian point of view, that the natural equals the good, that the great natural instincts that well up out of the subconscious depths of men—and particularly the sexual instinct, whatever form it may take—are to be trusted absolutely. But Williams is too strong a moralist, far too permeated with a sense of sin, to be able to accept such an idea with equanimity. However pathetic he may make the martyred homosexual, however seemingly innocent the wandering love-giver, the moral strength that led Williams to punish the guilty Blanche impels him to condemn Brick and Chance. But because he is condemning what he most desires to pardon, he must sometimes, in order to condemn at all, do so with ferocious violence.

When the conflicts among Williams's sympathies are at a minimum, when his morality is clearly focused and has some recognizable relation to one that most men find intelligible, as in *Streetcar*, he is at his best. When, however, his mind is confused, when we cannot tell whether the central figures of his plays are innocent or guilty, as in *Cat*, or when we are asked to believe that the obviously guilty have in some mysterious way retained their innocence, as in *Sweet Bird*, our credulity is strained, and the desperation of the most powerful moral playwright of our time becomes painfully visible.

XV

HENRY POPKIN

Authur Miller: The Strange Encounter

Arthur Miller's regular practice in his plays is to confront the dead level of banality with the heights and depths of guilt and to draw from this strange encounter a liberal parable of hidden evil and social responsibility. Each of his mature full-length plays (*All My Sons, Death of a Salesman, The Crucible,* and *A View from the Bridge*) exhibits the same basic pattern: each one matches ordinary, uncomprehending people with extraordinary demands and accusations. The characters are like the man in the old Jewish story who asks the price of bacon and then shudders at the sound of thunder out of the heavens; he protests meekly that he was only asking the price. Thunder sounds abruptly for Miller's people too. From day to day they live their placid, apparently meaningless lives, and suddenly the eternal intrudes, thunder sounds, the trumpet blows, and these startled mediocrities are whisked off to the bar of justice. In the midst of banality, guilt appears: "You killed twenty-one fliers. You lived your life by false standards. You betrayed your wife and thereby caused her to be charged with witchcraft. You have condemned a family to starve." The little man protests: "What is the cosmos doing in my tacky living room? Must I decide the fate of the world? Am I my brother's keeper?" The crime is betrayal, the verdict is guilty, and the sentence is death. Punishment is imposed, directly or indirectly, by the victim himself. In Miller's first Broadway play, *The Man Who Had All the Luck,* betrayal and guilt are present, but retribution is nowhere to be found. The chief character spends most of his time feverishly searching for it. Miller's novel, *Focus,* has two crimes—being anti-Semitic and being Jewish; the chief character atones for the first by confessing to the second, of which he is not guilty.

Reprinted from *The Sewanee Review*, LXVIII (1960), 34–60, by permission of the author and the publisher. Copyright 1960 by the University of the South.

At the center of each play is the tension between little people and big issues, and each play confirms our belief that little people cannot live up to big standards. Miller always goes to some pains to make his people sufficiently small. The banality is deliberate and dramatically effective; it belongs to the characters and not to Miller himself. His best-known hero, Willy Loman of *Death of a Salesman,* is even labeled a little man by his name: he is society's low man. Ideally, the little men are stripped of concreteness, intelligence, and literacy. If farmer John Proctor of *The Crucible* seems to be a superior human specimen, he is benefiting from the enchantment lent by a distance of three centuries. Joe Keller of *All My Sons* is a manufacturer, but a special point is made of his ignorance, so much so that we may doubt even the presence of the crude intelligence that made him a success in the first place. He wonders at his son's interest in the Sunday book section, asks if books come out every week, "brooches" subjects, and amiably parades his illiteracy. Willy Loman, the archetypal salesman, and Eddie Carbone, the longshoreman of *A View from the Bridge,* are equally inarticulate; disaster renders them speechless. Their plain talk is matched by their plain appearance. Most of the men and women of Miller's plays are not beautiful, nor have they ever been. To name the actors who created the roles is to read the catalogue of honest careworn plainness: Lee J. Cobb, Ed Begley, Mildred Dunnock, J. Carroll Naish, Eileen Heckart. Even the younger leading men tend to be rugged and weatherbeaten: Arthur Kennedy, Van Heflin. To be exceptional is more dangerous than to be honestly homely: Happy, in *Death of a Salesman,* is, like Narcissus, seduced by his own beauty, and Rodolpho, in *A View from the Bridge,* is inevitably a victim of jealousy. If Abigail, of *The Crucible,* is "strikingly beautiful," she is also the devil incarnate.

In their language, their culture, their incapacity for comprehending their fates, these people may well possess as little imagination as any characters ever brought to the stage. By way of contrast, Odets gives his characters colorful language, and some of them have cultural aspirations. Even Hauptmann's proletarians aspire to change their lives, and Gorki's derelicts at least have interesting vices. But Miller's people inhabit the dead center of dullness as they sit and wait for the voice of doom. Or, if they don't sit, they go about the daily round of their lives— washing cars, eating late snacks, playing football, picking up girls, going to movies, as if destiny would never come calling. And, incidentally, we may wonder how unspeakably banal their whole lives would be if it were not for that timely trump of doom. In the shadow of crisis, they reminisce about the past, when life was happier without being essentially different. *All My Sons* contains some happy recollection of the prewar past suitably summarized by the play's heroine: "Gosh, those dear dead days beyond recall." Much of *Death of a Salesman* is devoted to recreating the happy past, when Willy's sales were bigger, when Biff stole footballs instead of suits, when trees grew in the Lomans' section of Brooklyn. Miller's short play, *A Memory of Two Mondays*, is an extended reminiscence of an uneventful past, in which life is colored by a vague, unexpressed good fellowship and crises occur only in the lives of others. Miller has described it as "a kind of letter to that sub-culture where the sinews of the economy are rooted, that darkest Africa of our society." He adds that it conveys "the need for a little poetry in life." But *Memory of Two Mondays* is no more prosaic or subcultural than the other plays. True, one character points up the sub-culture by reading *War and Peace*, but the real difference is in the atmosphere of friendliness unspoiled by pressures from outside. Hitler is just a name in the newspaper, Roosevelt inspires hope as well as hostility, and, best of all, no one is capable of malice or of zeal for personal success.

Except for the boy who reads Tolstoy, none of Miller's characters, not even a "good" one, is capable of the sort of cultural reference that used to dot Odets's plays of middle-class life; Marx, Rouault, Verdi are names all equally unknown here. The only significant objectives are to earn a living and to kill time between working hours. The need to kill time may inspire some gala celebrations which are rather telling in their flatness. Willy Loman's wife tells him his sons are "gonna blow him to a big meal." This phrase is so catchy that she says it twice. Of course, going out for a big meal is also Joe Keller's idea of a bacchanalian revel. But the favorite activity is sitting home and putting strains on the family tie. Son accuses father, uncle desires niece—but they have little identity *beyond* the family tie.

The families of *All My Sons* and *Death of a Salesman* do not belong to any discernible ethnic group. They are deliberately made the washed out, colorless representatives of society in general. Miller himself was apparently endeavoring to assert the non-sectarian universality of *Death of a Salesman* in his remarks to the press when Thomas Mitchell succeeded Lee J. Cobb in the role of Willy Loman. Finding himself impressed with Mitchell's performance, Miller remarked that he did not realize he had written a play about an Irish family. Did he think he had written a play about a family with any kind of ethnic identification? Ostensibly, not at all. Still, in an ingenious *Commentary* article of a few years ago, George Ross made a good case for the underlying Jewish elements in *Death of a Salesman*. One recognizes a possibly Jewish problem in the anger of the father whose authority is threatened and in the exaggerated Americanism that might logically belong to a second-generation family. Joe Keller has a son named Chris; that seems to de-Semitize the rather similar family in *All My Sons*. And yet, in Miller's earliest plays (extant but unpublished and never professionally produced), the families which encounter comparable problems are frankly Jewish. Miller's first Broadway play, *The Man Who Had All the Luck*, is transitional in this respect. It has an all-American setting, a small midwestern town, but in the published version (in *Cross-Section 1944*) the hero is named David Frieber. By the time the play was produced, he had become the brother of another character and had thus acquired the name of Beeves. In the novel *Focus*, published the following year, an anti-Semite gets accustomed to being taken for a Jew and finally identifies himself with the Jews. The character bears a suitably ambiguous name, Newman—as ambiguous as Miller's. Like Laura Hobson's *Gentleman's Agreement* (published soon after), *Focus* carries an odd implication—that Jewish identity is external, that it can be put on at will, that all that is essential to it exists only in the eye of the beholder. On the dust-wrapper, Miller seems to be playing his character's game in reverse; here he is quoted as telling how he was taken for "an Italian, a Pole, an Irishman," even for a Jew. This account is in keeping with the implications of the novel and the plays: *anyone* is in danger of being taken for a Jew. True, the novel has a Jewish shopkeeper named Finkelstein, but, when ethnic identification is applied to *you* (Miller, Newman, Keller, Loman), it is a curious error. *You* don't belong to any group except the amorphous majority, and that makes *your* problem universal. But, as the characterizations in *Focus*, *All My Sons*, and *Death of a Salesman* reach for universality, they run the risk of being so general that they are, in some respects, nebulous.

Keller and Loman are made as general as possible so that they may play the role of Everyman in their dramatic parables. Eddie Carbone, of *A View from the Bridge*, is at least a cousin to Everyman; he is an Italo-American longshoreman, and his ancestry is significantly Sicilian. The Greek associations of Sicily encourage Miller to call the play a tragedy and even to employ a chorus. Also Eddie Carbone speaks verse of a sort; Eric Bentley wrote that when the printed version revealed "that a lot of dialogue was in verse, you could have knocked me over with a feather." Miller retreated to prose when *A View from the Bridge* reappeared in the *Collected Plays*. But he had written in his preface to the earlier text: "Verse reaches always toward the general statement . . . it is the most public of public speech." He found a corresponding wideness of reference in the kind of play he was writing, "social drama," a genre which he takes to include Greek tragedy: "To put it simply, even over-simply, a drama rises in stature and intensity in proportion to the weight of its application to all men." In this play, as in his other serious dramas, Miller had written a parable which was intended to apply to everyone. Joe Keller is every man facing a responsibility to his nation in wartime. Willy Loman is every low man in our economic order. *The Crucible*, written at a time when many spoke of witch hunts directed against political heresy, was obviously designed to display a political parallel to our time in the Salem witch trials. And *A View from the Bridge* is Greek, poetic, and therefore all the more public in its object lesson on the folly of betrayal. The plays are dramatic parables or fables; their characters are as typical as the prodigal son or Aesop's lambs and wolves. They are as unattached and as non-sectarian as the medieval Everyman, and that is why they cannot be individuals.

But where ethnic associations may be vague, the characters' occupations are loaded with symbolic usefulness. Joe Keller must be engaged in war work, and it must be possible for his son in the air force to make use of the products he manufactures; the son's suicide is a public acknowledgment of guilt. There can be no more suitable emblem of our commercial society than the salesman Willy Loman, especially since we are never told what he sells. In a sense, he sells himself, but the product wears out. The waterfront is a suitable setting for *A View from the Bridge* because it had recently been the scene of a film in which Elia Kazan had apparently justified betrayal, in certain circumstances; with the evident intention of replying to Kazan, Miller returned to the waterfront.

Whatever else these plays may be, then, they are instructive. They argue cases; they prove points. Each play is constructed to expose a pattern of guilt, to find out who is guilty and to impose the penalty of death. The plot drives us from one to another of the devastating points which the prosecutor-dramatist makes against his characters. The purpose of *All My Sons* was, according to Miller, "to bring a man into the direct path of the consequences he had wrought." Up to the time of the play's action, Joe Keller has avoided consequences by avoiding the discovery of his guilt. By the end of the second act, his guilt is established, with the help of a clue that any respectable mystery writer would be ashamed to use. Keller had pretended illness on the day his company approved some cracked cylinder heads for the Air Force. He gives himself away by inadvertently referring to his unfailing good health. The case is nearly complete, but Keller still refuses to take personal responsibility. In the last act, his son produces a letter—what is so telling as documentary evidence?— in which another son reveals that he committed suicide because of his father's misdeeds. Keller quits arguing and shoots himself, just in time to prevent his son from turning him over to the authorities. The case is, as they say in the law courts, proven, and it is as airtight a case as any stage detective could hope for. But like all the proofs offered by stage detectives, it proves a *fact*. Miller's goal is to demonstrate an *idea*, but his method is too rigid for exposition; it is suitable only to proof, and that implies simplicity on the part of the idea, the characters, or the author. The idea in *All My Sons* is the most elementary conception of social responsibility; as for the characters, Miller has informed us that he knows "how rarely the great issues penetrate such environments." Two simplicities collide—the idea and the man— and we recognize that on this dramatic railroad, Miller has constructed only one track.

Death of a Salesman is a play of a looser sort but is also to a degree constructed as an investigation—a word which, by the way, Miller applies particularly to *The Man Who Had All the Luck*. Willy Loman hunts the secret of his failure; he wants to know the right path. His mistake is that there is no right path; there is, however, a wrong path, and Willy has traveled on it for most of his life. He asks his brother Ben and his neighbor

Charley for the secret; they can not tell him, and he cannot guess that it does not exist. He stumbles upon telltale clues and significant discoveries, but he manages to ignore most of them. It is his son Biff who plays detective more successfully. Present events make Biff see his lies about the past; he perceives the hollowness of the dream of success from the start. The real hostage of success, Willy Loman, remains unaltered. But once more, the terms of the courtroom apply to this play. Willy's offences against his wife, against his sons, against society are exposed so that sentence can be passed. Miller himself describes Willy as a man who "has broken a law" in which he deeply believes. This time, however, it is the play's purpose to show that the law requiring success is not or should not be valid.

The Crucible, too, turns upon a law which we should not respect: "Thou shalt not permit a witch to live." It takes the form of an investigation, for it begins with the arrival of the great investigator of witches. Our pursuit of the facts takes us over two paths; while the witch-hunters make their efforts to measure the extent of witchcraft in the community, we follow John Proctor's attempt to weigh the guilt in his infidelity to his wife. The question of Proctor's guilt peters out since his guilt is nothing beside the community's. The issues are made a good deal simpler than those of the earlier plays. In our eyes, the community condemns itself, totally and without qualification, as it builds its airtight case against John Proctor. Contrasting his crime with the court's, the defendant justifiably thinks better of himself: "Now I do think I see some shred of goodness in John Proctor."

The play sustains considerable dramatic interest as the witch-hunters descend upon the Proctors, but it surely falls short in the realm of ideas—and especially by pressing so hard to make a particular judgment prevail. The actions of the witch-hunters are evidently to be attributed to the invincible evil of their characters. Notes to the printed version qualify this interpretation by strengthening the hints that these villains are motivated by greed, but Miller himself states that he did too much to mitigate the evil of the judge. At the same time, we require Proctor to be a model of good. Since we regard his adultery as a sin against his wife alone, he expiates it easily enough by sacrificing his life for hers. But Miller unintentionally reminds us how hard he is working to set up this adequate expiation for Proctor.

Only Proctor and his wife are taken seriously. Abigail, who corrupted Proctor and now accuses his wife of witchcraft, could have been no more than seventeen when Proctor was her lover. She tells him he "put knowledge in her heart," and she continues to protest her love to him. But she is totally vile, she seduced him, he feels no obligation toward her, and evidently we are to regard her becoming a prostitute as a fitting result of her total depravity. Surely she needs more careful attention, and so does Proctor's responsibility toward her. Something is seriously at fault here. Miller no doubt began with the intention of creating an ulterior motive for the charges of witchcraft and also with the purpose of giving Proctor a less than mortal sin to expiate. But, giving his closest attention only to Proctor and to the main issue of the play, he lost sight of Abigail as a participant in a human relationship.

A View from the Bridge also has at its core the proving of a case. Eddie Carbone desperately endeavors to conceal from himself and from the world his incestuous passion for his niece. He bitterly resents Rodolpho, the young man she favors, but he feels obliged to make his hatred publicly acceptable by proving Rodolpho to be a homosexual. He seizes Rodolpho and kisses him, then goes to a lawyer to offer this incident as proof that "the guy ain't right." Ultimately, Eddie uses the assumption of homosexuality and opportunism to justify him in turning Rodolpho and his brother in to the immigration authorities. To his death, he continues to plead his case, protesting the pure motives behind his treacherous action. But, obviously, we must conclude that informers, like the accusers of witches, must themselves be brought to judgment and that a verdict must be returned against them. Miller is more compassionate toward this informer, who is proved to be merely sick and not, like Abigail in *The Crucible*, totally depraved.

Each of the full-length plays, then, argues a case in public; structure and content are determined by rules of evidence appropriate to the theater. The characters themselves remind us that the case is fought in open court and not in the judge's chambers. Each protagonist fights for his good name, for the respect of his community, for a public verdict that will exonerate him. If Joe Keller, of *All My Sons*, fights the idea that he owes anything to society, he is won over by his sons. One has killed himself because he joins in the public condemnation which his father has ignored. The other son lives by his star, "the star of one's honesty"—a fitting symbol for the character the world attributes to him. Joe recognizes, as his sons have done, that he cannot live for his family alone, that he and his family belong to the world, and therefore he commits suicide because he cannot live without his good name.

Willy Loman also plays to an audience; he is a salesman who must require to be approved, to be well liked. His life, however, suggests the public role he really plays:

His name was never in the paper. He's not the finest character that ever lived. But he's a human being, and a terrible thing is happening to him. So attention must be paid. He's not to be allowed to fall into his grave like an old dog.

As the drama progresses, Willy's faltering claim on the respect and affection of others is matched by his new role as a horrible example, a public instance of the man for whom society has no further use.

John Proctor and Eddie Carbone die for their good name and make no bones about it. Proctor refuses to put his name to the lies he has told to save his life. He will lie privately, but he will die rather than compromise his public integrity: "How may I live without my name? I have given you my soul; leave me my name!" In a much worse cause, Eddie Carbone demands his good name from the man he has ruined: "I want my name! . . . Marco's got my name—and you can run and tell him, kid, that he's gonna give it back to me in front of this neighborhood, or we have it out." These are no private dramas; each frustrated, ruined hero compels attention, demands that some meaning be found in his catastrophe. Rightly or wrongly, he wants respect for his good name, even in defeat. For Eddie Carbone, it should be added that, although the action of the play indicates a self-created disaster, Eddie's wife tries to mitigate his guilt: "Whatever happened we all done it." This is no more than a plea for pity; it's too bad about Eddie, but, like Willy Loman, he has to be held responsible for what he does. And yet responsibility is somehow divided, not just in the sense that "we all done it." Guilt lies finally at the door of a more selective group of culprits, the secret rulers who exercise authority among us.

Whatever personal contributions Miller's heroes may make to their misfortunes, the main burden of guilt is usually borne by the dominant forces in their society. Miller begins by indicting parents. The revolt of a son against a father is at the center of both *All My Sons* and *Death of a Salesman*; in each play, a son painfully discovers his father's weakness and dishonesty. In his lecture before the New Dramatists Committee, "The Shadows of the Gods" (*Harper's Magazine*, August, 1958), Miller identifies this conflict with parental authority as the starting point of lives as individuals:

> Be it Tolstoy, Dostoevski, Hemingway, you, or I, we are formed in this world when we are sons and daughters and the first truths we know throw us into conflict with our fathers and mothers.

But he speaks also of the need to discover that "the parent, powerful as he appears, is not the source of injustice but its deputy," and to extend dramatic conflict to "that realm where the father is after all the not final authority . . . when we see beyond parents, who are, after all, but the shadows of the gods." Above and beyond the parents are the "hidden forces" against which the ultimate accusations must be directed. The sinister hidden forces palpably contribute to the weakness of the corrupt parents in the early plays; they are present in the callous business world which creates the ideology of Joe Keller and Willy Loman. In *The Crucible*, the hidden, evil forces are visible in the courts; in *A View from the Bridge*, they manifest themselves in the heartless immigration authorities and in Eddie's desperate passion for his niece. Invariably, a large share of the blame falls upon the people in power, father's surrogates. Authority, the government, the courts, the community's official values all conspire to crush Miller's lonely, hapless tragic hero.

But if Miller's hero is lonely, he is still not altogether alone. Good as well as evil has hidden forces on its side. In *All My Sons*, the cynicism at the top is being publicly challenged by the united devotion of a nation at war, but, in the other plays, the forces of good form a sort of secret underground, a real community whose values are worth sharing. The good which this decent underground embodies is deep and instinctive; it rarely finds any verbal expression. In fact, if we do not look sharply, we may not find the hidden forces of good at all. The good people have no theories, no ideologies, except for their goodness. Their practice and their faith are the same—doing good. Their virtue needs no legal or official sanction, and, in practice, it may defy the official world.

The good society is present in the neighbors of whom we

often hear in *All My Sons*. They help out when they are needed —"the day you were born and the water got shut off. People were carrying basins from a block away—a stranger would have thought the whole neighborhood was on fire!" But they also express their collective disapproval of the man who manufactured faulty equipment for the air corps—even when the courts exonerate him. We see this society more plainly in *Death of a Salesman* in the form of those inveterate good neighbors, Charley and his son Bernard. They are inexplicably—that is to say, naturally—plain, honest, and kind. Charley prospers in business without being hoodwinked by the ideology of salesmanship. Bernard wins glory by pleading before the Supreme Court, but he does this without any pushing from his father. Willy marvels, "You never took any interest in him," and Charley tells him, "My salvation is that I never took any interest in anything." How do they get this way? How do they manage to be so decent and so happy? Apparently they do it by following the natural bent of their virtue, by not listening to the voices of greed, of selfishness, of private ambition. When necessary, they break the rules to do good. Bernard helps Willy's son Biff to cheat on his exams. As he later admits to Willy, he loved Biff, although Biff always took advantage of him. Charley aids in another deceit; when Willy is put on straight commission, Charley gives him fifty dollars each week so that Willy can pretend to his wife to be earning money. The purity of these good deeds is further indicated by Willy's failure ever to say even a moderately friendly word to Charley. Obviously, good deeds are not to be explained or to be measured by simpleton standards of law, honesty, or reciprocation. In the authorities defied here—the teachers who give exams to Biff, the company which withholds a salary from Willy—we have a foretaste of the wicked authority which governs Salem in *The Crucible* and the hard-hearted bureau of imigration in *A View from the Bridge*. Defying such authority is a prerequisite for a clear conscience.

The Crucible, too, has its kernel of good people who oppose the witch trials but become the victims of the courts. They are paragons of virtue. Even the visiting investigator of witches remarks, of the most improbable defendant: "If Rebecca Nurse be tainted, then nothing's left to stop the whole green world from burning." No merely personal resentment could turn their accusers against them; the principal motive is greed. The parson wants gold candlesticks and better living arrangements; a fellow conspirator grabs other men's lands. If the play itself leaves any doubt on this matter, Miller removes it in his notes. A final note gives us the consoling knowledge that the subterranean good society won out in the next century: "To all intents and purposes, the power of the theocracy in Massachusetts was broken."

The good society is equally strong and silent in *A View from the Bridge*. Informers may be technically obedient to the law, but good people ostracize them. We hear first of a neighbor who betrayed his uncle and was brutally beaten by his family: "You'll never see him no more, a guy do a thing like that? How's he gonna show his face?" This is Eddie Carbone's fate: no neighbor will speak to him, and the cousin whom he has betrayed, the honest and sober Marco, justly kills him.

The line between good and evil, between the good society and the oppressors, is always clearly drawn in Miller's plays. Biff Loman may not perceive the distinction soon enough, and Willy Loman may never see it, but *we* are never permitted any doubts. Miller's bold certainty is best illustrated by his comments on *The Crucible*. Charged with making his witch-hunters too wicked, Miller replied that he did not make them wicked enough: "I believe now, as I did not conceive then, that there are people dedicated to evil in the world. . . . Evil is not a mistake but a fact in itself." Like the young man in Shaw's *Major Barbara*, Miller is sure he knows "the difference between right and wrong," and he permits his heroes—Chris Keller, Biff Loman, and John Proctor—to stand at last foursquare for righteousness. Even when he adapted Ibsen's *An Enemy of the People*, Miller permitted his hero no shillyshallying as he approached the firm distinctions between right and wrong. The play's Dr. Stockmann is, as Ibsen himself said, "muddle-headed." Leaping rapidly from one attitude to another, he briefly adopts the view that breeding can produce superior individuals. In the next act, he has flown off in the opposite direction and has decided to educate the town's riffraff, and he has thus exhibited his mercurial temperament. But Miller would not permit him to be quite so mercurial. His free-wheeling cerebration was evidently rather appalling to a dramatist who knows exactly how far "good" characters may stray from the cause of right. Consequently, Miller omits the references to the importance of breeding. Explaining the change in his preface, Miller consistently fails to distinguish between Ibsen and Dr. Stockmann; he considers a "good" character to be a spokesman for the author, with no serious deviation. Apart from his consistent identification of the character with the author, Miller stumbles into some strange self-contradictions. First he assures us that Ibsen did not really believe in the efficacy of breeding: "That Ibsen never really believed that idea in the first place is amply proved." Then he tells us that Ibsen would never have adopted this heresy *in our time*—"In the light of genocide . . . it is inconceivable that Ibsen would insist today" on this odious theory. The implication now seems to be that Ibsen believed in Dr. Stockmann's heresy but would have rejected it in our century because of its sinister associations: "It is impossible, therefore, to set him beside Hitler." And remember, all this is about Ibsen, not Dr. Stockmann. There could be no clearer demonstration of Miller's insistence that a play is a parable of right and wrong, a parable in which no blurring of distinctions is permitted.

Miller's ideas and his technique are best illustrated in his most successful play, *Death of a Salesman*. This play exhibits all the most characteristic traits, in their plainest, most emphatic form. Plainness is achieved because Miller makes a principle out of his usual vagueness. The principle is Expressionism. The vague, typical hero becomes the embodiment of typicality, Willy the low man, who carries his status in his name. His friends Charley and Bernard—the only other family we see—have no last name at all, and neither does Willy's employer. Furthermore, the salesman is, as we have observed, the most representative member of our commercial society; in a sense, when the salesman dies, this society dies. Every strand of evidence, in and out of the play, points to the symbolic reading of the salesman's role. Replying to the many salesmen who thought they saw their own story writ large in the play, Miller has insisted: "I have and had not the slightest interest in the selling profession." The mystery of the salesman's product is preserved for symbolic reasons. Miller tantalizes us with references to stores in Boston and to Willy's eye for color, but, in response to questions, he invariably answered that the product Willy was selling was himself. Preserving the mystery keeps Willy the archetypal salesman of our time.

The details of Willy's origin are equally vague—or universal.

Even if we recognize some of the stresses of Jewish family life, what is more highly visible is Miller's determined effort to iron out these specific elements, to make the family Everyfamily or Anyfamily. The Anyfamily quality is reflected in Miller's delight with Thomas Mitchell's Irish Willy Loman, and it is manifest also in his obvious intention of making the Loman family history recapitulate the history of the nation. Willy's father used to set out across the continent from Boston; Willy remembers sitting under a covered wagon in South Dakota while his brother Ben went on to look for their father in Alaska. Somehow, this sounds like an improbable origin for Willy Loman, salesman, of Brooklyn. The point is, I think, that Willy is not the product just of this family but of the adventurous American past. The colorful background helps to make Brooklyn's hapless Willy as commonplace as he is required to be. The shabbiness of Willy's life is made abundantly clear when his colorful brother stops off on his way to the gold fields and asks, "chuckling," "So this is Brooklyn, eh?" The very presence of the daring entrepreneur is enough to show up the salesman who has been playing it safe all his life.

Willy is much more emphatically a representative figure, an American Everyman, than any of Miller's other characters; accordingly, his problems are much less personal dilemmas than they are public issues. Willy is a useful instrument for Miller's social criticism. This quality of his is the first trait by which we identify this play as an example of Expressionism. Certainly this concern with large social issues is the key to Miller's definition of Expressionism in his Harvard lecture ("The Family in Modern Drama," *Atlantic Monthly*, April, 1956): "It is a form . . . which manifestly seeks to dramatize the conflict of either social, religious, or moral forces *per se*." In his most recent article, Miller finds that the Greeks and the Expressionists are alike in their effort "to present the hidden forces."

The hallmarks of Expressionism are its employment of symbolic characters—The Man, the Woman, the Nameless One (all three in Ernst Toller's *Man and the Masses*), Elmer Rice's Mr. Zero, Miller's Loman—and its presentation of dream states in which hidden forces of every variety become plainly visible. It was against the pioneer Expressionist, August Strindberg, that Zola lodged the complaint that he did not know the last names of the characters in *The Father*; the characters of this play are like

Miller's Charley and Bernard in this respect, but no one complained about Miller's rootless figures. Perhaps the audience took it for granted that their name was Everyman. Certainly the acquired taste for Expressionism has made headway since the first American experiments in the 1920's. The dramatic *genre* had been in vogue among *avant garde* audiences for half a century before Miller adopted it. What is new is its presence in a popular success of fabulous proportions. If Strindberg won the connoisseur's attention with *The Dream Play*, O'Neill with *The Hairy Ape*, and Elmer Rice with *The Adding Machine*, what popular fame these writers earned rested on other plays. But with *Death of a Salesman*, Expressionism descended, in a slightly watered-down form, to the mass audience.

The Everyman element is ovious enough. To locate the dream-elements of the play also requires no great effort. Willy Loman's dreams occupy half the play; they are the dreams of all the world, the dreams of a happy, hopeful past and the inescapable dream of past guilt. The recollections are not straight flashbacks in the manner of the films, but they are distorted, speeded up, heightened by repetition and selection. The accompanying music and the distinctive lighting of the original production compelled us to set these remembrances apart from objective reality. Further testimony of unreality is to be found in one figure who appears in them but seems to have no existence in the real world—Uncle Ben, the embodiment of the American will to succeed. He is the fantastically rich relative who shuttles between the outposts of imperialism, Alaska and Africa. Long ago, he set out for Alaska to dig gold; he found himself on the way to Africa instead, and so he made his fortune in diamonds. When Willy last sees him, he is heading for Alaska. During the dream sequences, Willy seems unable to tell truth from fantasy, the present from the past. He loses himself in his recollections, interrupting a conversation with his neighbor Charley to address the absent Ben, losing all sense of the present in a men's room while he recalls his past exposure by his son. Willy is sick; his mental breakdown is certified by the hold his recollections have on him and by the great amount of obvious distortion in them. He has symptoms of schizophrenia, but his sickness is not his alone. His identification with Everyman assures us that, as in other Expressionist plays, we are examining the malady not of an individual but of society.

Willy is drab and average; the surest guarantee of his drabness is in his commitment to the standard ideals, the standard commercial products, and even the standard language. His fidelity to the great American dream of success is at the very heart of the play. He believes in this dream in its simplest, its final form. Years ago, Horatio Alger preached that success was the reward of virtue, while Herbert Spencer and his American disciples preached that it was the reward of strength; Willy's brother Ben would seem to belong to the Spencerian or Social Darwinist school of success through strength. But Willy himself subscribes to a different and later form of the dream; he believes, with Dale Carnegie, that success is the reward of making friends and influencing people—being impressive, being persuasive, being well liked. One becomes successful by being confident, by thinking of success, and therefore success is all Willy knows, all he believes. The cultural heroes whose names are heard in Willy's household are without exception figures from the world of well-publicized triumphs. Where Odets dots his dialogue with references to exponents of high art, low art, mass culture, the world of wealth, the world of politics, Miller has only these comparable references—B. F. Goodrich, Edison, Red Grange, and J. P. Morgan (the last of them cited to Willy by his neighbor). Like certain characters in Saul Bellow's recent fiction, Willy feels that successful men possess a secret which could be passed on to him; in vain he asks his brother Ben and his friend Charley to tell him the secret. Ben replies: "William, when I walked into the jungle, I was seventeen. When I walked out I was twenty-one. And, by God, I was rich!" That is to say, the riddle remains a riddle.

Willy Loman's catastrophe is one of the poignant and inevitable misfortunes of our society and our time. The various formulations of the idea of success, whether created by Horatio Alger or Herbert Spencer or Dale Carnegie, have contributed to the state of mind that makes failure a crime. Success is a requirement that Americans make of life. Because it seems magical and inexplicable, as it is to Willy, it can be considered the due of every free citizen, even those with no notable or measurable talents. One citizen is as good as any other, and he cannot be proved to be a natural-born failure any more than he can be stripped of his civil rights. The citizen may justly and perhaps even logically ask—If Edison, Goodrich, and Red Grange can make it, why not me, why not Willy Loman? In effect, this is the question Willy asks his brother Ben. It is unanswerable; the consequent disappointment that Willy feels is one of the great American exasperations. He postpones his anguish by transferring his ambitions to his sons, and so the play's free use of time permits us to observe aspiration and failure in both generations. The problems, the exasperation, and the pathos of this family were sufficiently serious and important to make *Death of a Salesman* a moving play and a spectacular success. As a resourceful and understanding treatment of a critical human problem, this play makes an unmistakable claim upon us. But to examine it as closely as it deserves is to discover that Willy transfers his qualities and his characteristic confusions to the play itself. This is a very subjective play; it seldom takes us outside the ideas, the aspirations, even the vocabulary of the doomed salesman.

Willy's language reflects his resoluteness in the pursuit of success. It is devoid of words for anything but the necessities of life and the ingredients or symbols of success. This world is full of aspirin, arch supports, saccharin (all the wrong cures for what ails Willy), Studebakers, Chevrolets, shaving lotion, refrigerators, silk stockings, washing machines. It is the only play I know that could stock a mail-order catalog. Everything but these commonplace objects is washed out of the characters' speech. In moments of excitement, they do not rise above "Knock him dead, boy," or "I'm gonna knock Howard for a loop," or "Knock 'em dead." In a context like this, phrases like "twist of mockery" or "masterful man" sound poetic, but the true fabric of language here is woven of the most ordinary stuff. Some dubious rhetoric is permitted on the few occasions when it is necessary to point a moral. This function is usually Linda's, but, at Willy's funeral, it comes to be shared by Charley, who speaks a eulogy not for Willy but, with striking appropriateness, for his calling: "A salesman is got to dream, boy. It comes with the territory." Buried under platitudes, Willy is allowed no more individuality in death than he has exhibited in life.

Willy is called to account by the crises of the play. He is weighed, and so are his values. There is some doubt as to just what tale the scales tell. Miller himself has made a recent contribution to this ambiguity. In a symposium on *Death of a Salesman* (in *Tulane Drama Review*, Summer, 1958), he replies to a critic who finds Willy "vicious": "The trouble with Willy

Loman is that he has tremendously powerful ideals. . . . The fact is he has values." Two pages later, he speaks of his play as "showing what happens when there are no values"; he explains: "I was trying in *Salesman*, in this respect, to set forth what happens when a man does not have a grip on the forces of life and has no sense of values which will lead him to that kind of grip." As the editor of the symposium observed, "Mr. Miller seemed to contradict himself." At least, Miller is very certain that values are involved. Miller himself is hammering out some values in the play, dramatizing them, recommending them to us. He seems to say: what Willy believes in is false, but it is a system of values nevertheless. On the one hand, the whole play is devoted to exposing Willy's errors. On the other hand, Willy has been so consistent and so conscientious in living by his false values that, at his funeral, his neighbor Charley (whom we are expected to take seriously) romanticizes the salesman's calling in the speech beginning: "Nobody dast blame this man." Although the values are real to Willy, they are so false that Miller can tell us in the symposium, right after he has insisted on their existence that they do not exist. This confusion is abetted by the greater clarity of the rejected values which are embodied in the dream of success. The false dream is fully and vividly sketched; positive values seem rather dim and conventional.

Prominent among the bad values is, as we have seen, the idea of personal success in a competitive society—not only the great American dream but also the great American subject. Miller makes the conventional equation between commercial competition and personal combat. Brother Ben has one lesson for Willy's boy: "Never fight fair with a stranger, boy. You'll never get out of the jungle that way." He illustrates his lesson by tripping Biff and menacing him with his umbrella. This view of our society is common enough in criticisms from the left; it is present in Odets' *Golden Boy*, in which the prizefighter here differs only by combatting his opponents more directly than the rest of us. But Miller's favorite indictment is a variation on Proudhon's "Property is theft." Miller revises this to read "Competition is theft." Biff is the particular exponent here: imbued by his father with the spirit of competition, he steals a football, a carton of basketballs, a suit, and, less deliberately, a fountain pen. The equation between competition and theft is made automatically by a waiter when Happy tells him he and his brother are going into business together: "Great! That's the best for you. Because a family business, you know what I mean?—that's the best . . . 'Cause what's the difference? Somebody steals? It's in the family."

Happy shows his competitiveness in another way. His "over-developed sense of competition" leads him into many sexual adventures. He is thus an authentic product of our competitive system. Stealing enters the picture because Happy shows a special interest in the fiancées of his company's executives; he has seduced three of them. Sex is in itself an evil, a false value, in this play, as it is elsewhere in Miller. In *The Crucible*, John Proctor's affair with his beautiful teen-age servant is the source of his undoing. In *A View from the Bridge*, Eddie Carbone is ruined by his incestuous passion for his young niece. The wife in each play is a fine woman who is not in the least sexually interesting. The same is true of Linda Loman, to whom Willy is unfaithful. Biff's discovery of this infidelity marks the crucial turning point in the relationship between father and son; thereafter Biff no longer believes in Willy. Significantly, Willy recalls the exposure—and it is played out for us—just as his sons desert him for two floozies they have picked up in a restaurant. These two exposures of illicit sex, one in the past and one in the present, double their force by coming at just the same moment in the play. Small wonder that Willy has earlier warned Biff to be cautious with girls. On the whole, Miller's implicit indictment of sex as a wicked influence is remarkably consistent and emphatic. We may suitably apply to Miller his own words, from the notes of *The Crucible*: "Our opposites are always clothed in sexual sin."

But Miller does more than criticize illicit sexual activity; he makes it both the root and symptom of his heroes' disorders in these three plays. Eric Bentley has suggested that, in *Death of a Salesman* and *The Crucible*, sex serves to mask social criticism and to offer an alternative explanation of the heroes' disasters. Thus, we have a double accusation. Willy and his son Happy are brought to account for their faulty social philosophy and also for their philandering. In the profoundest sense, Willy is destroyed by his false ideals. But the greatest single disaster in the play's present events may well be his sons' flight with the floozies while he is in the men's room. Sex has undone him, and society has undone him: you take your choice. This double interpretation is accurate, but it does not prevent Miller from doing something else—from dramatizing, with telling consistency, a Puritanical, repressive attitude toward sex. What is bad in society, illicit sex for instance, is directly and plainly shown. The positive values, if any exist, are dimly and imperfectly seen. The muscular, proletarian life is recommended as a healthy alternative to commercialism. Willy is most himself when he works with his hands, putting up ceilings, "making the stoop; finishing the cellar; putting on the new porch." At the funeral, Biff underscores the thematic use to which Miller puts Willy's neglected talents: "You know, Charley, there's more to him in that front stoop than in all the sales he ever made." Biff himself has the good sense to turn his back on a life of making sales and to work with his hands as a cowboy. He tells Happy, "We should be mixing cement on some open plain, or—or carpenters." The naturalness of such activity as this is associated with nature itself. We can be sure the Lomans are on the right track when they add to their manual dexterity a love of nature. Biff rhapsodizes about the inspiring "sight of a mare and a new colt" and about spring in Texas. When Willy loses his grip on himself, his salesman personality becomes submerged, and he can release his latent love of nature. He guiltily recalls that, driving along in a sort of trance, he found time to admire the scenery: "You can imagine, me looking at scenery, on the road every week of my life." Later, he complains that brick buildings have blocked him in, and he fondly recalls the elm trees, lilacs, wisteria, and daffodils of the past. When he finally cracks under the double strain of present disappointment and unhappy recollections of the past, he dashes to a hardware store and buys seeds which he begins planting at night by flashlight.

These bits of talk and action which recommend nature and manual labor to us are brief and not entirely coherent, but they form the main repository of Miller's positive values. Their brevity and incoherence imply that Miller finds it difficult to come out for the good, in any form. The leftist dramatists of the thirties spoke more boldly of the good life and of the way to attain it. In the forties the proletarian mystique was less accessible; however, its previous authority in drama and other writing had helped to create an aura of vague proletarian *bonhomie*, based on instinctive faith in manual labor and the simple things. The "positive" references of *Death of a Salesman* reinterpret the proletarian mystique but in a hesitant and tentative fashion. Miller barely *tells* us what the good is, but he is able to *show* us the bad.

The political vagueness of *Death of a Salesman* had much to do with political circumstances in the world outside. The play was written in a period of popular-front progressivism; three months before its opening Henry Wallace wound up his Presidential campaign. Wallace's Progressive faith united many who were destined to take divergent political directions; the Progressive Presidential candidate himself now supports a Republican President. Basic differences were obliterated by a unifying emphasis on grass roots and on simple, direct human relationship. Vice-Presidential candidate Glen Taylor twanged his guitar, and hootenanies responded throughout the land. A favorite campaign song described the leading candidate as "friendly Henry Wallace." Wallace once observed that the main issue of the campaign was whether he would be permitted to play tennis in public with his friend the Negro singer Paul Robeson. Asked if he were supported by Communists, he would characteristically answer a question with a question: "What is a Communist?" The great distance between the Wallace movement and the seats of power, a distance reflected by Wallace's small vote in 1948, suggested to his followers that the good folk at the grass roots had gone underground, that being good was a surreptitious and sometimes illegal activity. Real, serious threats to civil liberty were already apparent in the beginnings of black-listing and of political prosecutions: ten Hollywood screen workers had been called before a congressional committee, and the leaders of the Communist Party were indicted. At just this time, radical toughness was replaced by the simplicity of Wallace's "What is a Communist?" and by the *bonhomie* which had been the chief stock in trade of the newspaper *PM* (by then defunct).

I consider the Wallace campaign to have been not an influence on *Death of a Salesman* but a parallel development, another instance of the decline of the revolutionary mystique into a combination of conventional proletarian gestures and vague belief in friendly good folks at the grass roots. Another parallel instance of submerged rebellion occurs in a play which opened two weeks after *Death of a Salesman*, Clifford Odets's *The Big Knife*, in which the hero's radical activities seem summarized by his statement: "I believed in FDR." In these post-Wallace plays, social criticism is put in such general terms that John Mason Brown, reviewing *Death of a Salesman*, was able to say of Miller: "He has the wisdom and the insight not to blame the 'System.' " But he does blame the "System." The trouble is that criticisms of the "System" were being muted and transposed that year.

Responding to the political climate, Miller's plays have moved steadily inward. Although each play has probed the impact of large, bewildering issues upon a simple man, the large issues have become increasingly dim. Some of the haziness is intrinsic, but some of it is induced by the simple man's mounting personal problems. In *All My Sons*, the issue is no less than the war itself. The play shares the weakness of its chief character, who finds it hard to make the war's values immediate and meaningful. *Death of a Salesman* strikes a balance between the social problem of the shattered myth of success and Willy Loman's sex and family problems. *The Crucible* shows us witch hunts, but the obvious contemporary reference is masked by the historical setting and by the very distinctive seventeenth-century speech; what remains is the tension between the incalculable malice of private individuals and the conscience of a guilt-ridden husband. With *A View from the Bridge*, Miller's focus moves still further within. Eddie Carbone is not only troubled and guilty; he is sick, and his symptoms resemble those that Tennessee Williams, the most typically "internal" of contemporary American dramatists, had made the common substance of Broadway drama—incestuous inclinations, psychotic sexual jealousy, frenzied hostility to homosexuality, and possibly incipient homosexuality. If these symptoms are present, it is less important that the immigration service also has its shortcomings; the play's main topic has become Eddie's troubles.

In the vagueness of Willy's identity and his occupation, in the mysterious success of Uncle Ben, in the inexplicable virtue of the good neighbors, in the incomprehensible magnetism of Willy's proletarian tendencies, we have not only the studied ambiguity of Miller's method but also the quality of the radical political climate. In more ways than the dramatist may know, his plays speak for the spirit of the time.

XVI

TOM F. DRIVER

What's the Matter with Edward Albee?

The nation's publicity media, desperately in search of a "gifted young playwright," and unable to practice that asceticism of taste which is the requisite of culture, have praised the mediocre work of Edward Albee as if it were excellence. They have made the author of six bad plays into a man of fame and fortune, which is his good luck. They have also made him into a cultural hero, which is not good for anybody. It is time to disentangle our judgments of his merits from the phenomenon of his popularity.

Four of Edward Albee's six bad plays are too short to fill an evening. Another is a dead adaptation of a famous story. The sixth is the most pretentious American play since *Mourning Becomes Electra*. In each of these works there are serious, even damning, faults obvious to anyone not predisposed to overlook them. To get Albee in perspective, we should examine first the faults and then the predisposition of the audience not to see them. As a maker of plots, Albee hardly exists. Both *The Zoo Story*, his first play performed in New York and *Who's Afraid of Virginia Woolf?*, his most successful, are built upon an unbelievable situation—namely, that a sane, average-type person would be a passive spectator in the presence of behavior obviously headed toward destructive violence. In *The Zoo Story*, why does Peter just sit there while Jerry works himself up to suicide? Why doesn't Nick, in *Who's Afraid?*, take his young wife and go home when he sees that George and Martha want only to fight the whole night through? In both cases, the answer is either that there is some psychological explanation that has not been written into the play, or that if Peter or Nick did the logical thing and went home the play would be over.

Sometimes it is argued that this objection is out of place. It is held that the passivity of Peter and Nick is allegorical and is supposed to point to our general passivity in the presence of destructive tendencies in modern life. But this is cheap allegory. A situation cannot function well as allegory unless it is a believable situation. Whatever allegorical element is present in the situation of *The Zoo Story* and *Who's Afraid?* is in conflict with the realistic convention that both plays assume.

Failure to maintain the chosen convention occurs in all the Albee plays, even in *The American Dream*, which does not pretend to realism but is more like the "theater of the absurd." It opens in such a manner as to suggest that Albee is imitating Ionesco, or perhaps will parody him. After ten minutes it is no longer clear whether any reference to Ionesco is intended, and it never becomes clear in the rest of the play. On the other hand, no different convention imposes itself. Toward the end of the play the comic mode is destroyed by a long autobiographical speech by the title character, a speech so full of Freudian cliché and self-pity that the only humane response to it is to be embarrassed for the author. No one could have written it who did not regard himself above his art. In the work of amateurs we expect this sort of thing, we forgive it. But we do not praise it, for to do so is to substitute indulgence for criticism.

Who's Afraid? displays another failure to maintain convention. This play is supposedly a realistic depiction of "how life is." I have yet to hear a reasoned defense of it on any other grounds, including that of its director, Alan Schneider (*Tulane Drama Review*, Spring, 1963). Yet we are shown a married couple who go through life as the "parents" of a twenty-one-year-old "son" who is purely imaginary. The play ends when this "son" is sent to an imaginary "death" by his "father."

To be sure, the message of *Who's Afraid?* is clear in spite of this confusion; too clear. In many marriages illusions grow and have to be "exorcised" (this pretentious, crypto-religious word is Albee's), in order to save what is left of the partners. But the device Albee uses to state such a truism is once again from Ionesco. Patched into a realistic play, it turns the whole into a crazy mixture of the obvious and the incredible. This is not, as some have said, a problem in the third act only. The flaw that ruins the third act is already present in the first two, rendering them unbelievable.

Patching and stitching is the mark of Albee's style, if bad habits may be called a style. Scarcely five lines go by without making one feel that something extraneous has been sewn in. The scenes have no rhythm. They give no impression of having developed organically from situations deeply felt or from ideas clearly perceived. Nothing is followed through in the terms initially proposed. There is no obedience to reality outside the playwright's head, nor much evidence of consistency within it.

If Albee's arbitrary manner puts an unnecessary and uninstructive burden upon the audience, it also gives the actors more to do than they can accomplish. The exhaustion that the actors, as well as the audience, say they feel at the end of *Who's Afraid?* does not come from having experienced too much but from having pretended to experience it. All acting involves pretense, but there is such a thing as being supported by a role. Albee's roles have to be supported by the actors.

The performances of Uta Hagen and Arthur Hill in *Who's Afraid?* are remarkable to see, yet they are pathetic. These two skillful people are forced to manufacture on stage, moment by moment, semblances of character which the script not only does not support but even undercuts. The more brilliantly they perform, the more anguish we feel. But it is anguish for the performers. Arthur Hill manages his tour de force by holding desperately all evening to a few mannerisms, such as his gait, the unbalanced carriage of his shoulders, and his operatic delivery of the lines. Uta Hagen, with more variety, pulls even more tricks out of her professional trunk. In the course of the play's three and a half hours, it is the actors rather than the characters who become hysterical. Faced with the same hurdle in *The Ballad of the Sad Café*, Colleen Dewhurst takes a more dignified recourse. Given no intelligible character to enact, she refuses to pretend to act. She poses. Hers is the most beautiful example of non-acting I have ever seen, and I applaud her for it. No slightest hint of emotion escapes to betray the purity of her refusal; she is on strike, declining to do the playwright's work for him.

The falseness of Albee's characters is also due to the fact that they are but surrogates for more authentic ones. The characters who could make psychological sense of *Who's Afraid?* are not the two couples on stage but the four homosexuals for whom they are standing in. Granted that George is not very masculine and Martha not feminine, still we are asked to accept them as a heterosexual couple who might love each other. Their mutual sado-masochism renders this request absurd. They maintain their fight with increased pleasure-pain all night long.

I do not deny that heterosexual couples engage in *some* of the same behavior and show *some* of the same psychology. They do. But a play built around such an orgy invites us to ask what part of life it most aptly refers to. The answer is not to marriages but to homosexual liaisons. The play hides from the audience its real subject. This is quite apart from the question whether Albee *knows* what the real subject is. I think he does, but if not his job as a playwright is to find out. And to make his play tell it. We are driven to saying that either Albee does not know what he is saying or else that he is afraid to say what he means.

The significant cultural fact we have to deal with is not the existence of Albee's six bad plays but the phenomenon of their popularity. The public has been sold a bill of goods, but there must be reasons why it is willing to buy. What are these reasons?

Whatever may be said against Albee—and I've only said the half of it—one must also say that his bent is wholly theatrical. All his mistakes are theatrical mistakes. He confuses theatrical conventions, but he does not, except in *The Ballad of the Sad Café*, confuse the genre of playwriting with that of film, novel, or television. This is rare in today's theater. I expect this instinct for the theatrical is what people really have in mind when they refer to Albee's talent. "Talent" is the wrong word, for the nature of a talent is to grow, and Albee shows no signs of that. He does show a theatrical instinct.

Although theatricality is an important component in all great drama, it can also characterize some of the worst. That is, it can be used imaginatively or it can be used merely fancifully. Albee's use is the latter. There is evidence that this is a direct cause of his success. The truly imaginative use of theatricality is found today in Samuel Beckett, Eugene Ionesco, and Jean Genêt, none of whom has ever caught on with the large New York theater audience. Critics on the daily papers either misinterpret these playwrights (the *New York Times* told us recently that Genêt's *The Maids* is a "social tract") or they find them "obscure." Albee is preferred not because he is better but because he is worse. Since his themes are obvious, even hackneyed, they cannot be obscure. And his reckless inventiveness can pass for complexity without forcing anyone to entertain a complex thought. In short, he provides a theatrical effect conveniently devoid of imaginative substance.

This accounts, I believe, for the so-called "involvement" of the audience at *Who's Afraid of Virginia Woolf?* Since the situation and the characters are false, the play provides an occasion for the display of pseudo-emotions: mock anger, mock hatred, mock envy, and finally mock love. These are provided on stage by the actors, with whom the audience enters into complicity. Thus the audience achieves, at no expense to its real emotions, a mock catharsis.

In addition, there is reason to suppose that the very roughness and the gaucheries that mar Albee's plays contribute to his success. Most of the values that operate in our society are drawn from the bourgeois ideal of domestic harmony, necessary for the smooth functioning of the machine. Yet we know that there are subconscious desires fundamentally in conflict with the harmonious ideal. Albee satisfies at once the ideal and the hidden protest against it. In his badly written plays he jabs away at life with blunt instruments. If his jabbing hit the mark, that would be another matter. But it doesn't, no more than does the child in the nursery when he tears up his toys. That is why Albee is the pet of the audience, this little man who looks as if he dreamed of evil but is actually mild as a dove and wants to be loved. In him America has found its very own playwright. He's a dream.

XVII

ROBERT BRUSTEIN

Why American Plays Are Not Literature

One of the unique features of postwar American drama is its cheerful isolation from a central literary tradition. A successful playwright today may think of himself as a craftsman, an entertainer, even a creative artist, but only in very rare cases would he call himself a literary man. He does not share at all in those common interests—few enough in our society—which unite the novelist, poet, and essayist. In his subject matter, his writing style, his associations, his attitudes, and his ideas, the dramatist is far removed, if not completely cut off, from the mainstream of intellectual and literary discourse.

This lack of communication with the other disciplines gives the drama a peculiar insularity. The typical American playwright is encouraged to write, not by the pull of literary ideals, but by the stimulus of successful Broadway plays, and it is unusual when he develops beyond a hackneyed imitation of what is current and fashionable. Making his friends mainly within the theatrical profession, he rarely ventures out of it to have his mind refreshed. Unlike the novelist, he is almost never represented in the literary periodicals, and when he does communicate with the outside world it is generally through a short piece in the *New York Times* advertising his coming play with a reminiscence about how it came to be written.

Even our most important dramatists, past and present, have tended to remain firmly fixed within the confines of their own experience and craft. Besides plays, all the great European playwrights of the past hundred years wrote poetry, epics, novels, short stories, essays, or criticism; and in modern times dramatists like Brecht, Duerrenmatt, Beckett, Giraudoux, Synge, and O'Casey have moved freely among the other literary disciplines. With the exceptions of Thornton Wilder, Tennessee Williams

Reprinted from *Harper's Magazine*, CCXIX (1959), 167–72, by permission of the author. Copyright 1959 by *Harper's Magazine*.

(both former highbrows), and Arthur Miller, few American playwrights have made more than token gestures in the direction of non-dramatic literatures, while even fewer are aware of what is being attempted or said there. Specialization in America, insofar as it has affected the arts, has hit the drama hardest of all, cutting it off not only from other literary traditions but from the very life which should be its subject matter.

This isolation can be partly attributed to the fact that American drama is a comparatively new expression, forced to create its tradition as it goes along. English playwrights like Wilde, Shaw, Eliot, and Osborne could draw on an already established dramatic heritage, one which includes the most distinguished names in literary history; in consequence, even minor dramatists like Barrie, Fry, Bridie, and Galsworthy, nourished by this strain, have created dramatic works which are eminently readable. The American drama, on the other hand—which seems to have sprung full-grown from the imagination of Eugene O'Neill —can still remember its own origins. In fact, O'Neill's persistent experimentation would seem to indicate that he was hurriedly trying to create a dramatic tradition for America which, like their gardens, took the English hundreds of years to produce. Borrowing from the drama of the Greeks, the Elizabethans, the Japanese, and nineteenth-century Europeans, O'Neill sought not native but cosmopolitan influences, and thus initiated a split from American literature which widens every year.

The split, of course, cuts both ways: American literary culture generally scorns the stage. In France, it is a rare thing when a novelist, poet, or philosopher does not express his themes in dramatic form, and it has long been the tradition for a French man of letters to include a volume or two of dramatic essays among his collected writings.

In America, on the other hand, theater criticism, abdicated by most intellectuals, has fallen into the hands of newspaper reviewers, while the drama itself is practically monopolized by commercial playwrights. Although the plays of writers like Camus, Sartre, Gide, Claudel, Mauriac, and Cocteau constitute an important part of their creative work, gifted American authors have up till now, usually either ignored the drama totally or written badly in it. The quality of Fitzgerald's *The Vegetable*, Hemingway's *The Fifth Column*, and Wolfe's *Mannerhouse*— so far inferior to these authors' non-dramatic works—would seem to indicate that, unlike their French counterparts, American writers have not regarded the drama as a serious alternative form for the expression of their deepest convictions and insights.

FINANCE AND TASTE

If the American literary man has generally been indifferent, patronizing, or hostile toward the drama, some of the reasons for this indicate why our plays are so often outside the boundaries of literature. For there is a widespread conviction among men of mind that the dramatist, writing for an audience with debased values, does not have very high standards himself—and anxious to please a wide number, he creates a contaminated work which gives literature a bad name. Since the very structure of the drama is dependent on climactic emotional effects, it has often been accused of a fondness for bombast and sensationalism and of lacking intelligence and restraint—"an unmannerly daughter, showing a bad education," wrote Sir Philip Sidney hundreds of years ago, which "causeth her mother Poesy's honesty to be called in question." More frequently content to follow public taste than to lead it, the drama has developed an unsavory reputation through its alliance with the market place.

These traditional objections have become more vigorous in our own time as the drama has sough' wider and less discriminating audiences. In the eighteenth century, when a play attracted a public for sixty-two performances, it was called the most prodigious success in history, while today a play must run for at least a year simply to make up costs. The non-creative unions—the press agents, managers, stagehands, and musicians— are squeezing the theater to death with excessive financial demands, and Broadway further exacerbates the situation with increasingly spectacular and expensive scenic effects guaranteed to excite spectator interest if all else fails. If union featherbedding were restrained, a play could again be successful after no more than sixty-two performances. And there is no telling how many honest works of imagination might see the stage without alteration. But the producer—rather than speculate on something risky and new—sticks to a tried-and-true formula based on the successes of the past. With the drama arbitrated by "show business," questions of finance overrule questions of taste, and it becomes harder to find financial support for anything which might "disturb" the audience.

The dramatist, as a result, discovers a number of non-literary partners looking over his shoulder as he writes, and this makes his work more than ever vulnerable to charges of artistic compromise. Compromise is not an essential of the collaborative enterprise—imagine the conductor of a symphony orchestra dictating elaborate changes in a musical composition for the sake of greater audience appeal. But it has now become second nature to Broadway, and few plays ever open there without having undergone strenuous revisions. While the novelist creates in the solitude of his own imagination, the dramatist re-creates with five or six worried production men at his elbow. Once paramount in importance, the playwright, in consequence, now finds his position overshadowed by the director whose power mushrooms every day; and even some of our most influential dramatists have been known to alter their work radically to retain the interest of a director who might insure its commercial success.

Since these alterations almost invariably result in a work of diminished honesty and complexity, writers whose artistic conscience demands greater satisfactions than commercial reward and the praise of newspaper reviewers view the theater with alarm and suspicion. Archibald MacLeish is one of the few authors, not a professional playwright, who has regarded his occasional stage experience as a happy one, but then he seems to have adjusted nicely to the values of the medium in which he worked:

"I thought I was going to weep [when I heard] the Atkinson review [of 'J.B.']," he writes in a published letter to Kazan, and adds that the critical reception of the play was "general evidence that the problems *were* solved." When a work is primarily evaluated—as it is in our theater—by the enthusiastic applause of the majority, this is evidence indeed, and the distortions and convulsions to which a playwright's original ideas are submitted can be justified by a long line at the box office.

TAINTED IMAGINATION

A very different response to theater experience comes from William Gibson, a literary man who looks on the success of his play, *Two for the Seesaw*, as a hollow achievement reached by suppressing his true capabilities. Gibson, primarily a poet and novelist, has recorded his agonizing experience in *The Seesaw*

Log, an illuminating account of the play's progress from idea to opening night. Like most serious writers, "it had been several years since [he] had taken a believing interest in the theater," but once having written a play his ultimate disenchantment was to come when he discovered as his collaborators not only the director, the producer, and the star, but the elevator man and probably the lavatory attendant as well. A writer to whom artistic integrity is a code of honor, he found that the perpetual revisions ordered in his play served only to cheapen it; and his original work eventually turned into a harmless diversion giving neither difficulty nor offense to anyone in the theater:

Fifteen years earlier, when my work consisted of unpublished poems and a magazine asked me to change a word in one, I would not change a word: the poem went unpublished; it was a far cry to the present spate of rewriting to please. . . . I felt this of all of us, that in outgrowing our guardian angelship, and becoming reasonable citizens, we had lost some religious component in ourselves and this component was the difference between art and entertainment. . . . The theater, in this country, in this decade, [is] primarily a place not in which to be serious, but in which to be likable.

Mr. Gibson has accurately defined not only what distinguishes art from entertainment but literature from current drama. The silhouette of show business imposes itself on almost every work for our stage, and Broadway maintains its compulsive need to send the audience home in an affable frame of mind no matter what violence is done to the line of the play. With the writer constantly badgered to turn his play into the theatrical equivalent of a best seller, honest works of the imagination invariably become tainted with sentiment and dishonesty.

The director, of course, has a duty to request clarification of an author when his work is muddy, but more frequently revisions are a surrender to commodity demands. The famous changes in the last act of *Cat on a Hot Tin Roof*, for example, had no bearing on the essential flaw of the play (which was the elusive ambiguity of the homosexual theme) but they did introduce into a bleak work a hopeful note of uplift compatible with Broadway's desire to remain well-liked. Since the trespassing of the director on the playwright's domain creates an atmosphere in which dramatic literature is very rarely produced, it remains the knottiest artistic dilemma of the American stage. It is not to be solved, as Tennessee Williams suggests, by having a "good psychiatrist in attendance at rehearsals," but rather by the playwright's strong resistance to commercial pressures when he is certain his work is being cheapened.

CULT OF INARTICULACY

Of course, this resistance alone will not guarantee a play of high literary value. American drama is plagued by internal problems as well as external ones, and the dramatist will have to revise a number of his own attitudes if he wishes to create works of lasting power. One of these is his indifference to language. American drama, no matter how serious in intent, is very rarely readable, for our plays are often stage mechanisms which seem oddly wan and listless on the printed page. Only Tennessee Wiliams has consistently created a dramatic language which a good novelist might not be ashamed to have written, and even his style deteriorated in his last play. Most of our other playwrights, including our greatest, Eugene O'Neill, are charter members of a cult of inarticulacy, communicating high moments of thought and feeling not through speech but through dashes and exclamation points.

Playwrights are generally aware of this problem but do not consider it very important. Ever since the Elizabethan age, dramatists have been embarrassed when their plays appeared in print, but in the past they apologized for literary failings—today they caution the reader to ignore them and concentrate on dramatic values. Elmer Rice, who holds that "literary excellence is not an essential criterion in the evaluation of a play," goes even further in declaring that "words are not even necessary for the creation and communication of drama." Arthur Miller writes: "It is necessary to separate the drama from what we think of today as literature. A drama ought not to be looked at first and foremost from literary perspectives merely because it uses words, verbal rhythms, and poetic images." And Tennessee Williams defiantly defends "the incontinent blaze of a live theater, a theater meant for seeing and feeling." It is not surprising that Eugene O'Neill once blamed the failure of an early play on the fact that the actors had not emphasized the *silences* in the last act where the meaning of the play was to be found.

Nevertheless, to emphasize the drama's distinctness from literature is a defensible position if not carried too far. It is certainly true that plays are written primarily to be performed, and that writers who put inordinate emphasis on language to the exclusion of other important dramatic values have invariably produced works which are lifeless and dull on the stage. (I am thinking not only of closet dramatists like Robert Browning, Thomas Hardy, and Henry James but also of working playwrights like Sean O'Casey, whose later plays bog down in succulent and bloated rhetoric.) But both the finely jeweled style of closet drama and the shoddy language of our current plays are extremes. The dramatic form has always seemed to me the greatest literary form because it combines action *and* language. All of the great working dramatists of the past and present have been able to articulate their works, and there is still no better stage device than language for the unfolding of character and the revelation of dramatic insights. By permitting some scenes to be built out of actors' improvisations, certain playwrights abdicate their function entirely; and it is partly because of the playwright's indifference to language that our most conspicuous stage hero is brutal, inarticulate, and incapable of reflecting on his condition. The failure of dramatic language leads to a situation where a great many of our plays, including two of Mr. Miller's, conclude on a question—"Why?"—when it has traditionally been the dramatist's job to answer this question.

In other words, the murky language of our plays is a serious failing only insofar as it reflects our drama's basic failing, its murky thought. American plays are difficult to read because they so often yield little sense when they are read; in the quiet of the study one stumbles on inconsistencies, disharmonies, and contradictions which are sometimes ignored in the rapid excitement of performance. Those dramatists who are aware of this make an oblique admission of it by employing extra-dramatic techniques in the published plays in order to obscure the flaws. In some of the early plays of Eugene O'Neill, for example, extravagant stage directions are provided to sharpen points which have not been suitably dramatized, and Tennessee Williams also is sometimes given to lengthy parenthetical discussions of purpose, especially when he realizes he has ducked the very questions that his play has posed. As George Orwell has proved so emphatically, there is an intimate connection between language and ideas, and inadequate writing is often a sign either of confusion or evasion. In his compulsion to "move" the spectator no matter what happens to credibility or coherence, the American dramatist is further cut off from a literary tradition which is in our time experiencing an authentic renascence distinguished by its love and feeling for ideas.

As a consequence, American drama often seems to be the most mindless form of legitimate culture since eighteenth-century sentimental comedy, a form to which it bears more than a little resemblance.* I know of few professional American playwrights—Arthur Miller is a prominent exception—who would not consider it very odd to be called a thinker. On the contrary, most playwrights are devoted to dramatizing sensations which grow more hysterical and rarefied with every passing year.

"FITFUL LIGHTNING"

In this, no doubt, they are trying to distinguish their work from what they consider the passionlessness of the English theater, and their vitality and energy have often had great value.

But this reaction can be carried too far. Tennessee Williams, for example—who calls himself a "feeling playwright"—is now indifferent to those dramatic works which, in embodying thought, are meant not only for performance but for reading and reflection, for he has developed an entirely different concept of a play:

The color, the grace and levitation, the structural pattern in motion, and quick interplay of live beings, suspended like fitful lightning in a cloud, these things are the play, not words on paper, nor thoughts and ideas of an author, these shabby things snatched off basement counters at Gimbel's.

Beginning with a distaste for the logical, the abstruse, and the tendentious, Williams concludes by rejecting ideas altogether. He thus turns a truth into a half-truth, for there is a fruitful area between the ideological play and the play of pure sensation. In this area, two of Mr. Williams's major influences, Strindberg and D. H. Lawrence, produced some of their finest work. In

* I quote from Oliver Goldsmith who, in attacking the sentimental dramatists in 1772, might have been describing American domestic plays like *The Dark at the Top of the Stairs* or *Raisin in the Sun:* "These comedies have had of late a great success, perhaps from their novelty, and also from their flattering every man in his favorite foible. In these plays almost all the characters are good, and exceedingly generous. . . . If they happen to have faults or foibles, the spectator is taught, not only to pardon, but to applaud them, in consideration of the goodness of their hearts."

fact, Mr. Williams's own place in the drama is secure not only because of his powerful "feeling" but because certain of his plays embodied provocative themes, while much of his later work is inferior because in relying too much on "fitful lightning" his thought is turgid and confused.

It should be clear that to introduce serious thought into the theater is not to rob it of passion; it is rather, by making that passion more meaningful, to impose greater burdens on the audience than a mere fingering of their emotions. I use the qualifying word "serious" because thought of one kind or another exists whether you like it or not—no work which uses words and action can be totally free from ideas. Even the most unintellectual forms—such as the farces of Labiche—have an idea at their base, if only a maxim by Rochefoucauld. Broadway is depressing not because ideas are not enunciated there but because these ideas invariablye *are* "snatched off basement counters at Gimbel's." Pretentious, evasive, and rarely free from formula, the falsification of Broadway thought inevitably results in the falsification of its passion. Our farces are no longer amoral and destructively funny but now embody homilies and sentiment while our melodramas revolve around drug addiction or the pernicious psychic influence of Mom. Our serious drama is informed by a debased Freudianism, our comedies are set in motion by man-chasing women, and our musicals—with one or two exceptions like *West Side Story* and *My Fair Lady*—are produced by people who write about Love while thinking about Money. There are hardly two plays each year which are not obsessively biological in their themes, yet for all this preoccupation none have any real sexual interest. Homosexuality, promiscuity, infidelity, incest—all these considerations are toyed with but always sentimentalized or evaded. The result is that we have a theater which will not admit the simple truths that everyone discusses in the living room.

Almost all of our drama, in fact, is equivocal or needlessly ambiguous, for our dramatists find it difficult to square the passionate aspects of their plays with their ideas about American life. One frequently finds, consequently, contradictions between the psychological and the social or the emotional and mental aspects of a play. O'Neill squeezes an attack on American capitalism into a romantic play about Marco Polo; Arthur Miller tries to document the effect of McCarthyism on the American public through an obfuscating treatment of the Salem witch trials; Tennessee Williams drags a Southern segregationist into the middle of a sexual nightmare; and Archibald MacLeish superimposes his feelings about the hydrogen bomb on a religious drama adapted from the Book of Job.

Though each of these dramatists is concerned with some specific fact of American life, none is able to speak concretely about it for fear that his work will somehow lose its "universality"; but as any good literary man can tell them nothing is more "universal" than a careful presentation of the particular. (Saul Bellow's Chicago Jew, Augie March, is more American in his special and concrete experience than any of the universalized figures of our postwar drama.) A direct confrontation of American life—banished from our stage—has had to find refuge in "illegitimate" theatrical entertainments like the monologues of Mort Sahl, the nightclub skits of May and Nichols, and an occasional review at the Downstairs Room.

There is, in other words, very little that is contemporary about our contemporary drama. Most of our plays, for all the light they throw on American life, might have been written by a Visigoth in the Year 1, while the others merely parrot the liberal prejudices of the audience or hide their meaning (if it is disturbing or controversial) under a mountain of allegory. In this self-imposed censorship, our dramatists demonstrate the most severe consequences of their alienation for intellectual discourse; for in our theater, as it is now constituted, there is little to stimulate the more ambitious playwright. Postwar American drama is stationary, and its fondness for formal experimentation (generally designed to obscure sentiment, banality, or sheer confusion) merely gives it an illusion of movement. America today has no theatrical *avant-garde*, only two dramatists worthy of note, and no one among the younger writers to ruffle a few feathers with radical and exciting new ideas. The intellectual ferment provided in the past by O'Neill, Odets, and Lillian Hellman is practically non-existent today, and our drama is daily growing more narrow and circumscribed, strangling itself in its own living room.

Coming Refreshment

Arthur Miller is the one American playwright with the ambition to write a mature drama which transcends the family crisis, the sexual conflict, and the individual psychosis; yet in his utterances about "the people" and "the common man" he sometimes sounds as if his social thinking has not yet progressed past the 'thirties. Since he is an artist with substantial gifts and a real affection for ideas, it seems a waste that some of his own plays should suffer from the very defects he observes in the plays of others; and it is very possible that these defects might have been avoided or overcome if there had been more opportunity for debate, conversation, and intercourse with his equals in the other disciplines.

I harp on these inter-disciplinary influences not just to make an academic point but because there is evidence that American drama may soon be refreshed from non-dramatic sources. The younger novelists of the 'fifties, whose work has such distinction and intelligence, are beginning to show some inclination to knock down the prevailing borders between literature and the drama. Norman Mailer and James Baldwin are both writing plays which are certain, in different ways, to be exciting and unusual; and Lillian Hellman and Lester Osterman are currently encouraging writers like Saul Bellow, Herbert Gold, and James Purdy to write plays as well.

If these writers can transfer to the stage some of the incisive knowledge of American life they display in their novels, if they can submit themselves to the fearfully difficult discipline of the dramatic form,* and if producers can be found who will support their works without trying to commercialize them, we may soon have a substantial group of exciting and controversial playwrights. Even more, we may soon have a drama which will set new standards of honesty, intelligence, and excellence for our practicing playwrights, and which will turn the theater once again into a place—not just to be likable—but serious and profound.

* Saul Bellow's excellent one-act play, *The Wrecker*, certainly indicates that he already has a native feeling for and understanding of the drama.

Contributors

JAMES A. HERNE (1839–1901), actor and playwright; author of *Shore Acres* and *Margaret Fleming*, early examples of naturalism in the American theater.

WILLIAM DEAN HOWELLS (1837–1920), novelist and essayist; drama critic of *Harpers Magazine*, beginning in 1889.

WALTER PRICHARD EATON (1878-1957), playwright, critic, and professor of playwriting at the Yale School of the Drama.

JAMES GIBBONS HUNEKER (1860–1921), author and critic of music, drama, and the fine arts.

ROBERT BENCHLEY (1889–1945), writer and comedian, drama critic of *Life* (1920-29) and *The New Yorker* (1929–40).

STARK YOUNG (1881–1963), novelist and critic; translator of the plays of Chekhov.

GEORGE JEAN NATHAN (1882–1958), essayist and critic (*American Mercury*, 1924–30); founder of the George Jean Nathan Prize for Dramatic Criticism.

H. T. PARKER (1867–1934), drama and music critic of the *Boston Evening Transcript*, beginning in 1905.

JOHN HOWARD LAWSON (born 1895), playwright and scenarist; author of *The Theory and Technique of Play Writing and Screen Writing* (revised edition, 1949).

MALCOLM GOLDSTEIN (born 1925), member of the faculty of Queens College, author of a forthcoming study of the American drama of the thirties.

VINCENT WALL (born 1906), member of the Department of English at Wayne State University.

FRANCIS FERGUSSON (born 1904), member of the Department of Comparative Literature at Rutgers, the State University of New Jersey; author of *Idea of a Theatre* (1950).

ERIC BENTLEY (born 1916), Brander Matthews Professor of Dramatic Literature at Columbia University, author of *The Playwright as Thinker* (1946), and *What Is Theatre?* (1963).

ARTHUR GANZ (born 1928), member of the Department of English at Rutgers University.

HENRY POPKIN (born 1924), teacher and critic, American correspondent for the *London Times*.

TOM F. DRIVER (born 1925), drama critic and member of the faculty of Union Theological Seminary.

ROBERT BRUSTEIN (born 1927), drama critic and member of the Department of English, Columbia University; awarded the George Jean Nathan Prize for Dramatic Criticism, 1962–63.

The editor wishes to acknowledge the assistance of Gary Scrimgeour and Jesper Rosenmeier in the research for this collection.